POPULAR MECHANICS DO-IT-YOURSELF ENCYCLOPEDIA

POPULAR MECHANICS DO-IT-YOURSELF ENCYCLOPEDIA

FOR

HOME OWNER, CRAFTSMAN

AND HOBBYIST

IN TWELVE VOLUMES

Volume I

Complete Index in Volume XII

J. J. LITTLE & IVES Co., Inc. ● NEW YORK

Foreword

POPULAR MECHANICS, a household word in America for more than half a century, proudly presents this encyclopedia of "do it yourself" knowhow for homeowner and craftsman. Here, in 12 handy volumes, is the information that will keep your household well-run, well-furnished and in good repair. Within these pages lie opportunities to save hours of time and labor and hundreds of dollars in money unspent.

This encyclopedia has hundreds of authors and illustrators. They are the same skilled craftsman, the easy-to-understand writers and the trained illustrators who produce the famous magazine, *Popular Mechanics*, and the host of how-to-do-it books published by Popular Mechanics Press. Each article in these volumes is written by a specialist in his particular field, and who has actually built the project or made the home repairs and improvements under discussion. In illustrating these articles, no expense was spared to have precisely the right drawings, photographs and charts necessary for easy understanding of the job at hand.

The variety of topics within these volumes is such that there is no household, homemaking, garage, workshop or garden task for which you will not find an easier way, a right way, an economical way. From Abrasives (how to use) to Youngster's Bed (design & construction), the handy alphabetical arrangement of these volumes makes it easy to find answers to a bewildering number of home problems. The complete index in volume twelve will act as a further aid to quick location of material. The home craftsman will find a wealth of information on how to better use his power tools, lumber and other materials; valuable knowhow on special jigs and attachments, and a treasury of projects he can make for his own use or for sale. The householder concerned with repairs and home maintenance will find approved methods for getting all these jobs done economically. There are sound and simple instructions for repairing your automobile and making it run better and longer. There are hundreds of household hints and scores of interesting hobbies for all members of the family.

Would you think it a rare encyclopedia which gave you practical information on basement moisture-proofing, bandsaw techniques, photography, archery, furniture building, welding, roofing, antique refinishing, air conditioning and how to read a blueprint? You would? You have such a rare volume in your hands.

THE EDITORS

THE A B C
OF COLOR

With paint you can change the apparent size of a room, inject life and gaiety, produce quietness, dignity and often greatly camouflage objectionable details

FOR THE COST of a few gallons of paint you can change the size of rooms, raise or lower ceilings, subdue objectionable furniture and, in general, give your home a pleasing and inviting appearance. It is all done with the correct use of color.

For example, notice the two pictures on this page. In the lower one, the davenport is a dominant feature against the pink wall and red drapes. In the upper picture on this page, the use of harmonizing colors and a change of drapes blend the davenport into the wall, making the room seem larger and more pleasing.

A similar idea is illustrated in the two views on page II . The fireplace at the left dominates the view and tends to pull the

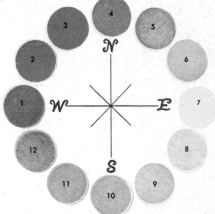

Key: 1. Violet; 2. Red violet; 3. Red; 4. Red orange; 5. Orange; 6. Orange yellow; 7. Yellow; 8. Yellow green; 9. Gr.; 10. Blue gr.; 11. Blue; 12. Blue violet

Illustrations above and at the right show how color treatment of the walls affects apparent size of the sofa. Largest areas of rooms usually carry dominating color scheme with harmonizing colors as accents

I

When it's desirable to emphasize or subdue a room detail, such as a fireplace, color-treat it as in either of the two views above, depending on which effect is wanted. Note variation in room atmosphere

wall inward. In the right view, it blends into the wall, which then gives the illusion of receding and thus increasing the size of the room. In the lower picture the door and wardrobe are not only "eyesores," but also dominate the scene, thus making the room seem smaller. The right scene shows what was done with paint.

Treatment for long, narrow rooms that give a feeling of being in a hallway is shown on page III . Here the room was "widened" by painting the ends a darker shade of the color on the side walls. The darker shades "pull" the end walls in.

High ceilings in narrow rooms that tend to make the room seem even narrower and give large rooms a barnlike appearance can be lowered by painting the ceilings a dark color that contrasts with the wall color. On page IV notice how much lower the ceiling at the top of the page appears than the one in the center picture.

While specific colors are unimportant in color-sizing of rooms, the color scheme usually being determined by unchangeable factors such as rugs or furniture, specific colors are important in the warmth or coolness of a room. Selection is made on the basis of sunlight exposure of rooms, cool colors, greens, blues, yellows, etc., for maximum sunlight and warm colors, reds, browns, etc., for minimum exposure. Intermediate color hues are used in rooms exposed to sunlight only part of the time. With warm colors in bright hues you can lighten dark rooms, or with cool colors add an illusion of refreshing coolness to rooms that are hot during summer months. In rooms where west light conflicts with east light use neutral tones, or warm and cool colors reduced in intensity.

A color wheel like that pictured on page I shows how it is possible to create a color plan for the home by intermixing the primaries of yellow, red and blue and build-

Outdated woodwork and badly proportioned cabinets are made less conspicuous by covering with the wall color as in lower right-hand view. Compare with view below and note how woodwork detail is emphasized

Room interiors above and at the right show how careful use of color contrast can fool the eye. Ends of long, narrow room are in contrasting color. Lines in rug and blind give smaller room better proportion

ing up almost any hue desired. A secondary color is made by mixing two primary colors. As an example, red and yellow primaries give an orange secondary color. Red and blue result in a violet secondary and blue and yellow mix into an attractive green. There are three general types of color schemes, the monochromatic consisting of shades of one color; the related harmony, or analogous scheme, is worked out with adjacent colors, while contrasting schemes are developed from color hues that appear opposite each other on the wheel. Of course, the shades can be changed somewhat from those pictured, by varying the pure hues with black, gray or white.

Certain colors are suitable for use as dominant hues in rooms of varying exposure. As an example, yellow is generally

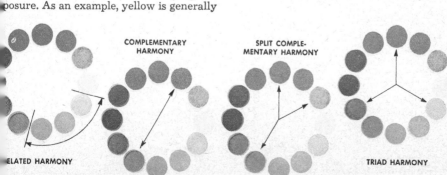

COMPLEMENTARY
HARMONY

SPLIT COMPLE-
MENTARY HARMONY

ELATED HARMONY

TRIAD HARMONY

selected as the dominant color in a room having an east or north exposure. The largest areas of the room—usually the walls and floor coverings—normally carry the dominating color scheme but it often is desirable to relieve this by combining two or more harmonizing colors to supplement the general plan.

As a rule the complementary colors should cover considerably less total area than the dominant color. Harmony also can be achieved in certain rooms by using two or more complementary colors. When windows of the room face southeast, south and southwest, bright sunlight enters both summer and winter. Such a room calls for the use of cool colors, blues and greens, to produce a restful effect. Of course, it still is possible to use complementary colors in such rooms. Your paint dealer will have more detailed color charts at hand from which you can make pleasing selections of colors for rooms with varying exposures.

Changing room atmosphere and details: When the room is situated so as to necessitate a monochromatic color scheme, gaiety and sparkle can be added by selecting complementary colors to accent room details. Sometimes a color scheme can be worked out by using the color of the living-room sofa as a starting point. The entire decorating scheme is then built up with this unit as the nucleus.

If it is desirable to emphasize interesting room details such as a fireplace, stairway or built-in, they can be "spotlighted" with a complementary color as in the upper left-hand view on page II . Often the complementary color applied to the interior of a bookcase or built-in cabinet gives just the right degree of emphasis.

Color can raise, or lower a ceiling in the manner shown in the two views above. A dark contrast on the ceiling tends to bring the ceiling down and move the walls out. Note opposite effect in lower view

Color for adjoining rooms: When adjoining rooms are connected by a wide passageway, or archway, using the same color scheme in both rooms will produce an illusion of much greater spaciousness.

When variety is desirable, complementary colors often can be used to advantage. Where rooms are separated by single doors of standard sizes, it is rarely advisable to use the same color scheme in both rooms.

Light reflectivity: The amount of illumination in a room depends on the ability of walls and ceilings to reflect light. Pure white is a common selection for ceilings as it is a complementary to almost any color on walls. However, experienced decorators favor a tinted white, or off-white, for ceiling treatment in rooms which require the maximum reflectivity. The sources of light, both daylight and artificial, must be considered in planning the decorative scheme, especially in rooms having south and north exposures, to get the full benefit of the colors. ★ ★ ★

ABRASIVES AND ABRASIVE TERMS

Aluminum oxide: An artificial abrasive, with a base of the natural clay-like mineral, bauxite. Color, brown-gray to black; in pure form, white. Hardness, 9.*

Bond: Clay or other substance which holds abrasive grains together to form wheels, etc.

Crocus: A natural abrasive formed from oxide of iron. Color, purple. Used for fine polishing. Hardness, 2.

Emery: A natural abrasive, being an impure form of crystalline alumina. Much softer than aluminum oxide. Color, dull black. Hardness, 8.

Garnet: A natural abrasive mined in the United States. Extensively used in woodworking. Color, red. Hardness, 7.

Glazed: Said of a wheel or stone which has become clogged with metal particles so that it will not cut.

Grade: The resistance of the bond in a grinding wheel to any force tending to pry the abrasive grains loose. Has nothing to do with the hardness of the abrasive itself.

Grit: The size of the abrasive grains, determined by the number of grains which, end to end, equals one inch.

Lime: A fine natural abrasive, used extensively in the final polishing of brass and nickel. Color, white. Hardness, 1.

Oilstones: General descriptive term applied to all abrasives when made into stones for bench use.

Pumice: A natural abrasive. Used for final polishing, cutting down finishing coats of varnish, etc. Several grades of fineness. Color, off-white. Hardness, 4.

Quartz: Commonly called flint. A natural abrasive. Least expensive of all abrasives but very soft. Color, yellow. Hardness, 6.

Rottenstone: A natural abrasive. Negligible cutting action but good polisher. Color, off-white. Hardness, 3.

Rouge: A natural abrasive in powder form. Graded fine, very fine, extra fine. Color, red; also, green (chromium oxide). Hardness, 0.

Silicon carbide: An artificial abrasive made by fusing silica sand. Color, gray, green or black. Hardness, 10.

Structure: The spacing of abrasive grains in a grinding wheel. Usually represented by a number from 1 to 12, the smaller numbers indicating close spacing of grains.

Tripoli: A siliceous powder consisting of tiny skeletons. Color, pink. Graded. Used in fine polishing. Hardness, 5.

*Numbers given in this table list the hardness of the abrasives in sequence, from 10 (the hardest) to 0 (the softest). The number has no grading value, but is simply used to indicate the hardness of the abrasives in descending order.

COMPARATIVE GRAIN SIZES

NO.	GARNET	FLINT	EMERY	NO.	GARNET	FLINT	EMERY	NO.	GARNET	FLINT	EMERY
400	10/0	...	...	150	4/0	2/0	$\frac{1}{2}$	40	$1\frac{1}{2}$	$2\frac{1}{2}$	...
320	9/0	...	FF	120	3/0	1/0	1	36	2	3	...
280	8/0	...	F	100	2/0	$\frac{1}{2}$	$1\frac{1}{2}$	30	$2\frac{1}{2}$	...	...
240	7/0	...	3/0	80	1/0	1	2	24	3	...	...
220	6/0	4/0	2/0	60	$\frac{1}{2}$	$1\frac{1}{2}$	$2\frac{1}{2}$	20	$3\frac{1}{2}$	...	...
180	5/0	3/0	1/0	50	1	2	3	16	4	...	...

COATED ABRASIVE SELECTION

MATERIAL	ABRASIVE	ROUGH	FINISH	FINE
Hard Woods	Garnet or Alum. Oxide	$2\frac{1}{2}$-$1\frac{1}{2}$	$\frac{1}{2}$-1/0	2/0-3/0
Soft Woods	Garnet	$1\frac{1}{2}$-1	1/0	2/0
Aluminum	Alum. Oxide	40	60-80	100
Bakelite	Alum. Oxide	36-40	60-80	100
Cast Brass	Silicon Carbide	36-40	60-80	80-120
Comp. Board	Garnet	$1\frac{1}{2}$-1	$\frac{1}{2}$	1/0
Copper	Alum. Oxide	40-50	80-100	100-120
Cork	Alum. Oxide or Garnet	3	1	1-0
Fiber	Alum. Oxide	36	60-80	100
Glass	Silicon Carbide	50-60	100-120	120-320
Horn	Garnet	$1\frac{1}{2}$	$\frac{1}{2}$-1/0	2/0-3/0
Iron (Cast)	Silicon Carbide	24-30	60-80	100
Ivory	Alum. Oxide	60-80	100-120	120-280
Paint (removing)	Flint	3-$1\frac{1}{2}$	$\frac{1}{2}$-1/0	...
Plastic	Alum. Oxide or Garnet	50-80	120-180	240
Steel	Alum. Oxide	24-30	60-80	100

ABRASIVES AND THEIR USE

IN BOTH finishing and refinishing procedures the preparation of the surface by sanding is one of the most important steps in the whole process. Hand-tool or machine-tool marks must be removed and the surface made smooth before finishes can be applied. It is important to use the right abrasives throughout the step-by-step procedure right up to the last finishing coat. The use of graded abrasives smooths the finishing material, removing and leveling such defects as small dust specks, air bubbles and the fine ripples which sometimes develop in finishing materials laid on with a brush. By making good use of abrasive know-how, the home craftsman will find that it requires a minimum of effort to prepare new wood for finishing and also to restore scuffed, scratched and chipped finishes to the original luster.

Whether you are sanding down an old varnish finish preparatory to refinishing or are sanding new wood, it's important to begin with the coarse abrasive and progress by separate steps to the fine and very fine grades. The reason for this is that the whole process is simply that of removing the coarse, medium and fine scratches made by the respective grades of paper until the surface feels satiny smooth to the touch and the scratches can no longer be seen. On the coarse and medium papers, each abrasive grain removes considerable material from the surface at each stroke. This cutting action leaves a tiny groove, or scratch, which casts a shadow in oblique light, making the scratches visible both on the bare wood and under any clear finish. If a stain is used on such a surface the pigment in the stain will "build" in the scratches and dull the grain pattern, giving the job a flat, unattractive appearance.

Packaged abrasive sheets in various grades ranging from very coarse to very fine make it easy for the home craftsman to keep on hand a supply of garnet, aluminum-oxide and silicon-carbide paper both for planned refinishing jobs and also for those which may turn up unexpectedly. Although the waterproof sanding papers are commonly used in industry for finishing operations on metals and metal-finish undercoats, they are comparatively new to the home workshop. In the finer grades, these papers are considered by most finishers as being superior to pumice for rubbing down final coats of lacquer, varnish and enamel. Now, many experienced home craftsmen use them exclusively for this purpose. Waterproof papers can be used with either rubbing oil or water (the procedure is known to finishers as "wet sanding"), and in final rubbing and polishing operations they will produce a low-luster finish of satin smoothness. If a high-luster finish is desired, add another step by using specially prepared polishing compounds.

Photos and technical information courtesy "3M" Coated Abrasives Division, Minnesota Mining & Mfg. Co., St. Paul, Minn.

In the preparation of new wood and the sanding of old finishes to produce a smooth surface for the application of either varnish or enamel, the step-by-step procedure is the same but the grades of abrasive used must be varied according to the nature of the surface and the age of the old finish. If the old finish is smooth, then a light, wet sanding with fine and very fine paper will do the trick. One important point should be kept in mind when sanding down old finishes: It's advisable always to use water as the sandpaper lubricant. Rubbing oil is rather difficult to remove entirely from an enameled or varnished surface which has been cut by sanding. As a rule, oil is used only on the final finish coat. If confronted with a refinishing job, such as a cabinet or table, on which the finish is very old and oxidized to the point where it is badly checked in addition to being marred and scratched from long use, it is up to the finisher to decide whether to remove the old finish entirely (complete refinishing) or simply sand the old finish down until it is smooth. Very often the latter procedure will produce satisfactory results, that is, so far as the quality of the finish goes. However, if the original finish was clear, or if it has been applied over stain, then the grain of the wood must be considered. Age darkens the wood on old pieces, sometimes to such an extent that the grain pattern is almost obliterated. In this case, it is necessary to

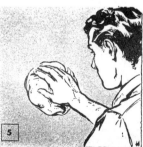

6

7

To furniture finishers, a complete refinishing job means taking off all the old finish down to the bare wood. The job starts literally "from scratch," with an old occasional table, marred, scuffed and scratched like this one is from long, hard usage

The first step is to apply a remover to soften and lift the old finish so that it can be scraped off easily with a wide-bladed scraper. When there are several coats of a pigmented finish, such as enamel, more than one application of remover may be necessary

8

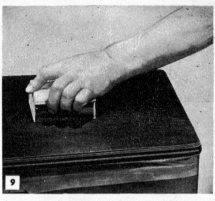

9

Above, the first sanding with coarse abrasive removes discolorations and exposes the wood in its natural color. Successive sanding steps prepare the surface for filler and sealer which are sanded down as in Fig. 9. Below, after applying, the final finish is wet-sanded between coats with very fine sandpaper

Above, after the surface has been prepared by sanding, Fig. 8, the stain and sealer are applied and allowed to dry. Then the surface is sanded lightly to prepare it for succeeding finish coats. If you want a fine high-luster finish, the final step is rubbing down the finished surface with a polishing compound, below

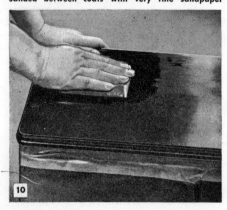

10

11

take off the old finish with prepared remover and sand the surface to bring out the grain.

It's comparatively easy to repair scratches on refrigerators, Fig. 3, metal kitchen cabinets, washing machines and ironers by a step-by-step procedure similar to that used on wood. The first step is to feather-edge the area around the scratch with waterproof silicon-carbide paper in the very fine grade. Water is used as a sanding lubricant and the sanding motion is made from the center of the damaged spot to the edges. This operation feathers the finish uniformly down to the bare metal, Figs. 1 and 2. When this step has been completed, the area is coated with metal primer, sprayed on. You can rent a sprayer from any well-stocked hardware store. When dry, the primer is lightly wet-sanded with very fine silicon-carbide paper, Fig. 4, the important thing being the sanding of the outer edges to level them flush with the surrounding surface. After the primer has been leveled, the finish coats of lacquer or enamel are sprayed on. Usually this is done by spraying a mist coat first, followed by a full coat. With the ordinary spray gun, the mist coat is produced by reducing the amount of enamel in proportion to the air volume. After the finish is dry, it is sanded lightly with very fine paper, using either water or oil as a lubricant and paying special attention to the sanding of the edges where the new finish builds onto the old. It takes very careful work here to reduce the finish to uniform thickness without ridges or ripples. Next, the spot is polished with a specially prepared polishing compound, working with a circular stroke and including all the area covered by the new finish, Fig. 5. Polishing blends the new finish into the old so that light reflections are equalized over the whole surface, thus hiding the repair.

Using very fine silicon-carbide paper and polishing compound, enamel finishes on re-

Above, sanding with coarse paper removes discolorations from the wood and levels the surface. Sanding with finer grades of paper smooths the wood and squares up edges of panels and frame. Below, after the rough and smooth sandings have been done, apply a sealer and, when this is thoroughly dry, sand smooth

This old door looks pretty messy as you see it here. Several coats of paint have been softened by a paint remover and are being scraped off to expose the bare wood. On some of the older, more difficult jobs, such as this, several coats of remover may be necessary

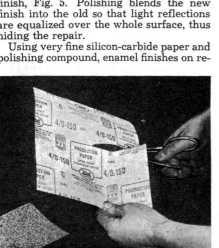

the garnet papers rather than silicon-carbide papers, which are more commonly used on enamels and other finishing materials applied over metals.

By use of abrasives which are now readily available, you can reclaim old work that looks hopeless in its present condition. The door, Figs. 12, 13 and 15, is a good example. First, the paint is removed as in Fig. 12. Then the preparatory sanding proceeds through the regular steps as in Figs. 13 and 15. Fill all dents and deep scratches with wood filler before the final sanding. Here is a good trick to know when sanding a door such as the one shown: Sand the rails (horizontal members) first, then take the stiles. This procedure will avoid scratches at the joints where the grain of the horizontal and vertical members meets at right angles.

Homemakers have discovered that very fine silicon-carbide paper is just the thing for cleaning blackened kitchen utensils, Fig. 16. A few strokes with the paper brightens the most stubborn discolorations and, after washing and wiping with a soft cloth as shown, pots and pans, skillets and teakettles look like new again. In some cases, it may be necessary to use a medium or fine paper, particularly on ironware. In any case, always finish the job with the very fine grade to remove the scratches left by the coarser grit. Do not use the coarser grits on copper or any plated kitchenware. In the homeshop, tools that have become rusted, such as handsaws and chisels, can be cleaned and polished with the fine papers as in Fig. 17. Use a few drops of oil to prevent the abrasive from clogging. Clean the bottom of a rusty hand plane by taping a piece of fine aluminum-oxide paper to the bench top and then stroking the plane lightly over it, with the plane iron raised. Cut abrasive paper into strips or squares with a small pair of tin snips as in Fig. 14. When cutting strips to fit a sanding block of the type shown in Fig. 18, it is advisable to cut the strip slightly wider than the block.

frigerators and other household appliances, which are discolored with age, can be made to look like new simply by wet-sanding and polishing uniformly over the whole surface. Wet-sanding removes a very thin film from the discolored surface, exposing new pigment. Polishing restores the original luster.

Figs. 6 to 11 inclusive picture the step-by-step procedure in refinishing a small table which has become badly scratched and marred by long use. This is a typical complete refinishing job, as the old finish is first removed entirely as in Fig. 7, using a prepared remover. Next the surface is coarse-sanded, as in Fig. 8, to remove discolorations and restore the original color of the wood. Then the sanding is continued through three more steps to smooth the surface. After the application of stain and sealer, the surface is sanded, Fig. 9, in preparation for the application of the finishing coats, which are sanded down as in Fig. 10. Then if you want a fine, high-luster finish, rub down the surface with a polishing compound as in Fig. 11. As a rule, finishers use polishing compound only on varnish and lacquer finishes. Also, it is better to use

Photos and technical service courtesy "3M" Coated Abrasives
Division, Minnesota Mining & Mfg. Co., St. Paul, Minn.

Most home workshops now are equipped with at least one power tool that can be adapted to sanding, either with ready-made attachments or with those you can make yourself. Hand-sanding methods can be relied upon to produce a very fine finish on cabinetwork, both on new projects and on old work, providing that the appropriate abrasives are used. For sanding by hand on bare (unfinished) wood, there are four sandpaper grades, or grits, in common use. These are commonly known as very fine, fine, medium and coarse. There also is a very coarse grade for special purposes, but this is not generally used in hand sanding because of the difficulty of removing the surface scratches with finer grades of sandpaper. Although it is still available, the flint paper has been largely replaced by the faster cutting garnet and aluminum-oxide abrasives for use in hand sanding. Most of the abrasives used in handwork are paper-backed and usually are designated as A, C, D and E. The first, or A grade, is known as "finishing paper." The C and D grades are referred to as "cabinet paper" and the E grade as "roll stock."

Although hand sanding is satisfactory for most purposes, machine sanding does the job faster and with less labor on your part. And in general application, the power sander is an aid in shaping, squaring and smoothing a variety of small parts made from wood or metal. Small portable and stationary sanding machines are available for use in the homeshop. These are of three general types, the disk sander, oscillating sander and belt sander. Disk and belt sanders are made in both the portable and stationary types, but the oscillating sander is made only in the portable type. Besides the power-driven sanders, there are a number

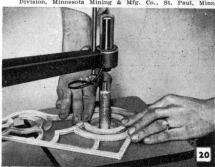

Above, this handy sanding attachment is available for small jigsaws. One face is convex and the other flat. Below, the small oscillating sander is just the thing needed to smooth narrow rounded edges

of attachments and accessories designed for other types of machines to adapt them to sanding operations.

In finishing new or old work by machine sanding, it usually is necessary to use the same abrasive-grit sequence as is used in

22

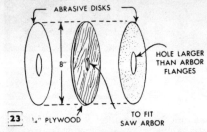

ABRASIVE DISKS

8″

HOLE LARGER
THAN ARBOR
FLANGES

23 ¼″ PLYWOOD

TO FIT
SAW ARBOR

It's easy to make a disk sander for use on your circular saw by gluing abrasive to a disk cut from plywood. Angular work is quickly smoothed and squared

24

Above, compound angles can be formed on a machine like this. Below, flexible-disk sanding machine is useful for preliminary operations on wood and metal

hand sanding, that is, begin sanding with the coarse grade and progress to the finer grade. However, it should be kept in mind that on the machine, regardless of type, the individual abrasive grains are driven across the surface at much higher speeds than is possible in hand sanding. Owing to the overlap of the cuts made by each individual abrasive grain on the same area of the surface, machine sanding with the coarser abrasives will produce a somewhat smoother surface than the same grade of abrasive when used in hand sanding. Because of this characteristic of the cutting action, it is possible to produce a very smooth surface by first using a coarse abrasive to level and true the work and then following with a fine abrasive. Thus it is possible to produce a creditable job in two passes instead of three or four, as required in handwork.

Fig. 19 pictures a combination disk-belt sander with the craftsman using the disk on a typical squaring operation on end grain. The rigid sanding disk is especially effective on this particular work, as it will square and smooth end grain ready for finishing in one operation if a medium grade abrasive is used. Fig. 24 shows the same type of combination machine with the disk being used to true a compound miter. Note that the machine table is tilted the required number of degrees. Home craftsmen who do not have this combination machine can utilize the circular saw as in Fig. 22. Simply cut a disk from plywood to 8 in. in diameter for an 8-in. saw and center-drill it to fit the saw arbor, Fig. 23. Then cut two abrasive disks and glue one to each side of the plywood disk. If desired, two different grades of abrasive can be used on the same disk. *Caution*: When operating this disk on the circular saw protect your eyes with goggles. Note in Figs. 19 and 24 that the sanding is done on the "down" side of the disk.

The flexible disk works close to a raised edge such as that found on recessed panels. Owing to high speed and flexibility of the disk, it cuts very fast

25

26

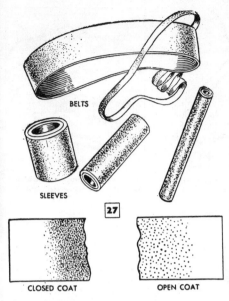

BELTS

SLEEVES

27

CLOSED COAT   OPEN COAT

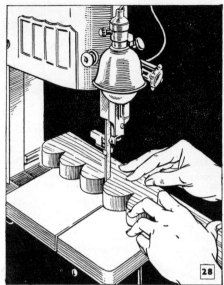

28

Although it is permissible to sand narrow pieces on the "up" side and it also is necessary to use both sides of the disk when sanding end grain on wide work, the surface produced will not be quite as smooth as that sanded only on the side of the disk going down.

One of the handiest accessories for the owner of a jigsaw is the tiny sanding attachment shown in use in Fig. 20. One side is convex and the other is flat so that you can sand concave, convex or flat surfaces with equal facility. Fig. 20 pictures a typical operation on scrolled work. The small size of the drum, less than 1 in. across the flat face, enables the operator to get into corners and small openings such as are found in fine scrolled work. Another handy

tool for the craftsman who specializes in fine cabinetwork and model construction is the small oscillating-type sander pictured in Fig. 21. The sanding pad on this little machine is driven by a vibrating coil housed in the body. The sanding stroke is about $\frac{1}{16}$ in. and the pad is driven at a speed of over 7000 strokes per minute. At this speed, fine abrasive produces a glass-smooth job either on edges, which are difficult to sand, or on flat work. It will work effectively on both metal and wood but is designed only for light work. Other oscillating-type sanders, which operate with the same sanding action but are motor driven, are shown in Figs 29 and 35. One, Fig. 29, consists of a frame and movable shoe, or pad, and is designed for attachment to a

This oscillating sander unit is designed to be driven by a ¼-in. portable electric drill. Machine leaves a smooth surface without ripples or long scratches

Small drum sanders are available as accessories in a wide range of sizes for use on shapers and drill presses. When driven at high speeds they sand fast

29

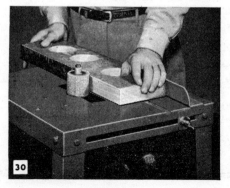

30

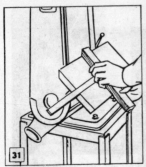

Stationary belt sanders of the type shown in the three views above are versatile machines widely used in small shops. The unit is fitted with a tilting table which is detached when sanding long pieces

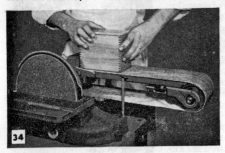

The combination machines are well adapted to finishing operations. The belt is used vertically also

Standard-size oscillating sander has direct drive. Here it is shown being used to smooth taped joints

small portable drill. The drill motor drives a special linkage which imparts an oscillating motion to the sanding pad. The other machine, typical of several which are available, has a direct-connected motor which drives a sanding pad of approximately the same size as that on the one just described. In the photo, Fig. 35, the machine is being used by a builder to smooth taped joints on plasterboard walls. Oscillating sanders are especially useful in preparing large surfaces for finishing, as they do a smooth job free from scratches or swirl marks.

Small rotating drum sanders with removable abrasive sleeves are designed for attachment to various machines such as shapers and drill presses. Fig. 30 shows one in operation sanding the edge of a piece of fairly heavy stock. The abrasive drum cuts very fast and the stock must be kept moving continuously while in contact with it as, otherwise, marks will be left on the surface. It can be worked on straight, flat surfaces or edges and inside any opening having a radius greater than that of the drum. The drums are available in various lengths and diameters, and suitable abrasive sleeves, Fig. 27, are readily obtainable.

Portable flexible disk sanders, such as those shown in Figs. 25 and 26, are widely used on a variety of sanding and grinding operations. The flexible disks with short built-in spindles for attachment to flexible shafts and drill chucks, are available as accessory units. Ready-cut abrasive disks are furnished in a variety of sizes for use with these units. In use, the flexible disk sander is tilted slightly so that only one side contacts the surface. It is moved over the surface in a dual motion, back and forth and forward simultaneously. The exception is shown in Fig. 26, where it is necessary to sand close to the edge in a recessed panel. Here the disk is tilted and the sanding progresses in one direction around the edge of the panel. Then the unsanded portion in the center is smoothed with the dual motion described.

The bandsaw sanding attachment in Fig. 28 converts the small bandsaw into a fast, accurate belt sander utilizing the narrow belt, or abrasive "ribbon," shown in Fig. 27. Belts, sleeves and disks for the various machines are quite generally available. On the open-coated type, Fig. 27, the abrasive grains are widely spaced to give the abrasive extremely fast-cutting and nonclogging properties. Belt sanders of the two types shown in Figs. 31 to 34 inclusive are widely used in industry and by home craftsmen for diversified finishing operations.

AIR COMPRESSORS

PAINT SPRAYING

SAND BLASTING

CLEANING SHOP TOOLS

OPERATING FORGE

PNEUMATIC TOOLS

H ERE is an air compressor that anyone can make inexpensively as it utilizes an old household refrigerator compressor of the piston type. It will handle any job requiring up to 65 lbs. per sq. in. pressure, such as paint spraying, sand blasting, air-blast cleaning, running portable pneumatic tools, etc.

Building a machine of this type is principally a job of assembling various purchased parts. However, some machine work will be necessary if the compressor unit is of the type that has the valve in the piston. If the valve is in the compressor head, the valve mechanism may be used without change. The compressor used in this unit is the valve-in-piston type. To convert it for use as an air compressor, the cylinder head and piston are removed and all the valve parts taken out of the piston. The valve hole is closed with a solid pipe plug and faced off flush with the top of the piston, which then is re-installed. A new valve body, cylinder head and valve retainers, as detailed in Figs. 1 to 5 inclusive, are turned from cold-rolled steel to hold the original flipper valve disks and valve springs. Care should be taken to provide smooth finished surfaces for the valve disks to seat against. Note in Fig. 3 how two narrow surfaces or rings are turned on the valve seat to contact the valve. These narrow surfaces provide better seals than one wide surface, and the center ring helps to prevent the valve disk from buckling under the increased pressure to which the compressor will be subjected. Two gaskets and longer head bolts complete the valve change-over. The parts are assembled as shown in the exploded view, Fig. 6A, and bolted to the compressor. The valve retainers are dimensioned to provide a 1/64-in. projection above the top surface of the valve body to assure an airtight seal and keep the retainers snug against the valve body. Fig. 7 illustrates how these valves operate on the intake and exhaust strokes. A pressure of 65 lbs. per sq. in. was obtained with a 1/3-hp. motor operating the compressor at about 550 to 600 r.p.m.

If your compressor unit is of a different make or model than the one shown, carefully measure the length of the valve

VARIABLE AIR REGULATOR CONTROLS PRESSURE FOR A WIDE VARIETY OF USES

springs as assembled in the piston and make the new valve head accordingly. This is important, as the strength of these springs has been calculated carefully by the manufacturer, and their compression in the new head must be the same as it was

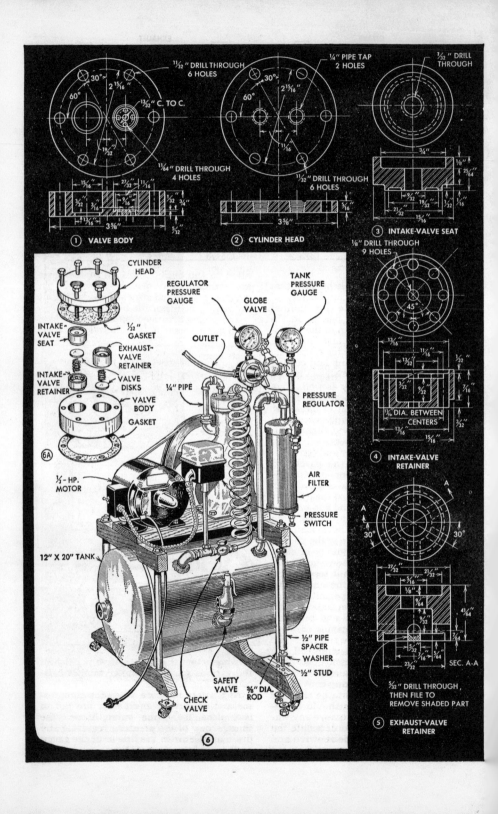

¹¹⁄₃₂" DRILL THROUGH 6 HOLES

30°
2¹⁵⁄₁₆"
60°
¹³⁄₃₂" C. TO C.

1⁹⁄₃₂

¹¹⁄₆₄" DRILL THROUGH 4 HOLES

15⁄₁₆" 27⁄₃₂" 1¹¹⁄₁₆"
³⁄₃₂ ⁵⁄₁₆ ⁹⁄₃₂ ⁷⁄₃₂ ³⁄₄
1¹³⁄₁₆" ⁵⁄₃₂
3⅝"

① VALVE BODY

¼" PIPE TAP 2 HOLES

30°
2¹⁵⁄₁₆"
60°

1¹⁄₁₆

¹¹⁄₃₂" DRILL THROUGH 6 HOLES

⁵⁄₁₆
3½"

② CYLINDER HEAD

¹⁄₃₂" DRILL THROUGH

³⁄₄"
1⁄₈" 25⁄₆₄"
⁹⁄₃₂ 1⁹⁄₃₂ ³⁄₃₂ ¹⁄₁₆
21⁄₃₂"
15⁄₁₆"

③ INTAKE-VALVE SEAT

⅛" DRILL THROUGH 9 HOLES

45°

13⁄₁₆" 1¹¹⁄₁₆" ³⁄₃₂
13⁄₃₂"
⁵⁄₃₂ ⁹⁄₃₂ ⁷⁄₁₆"
1⅛" DIA. BETWEEN CENTERS
13⁄₁₆" ³⁄₃₂
15⁄₁₆"

④ INTAKE-VALVE RETAINER

A
30°   30°
A

27⁄₃₂" 21⁄₃₂"
⁵⁄₁₆
⅛" ⁵⁄₆₄
⁹⁄₃₂ 4¹⁄₆₄"
⁷⁄₆₄
⁵⁄₃₂"
1⁷⁄₁₆" ⁵⁄₆₄ **SEC. A-A**
23⁄₃₂"

⁵⁄₃₂" DRILL THROUGH, THEN FILE TO REMOVE SHADED PART

⑤ EXHAUST-VALVE RETAINER

CYLINDER HEAD

REGULATOR PRESSURE GAUGE

TANK PRESSURE GAUGE

GLOBE VALVE

INTAKE-VALVE SEAT

½" GASKET

OUTLET

EXHAUST-VALVE RETAINER

INTAKE-VALVE RETAINER

VALVE DISKS

¼" PIPE

VALVE BODY

GASKET

PRESSURE REGULATOR

6A

⅓-HP. MOTOR

AIR FILTER

PRESSURE SWITCH

12" X 20" TANK

½" PIPE SPACER

WASHER

½" STUD

SAFETY VALVE

⅜" DIA. ROD

CHECK VALVE

⑥

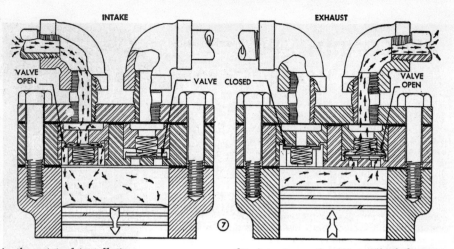

INTAKE   EXHAUST

VALVE OPEN —   — VALVE CLOSED   VALVE OPEN

(7)

in the original installation.

When purchasing the tank be sure that it conforms to the American Society of Mechanical Engineers code for unfired pressure vessels of 150 lbs. per sq. in. In mounting the machine shown in the photographs a welded steel base and mounting plate were used. However, for those who do not have access to welding and cutting equipment, the arrangement shown in Fig. 6 will hold the parts equally as well. Two $\frac{3}{8}$-in.-dia. rods threaded on both ends encircle the tank and anchor it to the lower cross members. The four pipe spacers all should be the same length and slightly undersize so the cross members will clamp the tank securely. The motor and compressor then are mounted on the baseboard which is bolted to the upper cross members. The compressor intake is piped with a 90-deg. elbow turned toward the cylinder wall as indicated in Figs. 6 and 8 to prevent clothing or hands coming in contact with the intake opening when the machine is running. Although not shown in the photos, the input line to the tank should be of high-pressure tubing coiled as shown in Fig. 6. This will cool the air before it reaches the tank and avoid fracture of the line due to vibration. A check valve permits air to pass through in the direction indicated by the arrows in Figs. 6 and 8 and prevents the air in the tank from escaping through the compressor when it is not running. The adjustable pressure switch shuts off the motor when the desired pressure has been reached. A safety valve is a must and can be connected to the tank in any convenient outlet. If the compressor is to be used for paint spraying, an air filter should be installed in the outlet line to remove any water, oil or dirt that would contaminate the paint. A pressure gauge, globe valve and air regulator with pressure gauge then are

fitted to the outlet line. All of the parts are standard and may be purchased in whatever types and sizes are needed to suit the requirements of the builder.

The piping arrangement shown in Fig. 6 need not necessarily be followed; however,

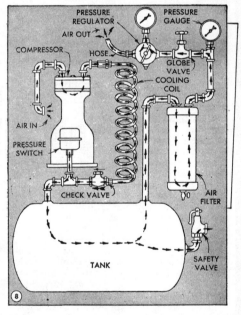

PRESSURE REGULATOR   PRESSURE GAUGE
AIR OUT
COMPRESSOR   HOSE   GLOBE VALVE
   COOLING COIL
AIR IN
PRESSURE SWITCH
   AIR FILTER
CHECK VALVE
TANK   SAFETY VALVE
(8)

it is important that the relative position of the various parts be similar to that indicated in Fig. 8.

As a safety measure when the compressor and air-driven equipment are not in use, close the globe valve, loosen the thumbscrew of the pressure regulator and drain off the air in the line until the gauge on the regulator drops to zero.

AIR CONDITIONING YOUR HOME

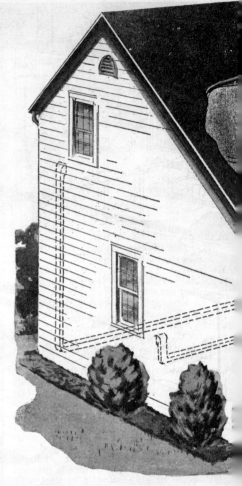

HOME AIR CONDITIONING is not "just around the corner," it is here in neat, packaged units available to any home-owner at a cost that approximates the cost of a forced-air furnace. This cost is for the unit alone, exclusive of installation. If, at first thought, an expenditure of this size seems rather high just to be cool on a few hot days during the summer months, consider the advantages of air conditioning which are much more than mere cooling. It enables you to keep your home closed and thus exclude dust and noise—an important consideration if you live in an industrial area. It controls humidity which, when excessive, is an enemy of health and home. Excessively high humidity not only aggravates certain human ailments, but it damages stored clothing, rusts metal parts and causes expansion and contraction of wooden parts which result in warped timbers and cracked plaster, as well as floor boards that spread or buckle at the joints.

In addition to its advantages, air conditioning floods your home with clean filtered air that reduces the misery of persons suffering from hay fever and other respiratory conditions caused by foreign matter in the air.

With these and many other advantages it can provide, air conditioning is rapidly becoming as much a part of the home as the heating plant or running water. In fact, many manufacturers are going into production of small year-round air-conditioning units. These range in size from 1 ton upward and consist of a forced-air furnace and an air conditioner individually packaged, but made to match so they can be used separately or as a unit. In this way, the furnace unit may be installed and the air-conditioning unit added later to produce a neat combination that takes little floor space. However, the conditioning unit may be added to any existing forced-air furnace.

In the belief that the small units could be installed in the average home by the owner himself, the Craftsman editors of *Popular Mechanics* commissioned a young couple, Mr. and Mrs. Henry Windsor III, to do the job themselves. Their home is pictured in cutaway view showing the original furnace and duct system. While this home is slightly larger than the average, being a story and a half and containing approximately 1500 sq. ft. of floor space as com-

pared to approximately 1100 for the average five-room home, it was typical in that it was several years old and had a forced-air heating system of the general type that could be found in thousands of homes over the country.

After consulting with air-conditioning engineers of General Electric Co., the Windsors (Hank and Mary) learned that the job would be relatively simple. Briefly, the job would amount to connecting the unit into one side of their furnace and into the furnace-duct system; running 220-volt current to the compressor motor of the unit and a water line to and from the compressor to cool it. There are many air-conditioning units on the market from which to choose. Hank and Mary picked the General Electric because it was small in size, took little floor space and seemed to fit their needs perfectly.

The next step was to obtain the correct

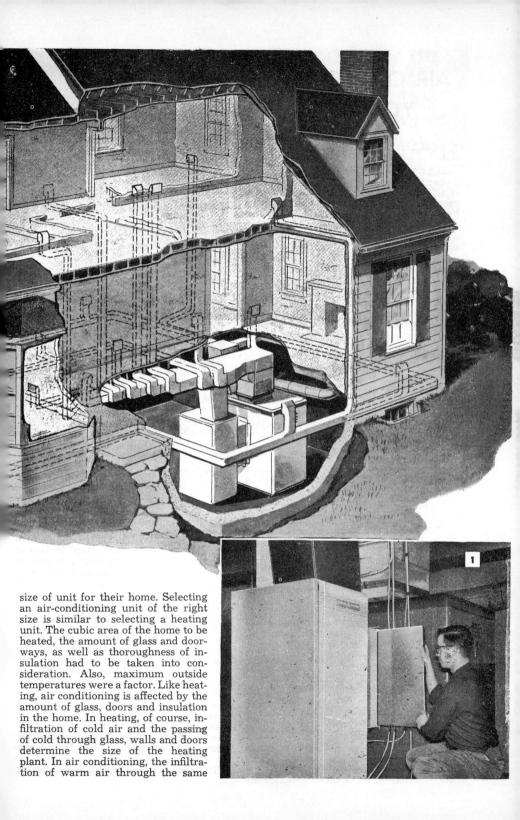

size of unit for their home. Selecting an air-conditioning unit of the right size is similar to selecting a heating unit. The cubic area of the home to be heated, the amount of glass and doorways, as well as thoroughness of insulation had to be taken into consideration. Also, maximum outside temperatures were a factor. Like heating, air conditioning is affected by the amount of glass, doors and insulation in the home. In heating, of course, infiltration of cold air and the passing of cold through glass, walls and doors determine the size of the heating plant. In air conditioning, the infiltration of warm air through the same

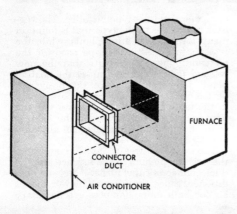

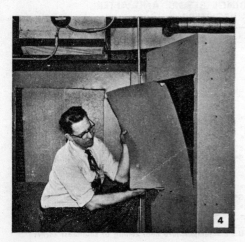

sources determines the size of the air conditioner. Since sizing the unit is rather complicated for the average person, although it is very important in industrial installations where large air volumes are dealt with, Hank learned that engineers had simplified sizing for homes by taking averages and building the units accordingly. In other words, if you had an average four or five-room home with average insulation, a 1 or 1½-ton unit would do. For a six or seven-room home, a 1½ or 2-ton unit would do the job. If you live in a climate having hotter and longer summers than the Chicago area, it likely would be necessary to increase the above sizes slightly. Your local air-conditioner dealer can aid you in picking the correct size. It is better to have the unit slightly undersized than oversized. If it is oversized, the air passing over the cooling coils will not keep their temperature high enough to prevent ice

FURNACE

CONNECTOR DUCT

AIR CONDITIONER

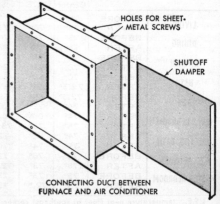

HOLES FOR SHEET-METAL SCREWS

SHUTOFF DAMPER

CONNECTING DUCT BETWEEN
FURNACE AND AIR CONDITIONER

forming on the coils. Hank found that a 2-ton unit would handle his home, which had the usual number of windows and doors for a house of that size.

Hank and Mary were now ready to go to work. They started with the register faces.

Existing registers were at floor level and shot the air straight out into the rooms. In order to get the air to rise, the register faces were replaced with a type that direct the air upward and to the sides. In other words, it blanketed the wall with cool air which was driven to the ceiling where it spread and fell to the floor. In this way, the room was cooled without evidence of drafts on the occupants. Figs. 2 and 3 show the type of registers used for the original equipment and the type installed. The register in Fig. 3 is of the type that is found in many forced-air heating plants, while the register in Fig. 2 is the type used for the air conditioner. To be sure that the new register faces would not upset the heating plant, temperatures were taken over a period of time as a check. These are shown in the table of Fig. 8. As you can see, the new registers even improved the heating of the home and distributed cool air without drafts.

The next step was to install dampers in the existing plenum of the furnace and the duct connecting the furnace and air conditioner. Since the furnace blower moves air for both units, dampers are necessary

8 **ROOM-TEMPERATURE READINGS BEFORE AND AFTER CHANGING REGISTERS**

		Center	L.S.E.	L.S.W.	L.N.W.	L.N.E.	U.S.W.	U.S.E.	U.N.W.	U.N.E.
LIVING	BEFORE	75°	75°	74°	74°	74°	78°	78°	78°	78°
	AFTER	75°	70°	71°	71°	71°	75°	75°	75°	75°
DINING	BEFORE	75°	74°	74°	73°	73°	76°	76°	75.5°	75.5°
	AFTER	76°	72°	72°	70°	70°	75°	75°	75°	75°
KITCHEN	BEFORE	76°	72°	72.5°	73°	72.5°	76°	76°	76.5°	76.5°
	AFTER	78°	73°	74°	71°	72°	77°	79°	78°	78°
BATH	BEFORE	70°	68°	68°	68°	68°	72°	72°	72°	72°
	AFTER	72.5°	67°	67°	67°	67°	74°	74°	74°	74°
DEN	BEFORE	72.5°	69°	69°	68°	68°	73.5°	73°	74°	74°
	AFTER	74°	72°	70°	70°	70°	77°	77°	74°	74°
N.W. BEDROOM	BEFORE	74°	70.5°	70.5°	70°	72.5°	74.5°	74.5°	74°	74°
	AFTER	75°	73°	73.5°	72°	75°	75°	75°	75°	75°
UPSTAIRS BATH	BEFORE	74°	72°	72°	72°	72°	76°	76°	76°	76°
	AFTER	79°	74°	74°	74°	74°	79°	79°	79°	79°
N.E. BEDROOM	BEFORE	72°	70°	72°	70°	70°	73°	72°	72°	72°
	AFTER	75°	73°	72.5°	73°	73°	76°	76°	77°	76°
MASTER BEDROOM	BEFORE	75°	73°	73°	73°	73°	75°	75°	76°	75.5°
	AFTER	75°	72.5°	73°	72°	75°	75°	75°	75°	75°

L.S.E.=temperature near floor at southeast corner. U.S.E.=temperature near ceiling at southeast corner

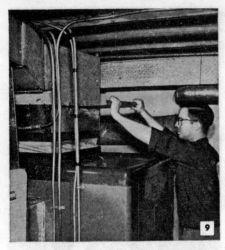

Above, Hank tests slide damper in plenum preparatory to starting up air-conditioning unit. Damper is part of sheet-metal unit shown in the detail below

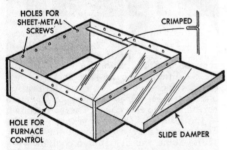

HOLES FOR SHEET-METAL SCREWS

CRIMPED

HOLE FOR FURNACE CONTROL

SLIDE DAMPER

Below, Mary lends a hand by driving sheet-metal screws to attach damper unit in plenum while Hank drills the pilot holes. Mary found many jobs on the project when Hank needed more than two hands

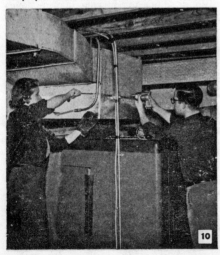

to control the flow of air through both the conditioner and furnace. The connector duct between the furnace and air conditioner is shown in details above Fig. 4 and to the right of it. This is made of sheet metal and fits over openings which you cut in the side of the conditioning unit and the furnace as pictured in Fig. 4. The duct can be made at your local sheet-metal shop. When you cut through the outer casing of the furnace, another casing, or baffle, will be exposed which also must be cut through. Be sure to cut the opening into the delivery section of the furnace, which is the section where the air is forced into the duct system.

Size of the connector duct will be determined by the size of the plenum that delivers air into the ducts. It should be of equal size or a little larger than the plenum if possible. The opening in the air conditioner is cut in the side next to the cooling coils so that when the air is forced from the furnace into the cooling unit it will pass over the coils and out the top of the unit to the duct system. Positioning of the opening in the unit will vary with different makes of units. In the General Electric unit, it was cut and positioned as shown in Fig. 4. As you can see in the details, the damper in the connector duct is nothing more than a piece of sheet metal that slides into a slot at one side of the duct to completely close the opening. This damper prevents air from passing through the cooling unit when the furnace is being operated.

In order to prevent flow of air through the plenum and into the duct system, thus bypassing the conditioner when it is in use, a damper similar to the one in the connector is installed in the plenum. To do this it will be necessary to cut a section from the lower end of the plenum and replace it with a connector similar to the one shown below Fig. 9. This connector also is made of sheet metal and is fitted with a slide. Fig. 10 shows the installation. Here Mary drives the sheet-metal screws while Hank drills the pilot holes.

The next step is to connect the conditioner into the duct system. This requires cutting an opening in the main duct as close to the furnace as possible and directly above the conditioner. This opening is shown in Figs. 6 and 7. A large sheet-metal duct is then connected between the opening and the top of the air-conditioning unit from which the cold air is exhausted. Shape and size of the duct will vary with different types of conditioners and different installations. However, the idea is to get a duct running from the top or exhaust part of the conditioner into the duct system, being sure the connection is made between the furnace and any branch ducts taking off from the main one. If you have ducts going in different directions directly from the plenum, it will be necessary to provide a duct to direct the air into the plenum above the shutoff damper.

Once all of these connections are made, you are ready to run a water line to the compressor of the conditioner to cool it, or carry away the heat absorbed from the house by the air being blown over the cooling coils. Most home air-conditioning units are water cooled, although some are now being manufactured to be cooled by air. Fig. 11 shows how the water line is connected into an existing water line in the basement. The new water line can be copper tubing or pipe, preferably copper tubing since it is much easier to install. Fig. 12 shows how the line comes in at one side of the conditioner housing and connects to the compressor. An exhaust line for the water is also connected at the compressor and then carried to a drain.

Since an air conditioner has a 1-hp. or larger motor, it will be necessary to use a 220-volt circuit in the house. If you do not already have this, one will have to be provided. Hank already had 220-volt current and had a friend who was an electrician install a circuit as in Fig. 15. Fig. 14 shows the wiring system. This may vary somewhat with various installations but, in general, you can follow the one shown. Likely, it will be necessary for an electrician to run the line and make the connections to the unit for you. Fig. 5 shows the original furnace-stack switch relocated and rewired to operate both units. Fig. 13 shows the two thermostats that are necessary.

With the job completed, Hank readies the conditioner for a test run by pulling the damper in the connecting duct, Fig. 1, and closing the one in the plenum.

Connecting the copper water line to the cooling unit into an existing water line in the basement

Above, copper water line being connected to the compressor. Below, 220-volt line to operate compressor is being connected into service fuse box of home

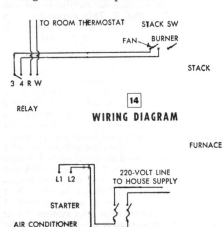

AIRFILTERS—WINDOW

NO matter where you live, an open window anywhere in the house lets in all kinds of airborne dust, soot and plant pollens. Homemakers, always beset with the dust problem, and especially hay-fever sufferers and those confined to the sickroom will appreciate these efficient air filters which use filtering units of the spunglass and honeycombed fiber type. They are easily made to fit in any double-hung window. The first type, detailed in Figs. 1 to 4 inclusive, is fitted with an electric fan and three spun-glass filter units of the type used in warm-air heating plants equipped with circulators. The fan is hooded for greater efficiency and is housed in a neat cabinet which projects only a few inches

beyond the window stool inside the room. Since the filter units come in standard sizes it's a good idea to have these at hand before you make the cabinet. Width of the filter units must be less than the width of the window. Also, it should be noted that dimensions given in Fig. 3 are only suggestions. They must be altered to suit the window frame and the fan and filter units at hand. The cabinet should be made of material that can be finished to match the woodwork. Birch plywood in ½-in. thickness is a good choice as it can be painted or stained and varnished to match almost any interior finish. However, for a painted finish, ½-in. fir plywood will do very well.

First, measure the window to determine

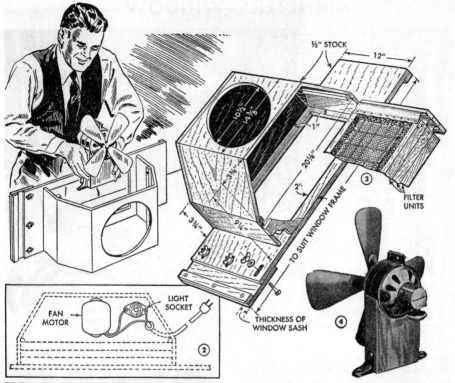

½" STOCK
12"
1"
10½"
14⅜"
3⅝"
20⅛"
2"
3¾"
9¼"
③
FILTER UNITS
TO SUIT WINDOW FRAME
THICKNESS OF WINDOW SASH
④

FAN MOTOR
LIGHT SOCKET
②

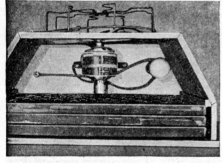

the length of the panel that fits under the raised sash. This measurement should be the same as the width of the lower sash. Note that this panel is made in two parts with a width adjustment so that it can be set in the opening between the inside sash stops and then widened to fit snugly in the sash grooves and against the pulley stiles. The extension piece, Fig. 3, is held in place with three small bolts which pass through slots cut in both members as shown. Wing nuts are used to provide a quick and easy adjustment. The outer ends of both members are built out to the thickness of the sash with cleats so that they fit snugly in

the sash grooves. The panel should be about 4 in. wider than the filter unit, and the opening should be about 1 in. smaller each way than the overall size of the unit. This provides a ledge or stop against which the outer unit fits when the cabinet is assembled. See Fig. 3.

Building the five-sided fan housing is mostly a matter of getting the angle joints cut to fit properly. If you don't have a circular saw, the best way to do this is to make the cuts outside the dimension lines with a handsaw and then finish with a plane to a perfect fit. The circular opening in the front member should be about ½ in. larger in diameter than the circle described by the fan blades. The opening can be covered by a fine-meshed wire grille or with the wire guard which is removed from the fan. Usually the guard is just about the right size and makes an attractive finishing detail as well as affording protection from the whirling fan blades. Generally it is necessary to alter the fan unit by removing the regular base and substituting another sawed from hardwood as in Fig. 4. Two sheet-metal compression bands, tightened with stove bolts, are used to hold the motor in place on the wooden base. This is anchored to the bottom of the cabinet with

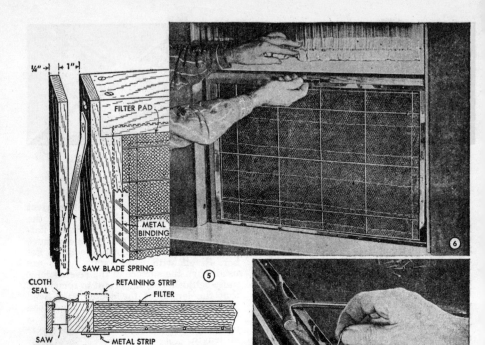

FILTER PAD

METAL BINDING

SAW BLADE SPRING

CLOTH SEAL

RETAINING STRIP

FILTER

SAW BLADE

METAL STRIP

two small steel angles as indicated. If a heavy rubber band cut from an inner tube is slipped over the motor frame before clamping it in place, the fan will be practically noiseless, and if you want a constant-speed fan to run slower than its normal speed, you can connect a porcelain light socket in the motor circuit as in Fig. 2. A 60-watt lamp in the socket will reduce the speed of a universal-type fan motor sufficiently for the purpose. The completed cabinet should have a snug-fitting cover.

Another type of air filter, detailed in Figs. 5 to 8 inclusive, utilizes the less expensive honeycombed fiber filter unit or pad. This comes in standard sizes, usually 2 by 16 by 20 in., 2 by 16 by 25 in. and 2 by 20 by 20 in. overall. The 25-in. length can be framed to fit nicely in the average window frame. Fig. 5 suggests one way of framing the filter unit so that it will be dust-tight yet can be removed easily. Note in Figs. 5 and 8 that a strip of cloth covers the space between the spring-mounted strips and the frame, thus forming an effective seal. The spring-mounted strip allows the assembled unit to be telescoped slightly so that it can be inserted in the window frame past the inside sash stops. The springs can be made from hacksaw blades, although any flat spring of sufficient strength will do. The inside of the frame is finished with linoleum seam binding as in Fig. 7. The

filter unit bears against a retaining strip screwed to the outside of the wood frame as in the lower detail, Fig. 5. A small metal handle attached to the top of the unit aids in removal. Where the unit is left in the window throughout the season it's a good idea to provide a cover to prevent driving rain from entering the filters. A strip of sheet metal screwed to the top member of the frame will serve this purpose. It should be about 4 in. wide and 1 in. shorter than the frame and should be bent down at an angle so that it sheds the water. Paint the metal strip to match the trim color.

ALUMINUM RIVETING

RIVETING aluminum sheets, either in factory production or in the home workshop, requires a specific procedure to produce maximum strength in the joint without any distortion of the material. In nearly all types of work the rivet pattern, Fig. 1, is important not only for decorative effect but for resistance to shearing or buckling of the joint. The type of rivet to be used is selected according to the nature of the work and the type of joint which is most suitable to the project in hand. The four rivet types shown in Fig. 2 will meet all ordinary requirements. If decorative value is a factor in the selection, then the round-headed and also the brazier-headed rivets usually are best. Use the round-headed type to join the heavier sheets where greater strength is required. The size and thickness of metal in the head is designed to strengthen the area around the rivet hole. When thin sheets are to be joined, a brazier-headed rivet is the one to use as its broad head gives a maximum grip on the

area surrounding the rivet hole. In places where the structural members are a close fit, the flat-headed rivet provides that extra clearance so often needed for bucking with a flat bar. Rivets with countersunk heads are used when the surface of the riveted joint must be flush. It is important to remember that the length of the countersunk-head rivet is measured from the top of the head while in all the others the rivet length is the length of the shank and not the overall length.

The length of the rivet in relation to the thickness of the work is illustrated in Fig. 3. Approved practice requires that when the head of the rivet is seated, the projection of the shank below the lower, or inside, surface of the metal should be 1½ times the diameter of the shank before upsetting, as in the right-hand detail, Fig. 3. In ordinary practice the rivet hole is made the same diameter as the rivet shank to give a very light press fit, but in production fabrication some specifications call for

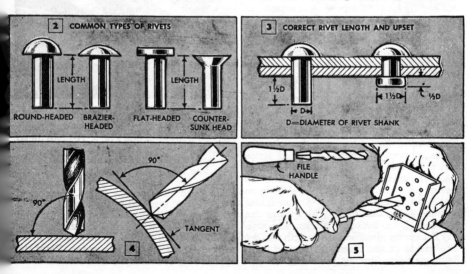

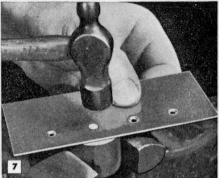

Rivets on dimples are upset in the usual manner. A rivet of the same size can be used as a dimpling die

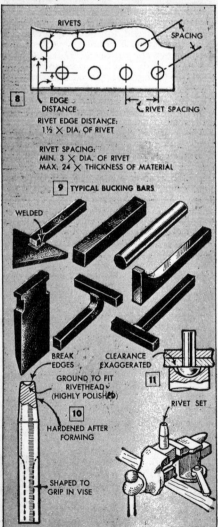

RIVETS

SPACING

8

EDGE DISTANCE

RIVET SPACING

RIVET EDGE DISTANCE: 1½ X DIA. OF RIVET

RIVET SPACING:
MIN. 3 X DIA. OF RIVET
MAX. 24 X THICKNESS OF MATERIAL

9 TYPICAL BUCKING BARS

WELDED

BREAK EDGES

CLEARANCE EXAGGERATED

GROUND TO FIT RIVETHEAD (HIGHLY POLISHED)

11

RIVET SET

10

HARDENED AFTER FORMING

SHAPED TO GRIP IN VISE

slight variations. In any case, the hole should be drilled with care to avoid undue burring. Be sure that the drill bit is properly sharpened for drilling aluminum. In breaking the hole through, care should be taken that the drill chuck does not spin against the metal surface and score it. After drilling, all holes are burred. In the small shop, this can be done with a burring tool made from an old square-shanked drill bit fitted into a file handle, Fig. 5. Be especially careful when burring thin metal to avoid depressing the metal around the hole. Good practice demands that, where the joints require a line of rivets, the holes be drilled in a precise pattern as in Fig. 8. Angle of the drill with the work, Fig. 4, should be uniform when drilling a series of holes. Both the lengthwise spacing and the edge spacing should be laid out to exact dimensions. If there are two lines of rivets, the holes are staggered and the lines are accurately spaced.

When riveting guns are used, the shank of the rivet is upset with a bucking bar, or dolly, Fig. 9. In some kinds of work, the bar also is used to bear on the head of the rivet while the shank is upset with a hammer. Bucking bars usually are made up in the shape required. In handwork, using round-headed rivets, the rivet set, or anvil, is used when upsetting. One end of the set is tapered as in Fig. 10 and the end is recessed to a radius slightly greater than that of the rivethead. This is done to give a clearance as in Fig. 11. Break the edges at the recessed end with a light beveling cut while the work is still in the lathe. The straight end of the rivet set can be shaped as in Fig. 10 so that it can be gripped in a vise or fitted in a hole drilled in a steel block as in the right-hand detail, Fig. 10 When using the set, be sure to hold the work square, otherwise the edges of the set may mar the work. Flat-headed and countersunk rivets can be upset neatly on any

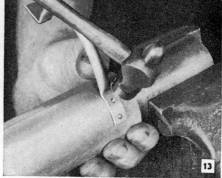

Automatic countersink assures uniform work. Tubing is riveted over a round bucking bar held in the vise

flat metal surface, but to assure that the rivethead will be flush after upsetting, it is necessary that the parts of the work be held tightly together. In order that countersunk rivets shall be perfectly flush when upset, it is necessary that the holes be countersunk to a uniform depth. Fig. 12 shows an automatic countersink in use. It is held in a drill chuck and can be set to countersink with exact uniformity at any average depth. Countersinking by hand will be less uniform of course, but with care it can be done with sufficient accuracy. In handwork, the tendency is to run the countersink too deep. When this happens, drill a hole in a small piece of steel and countersink it slightly undersize. Then spread the rivethead as shown in Fig. 15 so that it will fill the countersink flush when the shank is upset. When using rivets with countersunk heads on thin material where the depth of the head will not permit countersinking the metal, the rivet holes are drilled and then the two thicknesses of metal are dimpled as in Figs. 16 and 17. Make a dimpling bar by drilling a rivet-sized hole in a piece of round steel. Countersink the hole and break the edge, as indicated in Fig. 16, by simply beveling the edge slightly with a large drill bit held in the hand. Then use a rivet as a dimpling die as in Fig. 7. Burr the dimples lightly on one sheet only and when joining the work upset the rivets on the dimples as in Fig. 6.

Fig. 14 pictures the most common faults in riveting thin material. Although any one of these will produce a poor and unsightly job, the most frequent errors are in drilling holes oversize, using too short or too long a rivet and, on round work, Fig. 13, tending to upset the rivet too flat. For better results some riveters round the upset slightly on this type of work.

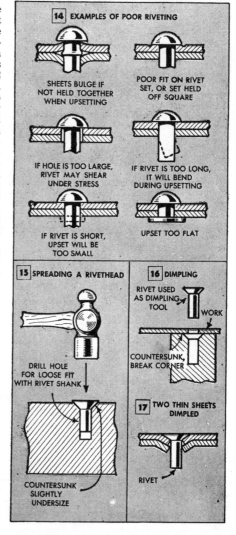

14 EXAMPLES OF POOR RIVETING

SHEETS BULGE IF NOT HELD TOGETHER WHEN UPSETTING

POOR FIT ON RIVET SET, OR SET HELD OFF SQUARE

IF HOLE IS TOO LARGE, RIVET MAY SHEAR UNDER STRESS

IF RIVET IS TOO LONG, IT WILL BEND DURING UPSETTING

IF RIVET IS SHORT, UPSET WILL BE TOO SMALL

UPSET TOO FLAT

15 SPREADING A RIVETHEAD

DRILL HOLE FOR LOOSE FIT WITH RIVET SHANK

COUNTERSUNK SLIGHTLY UNDERSIZE

16 DIMPLING

RIVET USED AS DIMPLING TOOL

WORK

COUNTERSUNK, BREAK CORNER

17 TWO THIN SHEETS DIMPLED

RIVET

ALUMINUM TUBING

ALUMINUM tubing is an excellent medium for quickly made, attractive projects. It is easy to work, readily available and inexpensive. Any one of these eye-catching items can be made in an evening.

An important thing to remember when working with aluminum tubing is to cut the end of the tubing perfectly square. This can be done by using a hose clamp as a marking guide, Fig. 4, cutting the tubing with a hacksaw and filing it to the guide line. If the aluminum is free from scratches, fine steel wool lubricated with a light oil will result in a good finish. Otherwise, use emery paper first and then finish with the steel wool. A fine "chrome" finish is obtained by buffing, and a satin finish may be put on

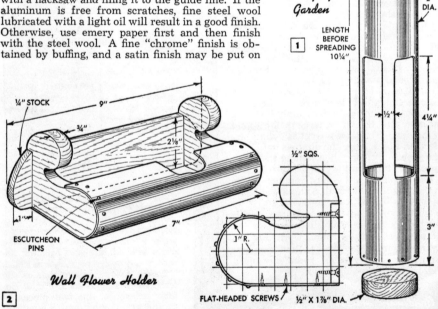

½"

½"

½"

Hanging Garden

1

LENGTH BEFORE SPREADING 10¼"

2" DIA.

½"

4¼"

3"

½" X 1⅞" DIA.

¼" STOCK

9"

¾"

2⅛"

½" SQS.

1" R.

1"

ESCUTCHEON PINS

7"

Wall Flower Holder

2

FLAT-HEADED SCREWS

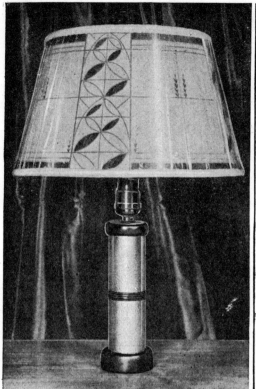

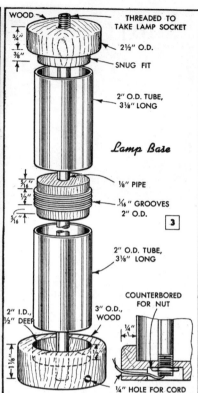

Lamp Base

WOOD

THREADED TO TAKE LAMP SOCKET

2½" O.D.

SNUG FIT

2" O.D. TUBE, 3⅛" LONG

⅛" PIPE

⅟₁₆" GROOVES
2" O.D.

3

2" O.D. TUBE, 3⅛" LONG

COUNTERBORED FOR NUT

2" I.D., ½" DEEP

3" O.D., WOOD

¼" HOLE FOR CORD

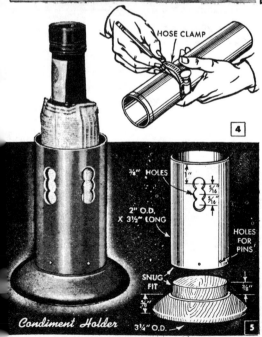

HOSE CLAMP

4

⅜" HOLES   1"
    ⁵⁄₁₆
    ⁵⁄₁₆

2" O.D.
X 3½" LONG

HOLES FOR PINS

SNUG FIT   ⅜"

Condiment Holder   3¼" O.D.   **5**

the tubing by using a wire brush.

Hanging garden: The tubing is cut to length and then cut out at the center as in Fig. 1. This can be done by drilling a hole in each corner of the cutout and sawing the tubing with a narrow hacksaw blade. Another way of cutting the openings is to slide the tubing over a piece of pipe and cut along the scribed lines with a small cold chisel. After this, the edges are smoothed with a fine file and the ribs in the cutout portion bent outward as shown in the photo. The wooden parts are turned, finished and attached to the tubing with escutcheon pins.

Wall flower holder: In this case, the tubing is slit lengthwise with a hacksaw. Then, approximately half the circumference is flattened by prying open the slit and hammering with a mallet. After the wooden parts are cut out and finished, the unit is assembled as shown in Fig. 2.

Lamp base: Construction of the lamp base is detailed in Fig. 3. Before assembly, the two pieces of tubing are slipped over a length of

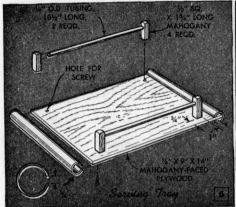

Attractive serving tray combines aluminum tubing with mahogany. Tubing is used to raise ends of tray and to provide decorative guardrails

bar stock or a piece of pipe and hammered with the rounded end of a ball-peen hammer. Wooden parts are turned carefully to size so the tubes fit them tightly. Note that the upper end of the ⅛-in. pipe is threaded for the lamp socket, and that the lower end is threaded for a nut which holds the assembly to the base. The bottom turning can be made larger or weighted with lead.

Condiment holder: The decorative holes in the sides of the tubing, Fig. 5, are drilled with a ⅜-in. bit and the wooden base is attached with escutcheon pins. The top edge of the tubing may be scalloped.

Serving tray: The tray, pictured in Fig. 7, is made as shown in Fig. 6. The lengths of

1-in. tubing used as endpieces are slotted to take the ends of the tray. This can be done by slitting the tubing and prying it apart ³⁄₁₆ in. to fit tightly over the ¼-in. plywood. An easy way to slit the tubing is to break off the ends of a hacksaw blade and mount it in a block of wood. The tubing is held against a wooden strip which guides the block and the blade is run back and forth along the top of the tubing. A brad driven at each end of the tubing will keep it from sliding and the fingers keep it from rolling. Four posts, drilled to take the rails, are fastened to the tray with countersunk flat-headed screws. Varnish all wooden parts.

ANDIRONS

Here's an attractive fireplace grate that differs from the ordinary in that both grate and andirons are all in one. It's primarily for holding logs, although it can be adapted for burning coal by placing a grille, such as a piece of expanded metal lath, over the bottom. All the parts can be hand-wrought cold from stock pieces of ¼-in. flat iron. The dimensions given in the drawing may have to be altered to suit the size of the fire pit. A machinist's vise will aid in making the sharp right-angle bends of the bed pieces, while the curved bends can be formed by working the pieces through the jaws of a monkey wrench. This is done with a slight sideward thrust as the metal is advanced through the jaws. In the case of the 3-in. pieces, the ends can be curved by clamping the work vertically in the vise, allowing about 4 in. to extend, and then grasping the end with an adjustable wrench. If necessary, a length of pipe slipped over the wrench handle will provide good leverage. All parts are riveted together. The andirons and the connecting horizontal pieces can be given a hammered finish, or the whole unit can be given a coat of flat black paint.

BUTT JOINTS

2"
2 7/16"

55°
35°

TYPICAL 4-SIDE 35° FIGURE

It's not what it seems!

TRUE HEIGHT 2 7/16"

TRUE HEIGHT IS SEEN WHEN SIDE IS ERECTED. ERECT POSITION ALSO SHOWS TRUE MITER ANGLE

TRUE MITER

60°

ERECT VIEW

FRONT VIEW

JOINTS 90° WHEN VIEWED FROM TOP

VIEWED IN TRUE PLANE, "SQUARE" CORNER IS SEEN TO BE LESS THAN 90°

ANGLE CUTTING

Now FOR SOMETHING ELSE that will demonstrate the versatility of the homeshop circular saw. Pictured on these pages are three projects—picture frame, console tabletop and colony birdhouse—all of which require variations of compound-angle joinery in their construction. When parts were joined to form four-sided units like the picture frame and the edging around the tabletop, oldtime cabinetmakers often called the corners "hopper" joints. Of course, this term does not include all types of compound miters, and moreover, these two projects feature only the simplest forms of the compound miter. Just take a look at the birdhouse roof. With only hand tools to work with this would be about the crankiest job in all woodworking joinery, but with a power saw fitted with tilt and miter-gauge scales graduated in degrees, it's a cinch. Naturally, to make the roof parts to a given size you must know the overall size of the structure the roof is to fit, but once the exact size of each part is known, the rest is easy. On the particular job pictured the miter gauge was set to 14 degrees and the saw table (or arbor) was tilted to 19 degrees. If you are careful in the measurements and in the setting of the saw, the pieces will fit together snugly.

A table of tilt and miter-gauge settings for compound-angle cutting on the circular saw will be found on pagefollowingthat with work angles ranging from 5 to 60 degrees, the table gives the angle settings for a 4-sided butt-joined unit, a 4-sided miter-joined unit, also for 6 and 8-sided miter-joined units. If you'd like to do a little experimenting on waste stock, begin with the 4-sided butt-joined figure and work it out through the various settings, from say, 5 to 45 degrees. You'll discover that work angles above 45 degrees seldom find practical applications but that the lesser angles are frequently used.

An example is the picture frame already referred

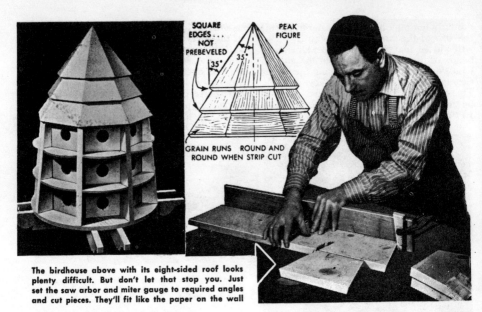

SQUARE EDGES... NOT PREBEVELED

PEAK FIGURE

35° 35°

GRAIN RUNS ROUND AND ROUND WHEN STRIP CUT

The birdhouse above with its eight-sided roof looks plenty difficult. But don't let that stop you. Just set the saw arbor and miter gauge to required angles and cut pieces. They'll fit like the paper on the wall

to. This is an extremely popular type of frame and is made in a wide range of sizes, using both wide and narrow molds and also flat stock like the sample pictured. Such frames are difficult to join at the corners with nails, or brads, in the regular way without making a special nailing jig. However, new quick-setting adhesives make it possible to join such a frame without use of either nails or clamps, provided, of course, the parts are small enough to be handled easily. In the upper right-hand photo and also in the two photos directly below, methods of cutting the parts for the birdhouse roof are shown quite clearly. Note in the lower photo of the three that the miter gauge is reversed in the groove. Keep this trick in mind, as it comes in handy when you have to crosscut wide stock on a small machine table. Another thing to note here is the height of the saw blade in relation to the thickness of the stock. In ripping, bevel ripping, or in bevel crosscutting as is shown here, always lower the blade so that the teeth just cut through the stock and no more. This is not only the safest position for the blade when you must work close to it, but makes for better work in ripping cuts as the blade is less subjected to twisting strains. Also, less dust is thrown on top of the machine table when the blade is operated in this position, as the teeth of the blade coming up through the table slot are covered by the stock.

In the details and the photo you see methods of joining the four-sided hopper by means of rabbeted joints A and B, and also how the same joint is miter-

FEED

FEED

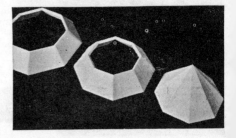

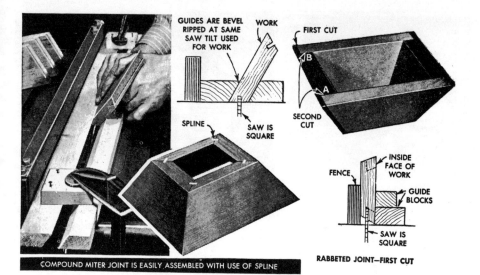

GUIDES ARE BEVEL RIPPED AT SAME SAW TILT USED FOR WORK

WORK

SPLINE

SAW IS SQUARE

FIRST CUT

B

A

SECOND CUT

INSIDE FACE OF WORK

FENCE

GUIDE BLOCKS

SAW IS SQUARE

RABBETED JOINT—FIRST CUT

COMPOUND MITER JOINT IS EASILY ASSEMBLED WITH USE OF SPLINE

joined and splined. Remember the splined joint pictured on previous page. Here it comes again in a different application. The photo at the left and also the upper center detail show how the spline groove is cut with the saw blade. Note that the blade is square with the table—only the stock is tilted in relation to the table surface. Although not essential on straight work, a jig like that pictured will aid accuracy in cutting spline grooves. Otherwise the angle corner of the stock must ride against the lower edge of the ripping fence, which is never flush with the machine tabletop. The slight space between the lower edge of the fence and the table is a necessary allowance for free movement of the fence. The guide members of the jig are ripped from 1⅛-in. stock to support the work firmly and hold it at the correct angle.

TILT AND MITER-GAUGE SETTINGS FOR COMPOUND ANGLES

FRONT VIEW

ANGLE

	4 Sides Butt Joint		4 Sides Miter Joint		6 Sides Miter Joint		8 Sides Miter Joint	
Work Angle	Tilt Table	Miter Gauge	Tilt Table	Miter Gauge	Tilt Table	Miter Gauge	Tilt Table	Miter Gauge
5°	½	85	44¾	85	29¾	87½	22¼	88
10°	1½	80¼	44¼	80¼	29½	84½	22	86
15°	3¾	75½	43¼	75½	29	81¾	21½	84
20°	6¼	71	42	71	28¼	79	21	82
25°	10	67	40	67	27¼	76½	20¼	80
30°	14½	63½	37¾	63½	26	74	19¼	78¼
35°	19½	60¼	35¼	60¼	24½	71¾	18¼	76¾
40°	24½	57¼	32¾	57¼	22¾	69¾	17	75
45°	30	54¾	30	54¾	21	67¾	15¾	73¾
50°	36	52½	27	52½	19	66¼	14¼	72½
55°	42	50¾	24	50¾	16¾	64¾	12¾	71¼
60°	48	49	21	49	14½	63½	11	70¼

FIGURES ARE IN DEGREES AND ARE FOR DIRECT SETTING TO TILT SCALE AND MITER GAUGE. SCALE PROVIDING TILT STARTS AT 0° AND MITER GAUGE AT 90° IN NORMAL POSITION.

Slip-feathering mitered frames makes the mitered joints stronger than the wood itself. The two illustrations above show how simple this job becomes when you use a tenoning jig on your circular saw. Use hardwood slips

Other methods of making splined joints with a tenoning jig are shown in Figs. 30 to 32 inclusive. In Fig. 32 the spline groove is being cut across the full length of the joint face, while in Fig. 30 the groove is being cut across the corner of the assembled joint. In Fig. 30 the assembled frame is held against a block by means of the clamp screw which is a part of the tenoning jig, but notice in Fig. 31 that the assembled frame is being supported in a separate corner block which is built up from two pieces. Note also that the clamp screw bears on the mitered frame and holds the whole assembly in place while the cut is run. This latter method is somewhat more accurate and is especially effective when handling large frames. Although the method is similar to that used in cutting full-length spline grooves, the corner-splining method does not produce a true splined joint, but rather what is more properly called a keyed miter joint, or slip-feather joint.

Slip-feathered joints have a number of practical applications, a random example of which is an old-style steeple-clock case. In handling such a job, first make a trial assembly to make sure that the angle joints fit correctly. Then assemble the case in an improvised jig, using a quick-setting glue in all angle joints (miter joints). After the glue has set (30 to 60 seconds) slip-feather the joints at the peak and at the shoulder miters. After setting the feathers in the grooves sand the feathers flush preparatory to finishing the wood. The joints will be stronger than the wood itself. Fig. 33 shows a good method of clamping splined and

Splining is similar to slip-feathering except that the groove is run across the edge, or stopped as shown

This is a sure way to clamp a mitered frame. Set the corner blocks right and draw up lightly on bench vise

slip-feathered joints in a frame assembled with 45-degree miters. Of course, you wouldn't do this to a good bench top but it's easy to improvise a frame on the bench top to hold the corner blocks.

Three kinds of angles

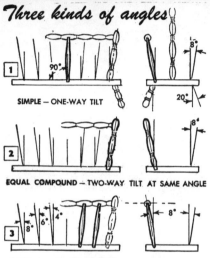

1 90°

SIMPLE — ONE-WAY TILT

8°

20°

2

EQUAL COMPOUND — TWO-WAY TILT AT SAME ANGLE

8°

3 8° 6° 4°

8°

UNEQUAL COMPOUND - TWO-WAY TILT, DIFFERENT ANGLES

4

ANGULAR DRILLING

IF YOU PLAN to build furniture, likely you will run into a job where holes must be drilled at an angle. Although angular drilling may seem complicated, it actually is quite simple.

Kinds of angles: There are three main kinds of angles as shown in Figs. 1, 2 and 3. All three types are required in construction of the magazine rack pictured in Fig. 4. The simple angle involves a one-way tilt only. Most used is the equal compound angle, Fig. 2, which involves a tilt of the same magnitude as viewed from the front and end of the work. The unequal compound angle, Fig. 3, is likewise a two-way tilt, but with one angle greater than the other.

The simple angle: A basic rule in drilling at a simple angle is that the work must be square with the table, Fig. 8. It will be apparent that if the work is off to one side, the hole will show a similar error as in Fig. 9. However, positioning of the work is not too critical at low angles so that placement of the work by eye alone usually is sufficiently accurate. Examples of the simple angle are shown in sketches A, B, and C above. Note that when one turning joins another turning, the angle is always a simple angle—a one-way tilt. Radial work, sketch B, is always a one-way tilt and requires only that a radial line from the center of the work to the drilled hole must be square with the drill table.

Work requiring a simple angle usually is specified at so many degrees of tilt. The simplest way to set the tilt is to use a circular-saw miter gauge set at the needed

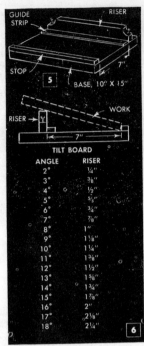

TILT BOARD	
ANGLE	RISER
2°	¼"
3°	⅜"
4°	½"
5°	⅝"
6°	¾"
7°	⅞"
8°	1"
9°	1⅛"
10°	1¼"
11°	1⅜"
12°	1½"
13°	1⅝"
14°	1¾"
15°	1⅞"
16°	2"
17°	2⅛"
18°	2¼"

angle, and sight the bar to the drill column while adjusting the table as in Fig. 10. Use of a T-bevel, as shown in Fig. 11, is obvious. Also, instead of tilting the drill table, you can leave the table level and make the tilt with a tilt board as indicated in Figs. 7 and 12. If the tilt board is made exactly 7 in. between stop and riser, Figs. 5 and 6, height of the riser needed for any specified angle up to 20 deg. will be ⅛ in. per degree. This is tabulated in handy form in Fig. 6. Over 20 deg., the progression of ⅛ in. per degree will show a constantly increasing

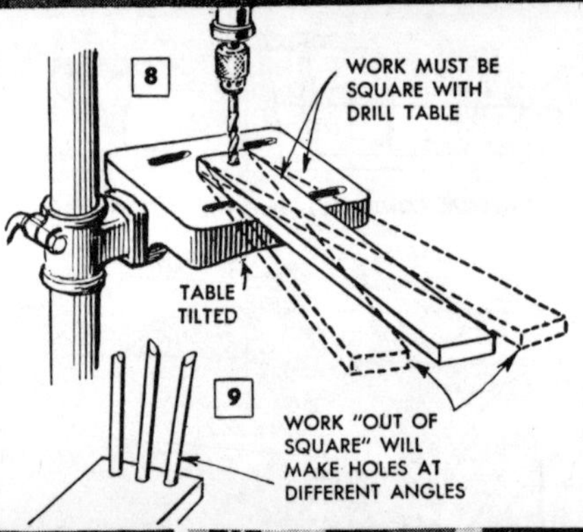

WORK MUST BE SQUARE WITH DRILL TABLE

TABLE TILTED

WORK "OUT OF SQUARE" WILL MAKE HOLES AT DIFFERENT ANGLES

Setting the simple angle

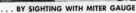

... BY SIGHTING WITH MITER GAUGE

... WITH SET BEVEL

... WITH TILT BOARD

14

EQUAL COMPOUND ANGLES CAN BE CONVERTED TO SIMPLE ANGLES BY USING THE TABLE SHOWN AT THE TOP OF THE PAGE. NOTE THAT THE DRILLING LINE IS ALWAYS 45° TO THE EDGES OF THE WORK SURFACE

EQUAL COMPOUND ANGLES			
WORK ANGLE	TABLE TILT	WORK ANGLE	TABLE TILT
2°	2¾°	12°	16¾°
3°	4¼°	13°	18¼°
4°	5½°	14°	19½°
5°	7°	15°	21°
6°	8¼°	17½°	24¼°
7°	9½°	20°	27°
8°	11°	22½°	30¼°
9°	12½°	25°	33°
10°	13¾°	27½°	36°
11°	15¼°	30°	39°

13

error, but within the limits of the table given is reasonably accurate.

The equal compound angle: On a drilling job like the one in Fig. 2, where the corner spindles tilt 8 deg. as viewed from the front, and 8 deg. when viewed from the end, you have an equal compound angle. Since the tilt is equal both ways, the drilling line is always at 45 deg. to the work, as in Fig. 15. Placement of the work is done easily by using a V-block. If the lower edge of the V-block is placed square with the table, the work and the drill will be in correct alignment. Tilt of the drill table itself, Fig. 14, is simplified by consulting the table in Fig. 13, which converts the equal compound angle to a simple angle. Thus, in the

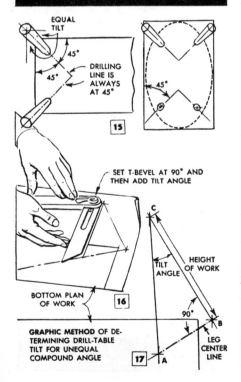

EQUAL TILT

DRILLING LINE IS ALWAYS AT 45°

45°

45°

45°

15

SET T-BEVEL AT 90° AND THEN ADD TILT ANGLE

C

TILT ANGLE

HEIGHT OF WORK

BOTTOM PLAN OF WORK

16

90°

B

LEG CENTER LINE

GRAPHIC METHOD OF DETERMINING DRILL-TABLE TILT FOR UNEQUAL COMPOUND ANGLE

17

A

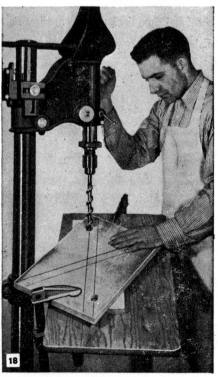

18

| | | 19 | 20 | 21 |

MOUNTING THE WORK CAN BE DONE BY ANY OF THE THREE METHODS SHOWN ABOVE. THE ANGLE VISE DETAILED AT THE RIGHT AND SHOWN IN USE IN THE LEFT-HAND PHOTO ABOVE, IS USEFUL FOR A VARIETY OF DIFFERENT JOBS

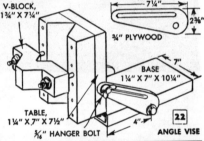

V-BLOCK, 1¾" X 7¼"
7¼"
2⅜"
¾" PLYWOOD
BASE 1¼" X 7" X 10¼"
7"
TABLE, 1¼" X 7" X 7½"
⅜" HANGER BOLT
4"
22
ANGLE VISE

example previously mentioned, Fig. 2, a two-way tilt of 8 deg. is a one-way tilt of 11 deg., keeping the 45-deg. drilling line square with the table. Sketches D and E also picture the use of the equal compound angle.

The unequal compound angle: This is best worked by actually making the two tilts required. The example in Fig. 3 shows that all turnings for the side of the magazine rack have a uniform tilt of 8 deg. when viewed from the end, but vary in tilt as viewed from the front. Set the 8-deg. tilt needed with the use of the tilt board. As shown in Fig. 6, this will require a 1-in. riser. Then, with the work placed on the tilt board, Fig. 7, the center spindle hole can be drilled as a simple angle. The two spindles on either side of center require a tilt of 4 deg. In the same way, set the 6-deg. tilt, and then, since you have the setup made, the equal compound angle required for corner spindles is made similarly, with 8 deg. on the tilt board and 8 deg. on the drill table. The work has to be square with the drill table for both tilts.

A drawing-board method of determining the drilling line and tilt for an unequal compound angle is shown in Fig. 17. From drawings of the project it is easy to make a bottom plan view, locating on this the leg center line, as shown by line AB. From B erect a perpendicular, making it as long as the height of the project. Join C to A. The angle at C will be the required tilt of the drill table. To take off the angle, set a T-bevel at 90 deg., as in Fig. 16, and then add the angle.

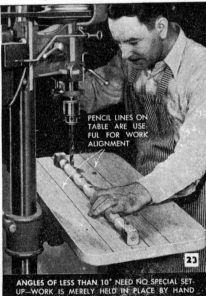

PENCIL LINES ON TABLE ARE USEFUL FOR WORK ALIGNMENT

23

ANGLES OF LESS THAN 10° NEED NO SPECIAL SET-UP—WORK IS MERELY HELD IN PLACE BY HAND

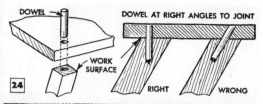
DOWEL

DOWEL AT RIGHT ANGLES TO JOINT

WORK SURFACE

24

RIGHT   WRONG

25

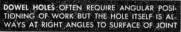
DOWEL HOLES OFTEN REQUIRE ANGULAR POSITIONING OF WORK BUT THE HOLE ITSELF IS ALWAYS AT RIGHT ANGLES TO SURFACE OF JOINT

26

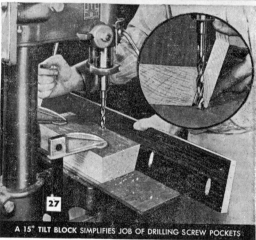

27

A 15° TILT BLOCK SIMPLIFIES JOB OF DRILLING SCREW POCKETS

Use the T-bevel, set in this way, to set the drill table, as shown in Fig. 11. Fig. 18 shows the job being drilled.

Mounting the work: Besides knowing how to set the angle, there is the job of mounting the work. A useful gadget for spindle work is the angle vise, shown in Figs. 19 and 22. Fig. 20 shows a simple handscrew mounting. The fluting jig, Fig. 21, is a good mounting for spindles, especially if spacing around the circumference is required. If the tilt angle is not over 10 deg., then simple placement of the work on the drill table as in Fig. 23, will do the trick. Note the pencil lines drawn on the table to help align the work. Note also how square sections are left uncut on turning. In order to keep the square sections on the table when drilling various holes along the turning, the drill table can be swung right or left as desired. This does not affect the drilling angle.

Curved work: When angular or straight holes must be drilled in curved work like the handle in example E, saw a jig block to fit the curve, keeping the opposite end of the jig block true and square. With the curved member held in the jig, you will have the equivalent of a square piece of work, and the tilt and positioning of work can be made accordingly.

Dowel holes: Angular drilling frequently is required in drilling dowel holes, but with the important difference that here you have a working surface. In Fig. 25, for example, a jig is made to hold the table leg in the required angular position, but the hole itself is no puzzle—it must be square with the work surface, Fig. 24. A similar case is the doweled miter joint, Fig. 26. Angular drilling for screw-pocket holes requires no calculation. A guide board with one edge cut at a 15-deg. bevel, Fig. 27, is clamped to the table so that the drill makes a hole at the extreme edge of the bevel.

ANTENNAS

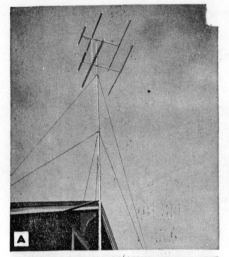

MANY homeowners wish to keep TV antennas off the roof if possible. Chimney mounts are not always practical for supporting the necessary high antenna-mast installations in fringe areas remote from television transmitting stations. Such TV antennas must be at least 45 feet from the ground, or higher in many locations.

Two practical solutions for this problem are illustrated and described on these pages. Both installations were made with metallic tubing extended from the ground up the side of the building to support the multiple-bay antenna arrays and only a few guy wires are required. The installation illustrated in photo A shows the tubing supported at the end of the roof ridge. A strap-iron bracket at the attic window provides another firm support as illustrated in photo B. This mast supports a two-bay Inline high-low TV antenna array with a single 300-ohm twin-lead lead-in. This is twisted and brought down through several TV lead-in standoff insulators attached to the tubing as shown in photo C.

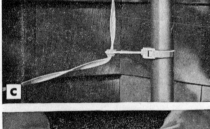

and brought down through several TV lead-in standoff insulators attached to the tubing as shown in photo C.

A much higher and heavier installation is illustrated in photos G, H, I and K. Photos G and I show the final steps in the completed installation, looking up from the ground.

The antenna array is a combination In-line double-stacked for the low bands, and a Yagi-type array for the high bands is mounted on top. Two twin-line lead-ins are used with lightning arrestors in each lead-in as shown in photo H. These are mounted on the side of the building and grounded; lead-ins enter the building through porcelain tubes. A double-throw switch is used at the receiver. The antenna array was assembled on the ground as shown in photo K.

In making this particular installation, the pipe assembly consisted of four 10-foot lengths of 2-in., one length of 1½-in. tubing and one length of 1-in. tubing. Since the top lengths overlap, the total length of the antenna mast is 56 feet. Photo J shows the lengths bolted together ready for installation. The 2-in. pipe was joined flush by using short pieces of pipe and additional split tubing inside the adjoining lengths and by bolting through the entire assembly above and below the joint with ¼ x 2½-in. bolts. Any similar method may be used. For the base, a 6-ft. length of 1½-in. pipe was driven 5 feet into the ground as illustrated in photo E to take the 2-in. pipe; the cement base block, photo F, is optional. Rings for the guy wires, photo D, were placed where needed on the top sections of the antenna mast, after the tubing was through the overhang opening. In both installations the guy wires were fastened to short lengths of angle iron screwed to the underside of the roof overhang.

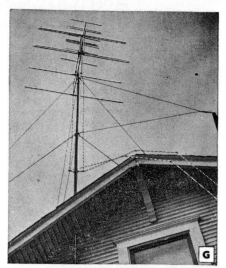

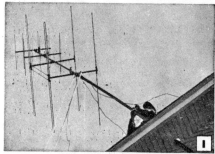

ANTIQUES–REFINISHING

A master craftsman, wise in the ways of refinishing antiques to the smoothness of old ivory and with a gleaming, rich luster, gave me the following tips: First, clean the work with a good paint and varnish remover, using a cheap brush to apply a generous coat over a small area. Let the remover stand about 15 min. and, without wiping it off, apply a second coat. Then mix a gallon of warm water with a cup of household ammonia and use the mixture with a stiff-bristled brush to scour the treated surface. Dip a rough cloth (an old towel is excellent) into the ammonia water and wipe the area. Rinse at once with clear water, removing all traces of ammonia and the work should be good and clean. Remember to clean only a small area at a time, for if varnish remover is applied over too large an area, it will harden into a cement-like finish. Should that happen, apply more remover—several coats, 15 min. apart—until you can wipe the surface clean. Before further refinishing is done, make any nec-

essary repairs to the work. Then sand with 1/0 or 2/0 garnet or sandpaper until very smooth. Wipe clean and apply the first coat of shellac, using a 4-lb. cut. Thin a pint of shellac with a pint of denatured alcohol. Use orange shellac on dark woods, such as mahogany, cherry and walnut, and white shellac on the lighter woods. Using a pure bristle brush, apply two coats of shellac with the grain of the wood, allowing 4 or 5 hrs. between coats. Between succeeding coats, allow 24 to 48 hrs. drying time. Sand after each coat using 6/0 or 7/0 garnet paper. Never apply shellac in damp or humid weather, and if the shellac gums up on the sandpaper, allow more drying time. When you have built up the desired number of coats, mix 3 heaping tablespoonfuls of fine pumice with paraffin oil to attain a creamy mixture. Then dip a pad of 000 steel wool in the mixture and rub the work briskly with the grain. When finished, wipe the surface with a soft cloth. Repeat this process twice.

ANTIQUING

SHADING plays an important part in the finishing of period furniture, and also has a considerable role in the decoration of other projects in both wood and metal. Briefly, the technique is simply a matter of lightening or darkening certain areas of the work to contrast with the general tone of the piece. Related terms include highlighting, glazing, antiquing, smutting, etc.

Spray shading: The spray gun is an excellent tool for shaded effects, and is capable of either sharp or soft shading. Sharp shading is confined largely to colored enamels, an example being the shading of a cream-colored chair with blue enamel, as shown in the photo at left. The color separation is strong and sharply defined—it is a kind of shading that is plainly visible. On the other hand, soft shading, as done on the average piece of furniture, is hardly apparent at first glance.

Various methods are used in spray shading. Most direct is to shade the work during the application of the stain coat, spraying lightly on some parts, heavy on others. Again, a first coat of stain, considerably diluted, can be allowed to dry, after which a second coat can be sprayed for shaded areas. Shading can also be done at any time during the finishing schedule by using special shading stains. These can be purchased ready-mixed or made by mixing powder stain with thin shellac or lacquer. Soft

Shading certain areas darker with stain or a different color with enamel is easily done with the spray gun, using a small pattern for good atomization to produce even blending

SHADING A PANEL

GOOD
NARROW RIM OF
DARKER COLOR

POOR
SHADED AREA
TOO LARGE

HIGHLIGHT

HIGHLIGHT BULBOUS
PORTION OF TURNING

NATURAL HIGH-
LIGHT CAUSED BY
WEAR

HIGHLIGHT
IMITATING
WEAR

Highlighting is easily done by wiping a pigment stain or glaze coat. Clean, sharp highlights can be obtained by sanding

Glazing is the term for a shading medium or technique. In the example above, the ground coat is blue, left photo. The white glaze is brushed on, center, and then wiped to expose the highlights, as shown in right photo

spray shading should be done with a small spray pattern and with the gun held 10 to 20 in. from the work.

Highlighting: If you don't have a spray gun—or perhaps even if you do—you can do shaded work by the reverse technique of highlighting. This is easily done with pigment oil stain, penetrating oil stain, and to some extent is practical with almost any type of stain. Cleaner wiping for highlights can be obtained if done on a second coat of wiping stain applied over a sealer. That is, you stain first for a uniform body color, not too dark. Then apply a sealer coat. Over the sealer coat brush on a second coat of pigment wiping stain. Clean this off rather thoroughly with a rag to leave the stain

only on areas which are to appear darker.

Highlighting can also be done mechanically on the first stain coat after it is dry by using fine sandpaper or steel wool, as shown in the photo. This is sometimes useful to obtain a few very sharp highlights. It has the fault that if overdone, patching by restaining is not always easy.

Glazing: Glazing is the term which most nearly describes the whole art of using a wiped, translucent shading medium. You can glaze a piece of work and then wipe it for highlights. You can glaze the work with the idea of antiquing it. Or you can use a glaze coat for a textured ground or to imitate wood grain. The glaze itself can be any wiping stain, any thin paint, etc., but is specifically a product called glazing liquid. This can be purchased ready made or can be made with varnish, 4 parts, boiled linseed oil, 2 parts, and turpentine, 1 part. Pigment colors in oil or japan are added as needed to obtain desired colors. The glaze coat is applied over a foundation coat of sealer or colored enamel. It is sprayed or brushed over the whole area and is immediately wiped with a cloth or blended out with a dry brush. It can also be applied with a cloth and wiped with the same cloth, a kind of rubbing-on process.

A soft-brown glaze on an off-white enamel ground (bone-white finish) is effective. The same on a cream ground gives a pleasing soft, shaded effect. For a clear finish, the glaze coat should be somewhat darker than the wood or the stained color of the wood. For colored enamel finishes, any of hundreds of color combinations can be used. An example is shown in the photos. For most work, the glaze should be wiped rather thoroughly. Graining effects can be obtained by wiping the glaze coat with a dry brush, whisk broom, combs and other gadgets. You can use your finger for tricky texture effects and designs. If a glaze coat becomes too tacky for clean working, it can be wiped with a cloth moistened with naphtha.

General technique: Regardless of how you do this shading, highlighting or antiquing, the work should not be overdone. On clear finishes especially, any shading or highlighting should be soft. A combination of methods is sometimes useful. For example, it is nearly impossible to spray-shade carvings, but it is very easy to apply pigment stain or glaze and then expose highlights by wiping. On the other hand, the spray gun is excellent for shading panels and table tops. Turnings are best treated by wiping since a simple run-over with a rag from end to end will automatically highlight the bulbous portions.

APARTMENT WORKSHOP

AFTER having had a complete basement workshop for many years, I was like a fish out of water when we moved into an apartment. Trying to carry on by using the kitchen table as a workbench and having to stow away everything each time

2

No one would suspect that this studio couch houses a complete "workshop." Just lift the cover and presto!—there it is all before you—everything in readiness to begin work. No time is wasted putting things away

3

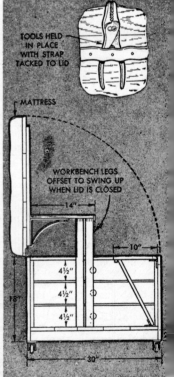

TOOLS HELD IN PLACE WITH STRAP TACKED TO LID

MATTRESS

WORKBENCH LEGS OFFSET TO SWING UP WHEN LID IS CLOSED

14"

10"

4½"

4½"

4½"

18"

30"

led me to build the portable, self-contained workshop pictured in Figs. 1 and 3. Not only does it solve the problem of a place to work with everything at finger tips, but it can be transformed quickly into a comfortable and attractive studio couch by simply closing the cover as shown in Fig. 2. There's really nothing to making it. Fig. 4 will give you a good idea of the construction which amounts to making a large box with a hinged cover and upholstering it with a mattress and slip cover. I used inexpensive, common-grade lumber, although ¾-in. fir plywood could be used. This would eliminate the work of building up the sides, top and bottom with battens. Notice that the bottom of the box rests on 2 by 2-in. sills, equally spaced, and that a caster is fastened to each corner.

Each end of the box is fitted with a removable three-drawer cabinet, which is made separately and slipped into place. For these you may be able to purchase a ready-made chest of the unpainted variety, such as is sold in large department stores, and adapt it to fit the box, or the drawer compartment of a discarded piece of furniture might do. It wouldn't be necessary for them to extend the full width of the box either. Regardless, the cabinets should simply set in place so that the whole thing becomes a knockdown affair to facilitate moving. I used flathead screws in assembling the box, and loose-pin hinges in attaching the cover so that it could be dismantled without too much trouble. The side view in Fig. 4 shows how both the workbench and seat are hinged to fold compactly. Regular metal shelf brackets support the bench top rigidly at right angles to the cover, and the legs are hinged offset to allow them to nest side by side when folded. Midget-type power tools such as a lathe, saw, drill press, etc., are ideal for use in this "shop." Mounting can be such as to allow the machines to be quickly interchanged, and there's ample room to store them in the bottom of the box. A piece of linoleum on the floor of the box will prevent sawdust from seeping through the joints of the boards.

The top is fitted with a standard cotton mattress, 30 by 74 in. This was spot-tacked around the edge to hold it in place and then covered with a slip cover having a pleated flounce. Note the hand holes that are cut in the top edge of the box at the front. This allows you to get a grip under the cover to raise it. Although not shown, a cleanout drawer in the bottom of the box, or a trap door, would facilitate removing shavings and sawdust. This necessitates raising the box higher off the floor to provide access for removal of the sweepings.

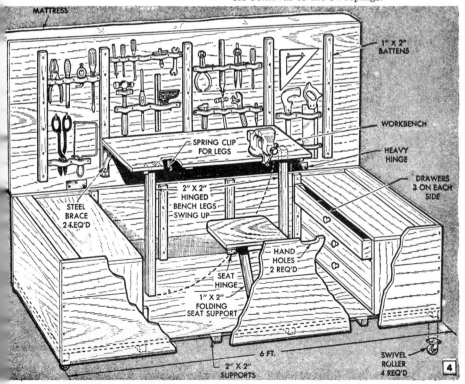

MATTRESS

1" X 2" BATTENS

WORKBENCH

HEAVY HINGE

DRAWERS 3 ON EACH SIDE

SPRING CLIP FOR LEGS

2" X 2" HINGED BENCH LEGS SWING UP

STEEL BRACE 2 REQ'D

HAND HOLES 2 REQ'D

SEAT HINGE

1" X 2" FOLDING SEAT SUPPORT

6 FT.

2" X 2" SUPPORTS

SWIVEL ROLLER 4 REQ'D

4

ARBORS

CAREFULLY planned placement of ornamental trellises can make a house appear wider, higher or lower, and the simple formality of an arbor lends interest and completeness to any garden. Trellises also are used to screen unsightly corners, conceal the garbage can, serve as a windbreak for delicate plantings, and to provide a patterned backdrop for a formal garden. The design of a trellis can be almost anything that suits your fancy or purpose, but the design and size of an arbor are less flexible because of the vertical and horizontal arrangement of the structural members. The architectural lines of even the simplest arbor make it necessary to plan the design of the structure and its location beforehand. If the arbor is to provide support and guidance for climbing vines or shrubs, then it is well to avoid fine structural detail and use only an open, slat-type construction. The arbor pictured above is a good example of the more practical design. This is just about the simplest saw, hammer and nail job possible, yet the secret of its attractiveness is in the pattern of squares which has been carried out in the construction of the side panels. Note that the supporting corner posts are placed the same distance apart each way, and that the height equals the length of the sides. The X-braces add both rigidity and an interesting structural detail.

A trellis of more formal design is pictured at the top of the opposite page. The architectural detail has been worked out with the purpose of extending the horizontal lines of the house, and the crisscross, or diamond pattern, above and at each side of the arch is obviously for the purpose of lowering the height of the opening in relation to its width. The gate arbor, or perhaps more properly, arch, shown at the lower right on the opposite page brings up another point in connection with arbor and trellis design. When building such structures, especially an arched gateway in a hedge, it's a good idea to stick to simple design. A heavy, ponderous structure decorated with detailed cornices or elaborate curved work appears rather out of place in the hedgerow. This one, you will note, is simple and effective as a decorative feature of the home grounds and, at the same time, serves the twofold practical purpose of providing rigid, permanent gateposts and a guide, or support, for training the hedge.

The formal trellis often is used to lower height of an opening or to make the house appear longer or wider

Small trellises, such as the fan type shown below, are easy to build. Bow is nailed to ends of fan slats

Stick to plain design when building a gate arbor in a hedgerow. This type is easy to build and maintain

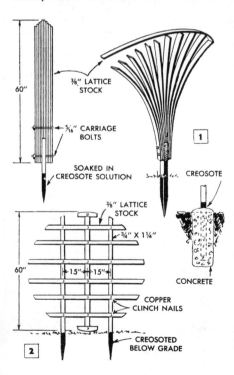

60"

⅜" LATTICE STOCK

5⁄16" CARRIAGE BOLTS

SOAKED IN CREOSOTE SOLUTION

CREOSOTE

⅜" LATTICE STOCK

¾" X 1¼"

60"

15"   15"

COPPER CLINCH NAILS

CREOSOTED BELOW GRADE

CONCRETE

1

2

Simple construction of bow-type arbor will appeal to homeowners having natural, or informal, gardens

Two popular types of simple trellises are detailed in Figs. 1 and 2. The fan trellis, shown in the upper detail, is pictured below in the right-hand photo. Here, two horizontal crosspieces have been added in addition to the bow top. The round trellis is made by nailing slats (lattice stock) to two spaced uprights of heavier material. The ends of the slats are cut off on a radius and are arranged in such a way that the structure appears circular in form when assembled. Addition of the center member with end blocks cut on a radius finishes the job. The trellises, arbors and gateways pictured on this and the opposite page are typical, and the various applications pictured are suggestive of the many uses to which these structures are adapted. The curved arbor shown at the left is detailed in Fig. 3. The dimensions given are merely indicative of the average over-all size. It can be built in any length up to 20 ft. and the arched members, or bows, can be installed in any number and spacing desired.

Above and below are two applications of trellises used to partially enclose open porches. Diamond pattern of one above screens a doorway effectively while squared design below lowers height of opening

Above, a typical application of the fan-type trellis placed against a red-brick wall to support a rambler rose. Below, diamond-pattern panels enclose hooded garage entryway and screen service door to kitchen

Three quite important construction details of various types are shown in Fig. 4. Another way of making the base for a large fan-type trellis is shown in the upper detail, and the method of anchoring the ends of the bow to the outside slats is covered in the center detail. When making flat, clinch-nailed joints such as are common in trellis and arbor construction, it's important to paint the joining surfaces with a prime coat before assembling. A still better procedure is to prime and paint all parts before joining. Parts driven into the ground or set in concrete below ground level should always be soaked in a creosote solution, Figs. 1, 2 and 3. Place the solution in a container and allow the lower ends of the stakes or posts to soak 48 hrs. or longer. A creosote solution is frequently used as a finish for the entire structure as it stains the wood a weathered brown and at the same time acts as a preservative. However, it should be remembered that oil paints cannot be applied over creosote.

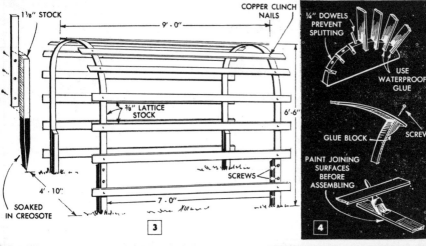

Build Your Own
ARC WELDER

Part One

BY REWINDING a discarded or burned-out service transformer and installing it in a housing mounted on a two-wheel cart, this portable a.c. arc welder, shown in the upper right-hand photo, was built entirely with hand tools for less than $25. It will handle metallic-arc welding rods from the smallest up to ³⁄₁₆ in. in dia. and can be regulated for use with a double-carbon arc torch for brazing, silver and soft soldering, and localized heating when bending, forging or heat-treating metal parts. In addition to welding, the metallic arc can be used for cutting metal and piercing holes when bolted construction is desired.

Selection of a transformer for rewinding is made on the basis of the output desired and the service current available. Where the welder transformer output required is approximately 150 amperes of welding current, the transformer should weigh at least 75 pounds exclusive of its cast-iron container or "pot." A welder of this output will handle almost any job on the farm or in the small shop and can be operated on a 220-volt circuit drawing a maximum of 30 amperes. Most shop or farm electric

TRANSFORMER PLATES
(26-GA. SILICON STEEL)

TABLE I	PLATE	100-Ampere Welder			200-Ampere Welder		
		Height of pile	Dimensions Width	Length	Height of pile	Dimensions Width	Length
50 to 60 cycle current	A	3½"	3½"	7"	4"	4"	8"
	B	10½"	1¾"	7"	12"	2"	8"
	C	7"	1¾"	3½"	8"	2"	4"
25 to 40 cycle current	A	4"	4"	8"	4½"	4½"	9"
	B	12"	2"	8"	13½"	2¼"	9"
	C	8"	2"	4"	9"	2¼"	4½"

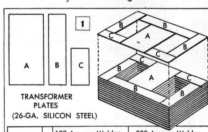

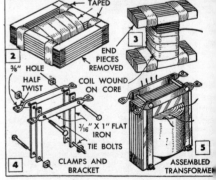

service will meet these requirements. However, check with your local electrician or power company as to the maximum load that may be imposed on the service line. Pole transformers, rated from 2 k.v.a. to 5 k.v.a., are recommended for making welders of approximately 150-ampere, 35 to 40-volt output. A smaller welder made from a rewound light industrial or X-ray transformer will deliver sufficient amperage for most welding jobs in the home shop and can be operated on 110 volts with less than 30 amperes. For light welders, the transformer alone should weigh at least 50 pounds. Pole transformers and X-ray transformers suitable for rewinding usually are of the shell type, and for compactness, a 3 or 4-part transformer is recommended. In buying a junked transformer, take only the transformer itself, as the pot which houses it is not needed. Usually, the transformer can be lifted from the pot by removing 4 or 6 bolts.

If a discarded service transformer cannot be found, you can build one from regular transformer iron of No. 26 to 29 gauge. Rectangular sections are cut to sizes indicated in Table I, Fig. 1, and these are tacked so that the pieces overlap one another in the manner shown. The core and the two sets of outer laminations are taped together tightly, Fig. 2, and then the end laminations are removed. The coils are wound directly on the core, Fig. 3, using

the same size wires and procedure given for rewinding a junked transformer as will be described later. The end laminations are then replaced and clamps and brackets, Fig. 4, bolted to the core to compress and hold it together. Fig. 5 shows the completed transformer.

Dismantling a service transformer is done by first removing the porcelain cap used to distribute the leads. The clamps which hold the core sections also are removed, Fig. 6. These clamps usually are bolted to a cast-iron bracket from which the transformer hangs inside the pot. Coils in a common service transformer designed to reduce 2300 power-line voltage to 220 or 110 volts, usually have half the secondary winding directly on the core in two or more layers. These layers are covered with a fireproof insulating material over which the primary wiring is wound. The primary is covered with another insulating blanket and the remainder of the secondary is wound over this.

To proceed with the dismantling of the transformer, remove the 4 sets of outer laminations. These are cemented to each other with an insulating varnish and it may be necessary to use a linoleum knife and pliers to separate them as shown in Fig. 7. On some transformers the laminations are L-shaped, with the short legs alternating from one end to the other. Stack the laminations in a pile in the order in

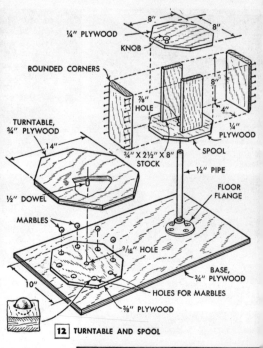

¼" PLYWOOD

KNOB

ROUNDED CORNERS

⅞" HOLE

TURNTABLE, ¾" PLYWOOD

SPOOL

¼" PLYWOOD

14"

¾" X 2½" X 8" STOCK

½" PIPE

½" DOWEL

FLOOR FLANGE

MARBLES

⁹/₁₆" HOLE

10"

BASE, ¾" PLYWOOD

HOLES FOR MARBLES

⅜" PLYWOOD

12 TURNTABLE AND SPOOL

which they are removed and number them to correspond with the side of the transformer from which they are taken. Continue to remove the laminations from the other three sides, keeping each group stacked and numbered separately. After removal of the outer laminations, there remains the central core upon which the coils are wound. Using a turntable and spool, the construction of which is detailed in Fig. 12, remove the outer insulation from the first, or secondary, coil. Fasten the end of the wire to the spool and carefully unwind the coil as shown in Fig. 8. Being of smaller-gauge wire, the primary winding is wound on another spool in the same way. The inner coil, which will be of the same size as the first coil, should be wound on the first spool. Thick layers of glass or mica insulation separating the primary and secondary coils are removed, as shown in Fig. 9, and saved for reuse. The binding around the core should not be removed.

For arc welders delivering less than 100 amperes, the secondary coil should be wound with a wire size not less than No. 6 gauge and the primary with wire not less than No. 12 or 14 gauge. For the welder described, the secondary should be at least No. 3-gauge wire and the primary of No. 8 or 10 gauge. Original transformer wire can be reused if it is miked for size and then "paralleled" to make up the required gauge. Paralleling is done by combining a number of small-gauge wires and connecting them at the taps, thus providing a cross-sectional area equivalent to a larger-gauge wire. Table II, below Fig. 12, gives equivalent wire sizes to determine the number

TABLE II — WIRE EQUIVALENTS				
WIRE GAUGE SIZE	NUMBER OF STRANDS AND WIRE SIZE NEEDED FOR SUBSTITUTE			
3	2 of #6	4 of #9	8 of #12	16 of #15
6	2 of #9	4 of #12	8 of #15	16 of #18
8	2 of #11	4 of #14	8 of #17	16 of #20
10	2 of #13	4 of #16	8 of #19	16 of #22
12	2 of #15	4 of #18	8 of #21	16 of #24
14	2 of #17	4 of #20	8 of #23	16 of #26

of any specific small wires necessary to make one wire of a desired size. Wires smaller than No. 16 gauge may be paralleled into a single strand by twisting them together with a hand drill. Larger sizes may be paralleled by laying them side by side on the coil.

The first portion of the secondary should be wound around the core by pulling out a lead about 6 inches long, and labeling it with a shipping tag, "A-start secondary." Then lay in the wire, using a single strand or several wires side by side as in Fig. 10. In most cases you should apply the first 15 turns in one layer. Wrap this portion of the secondary with two layers of cotton cloth and shellac it, Fig. 11. The cloth should be completely saturated. Next, wind another 15 turns over the first layer and tag the end of this coil, "B-1 secondary, 30 turns." Now, replace one of the insulating blankets over the secondary turns as in Fig. 13. Wind one layer of the primary over this blanket, first taking off a lead and labeling it, "primary start." Fig. 14 shows 5 strands of the original primary wire twisted together. Wrap this layer with one thickness of cotton cloth and shellac. Continue with the primary winding, insulating each successive layer with cloth and shellac. Take off taps at 110 turns, 165 turns and the final tap at 220 turns. Label these taps, "1 primary, 110 turns," "2 primary, 165 turns" and "3 primary, 220 turns." After this, replace the other insulating blanket and begin the second section of the secondary coil. Label the starting end of this secondary lead, "B-1 start, 3rd layer secondary," and after 15 turns, tap and label, "C-2, 3rd layer secondary, 15 turns." Insulate this with two layers of cloth and apply shellac. Continue on the fourth layer of the secondary, tapping after 5 turns and labeling the tap, "3 secondary, 5 turns." Make 5 more turns and tap, labeling, "4 secondary, 10 turns," then make 5 more turns or a total of 15 turns, and label the final tap, "5 secondary, 15 turns." After this, replace the laminations, driving the pieces into place with a softwood mallet as in Fig. 15. Finally, replace the yokes and brackets, using C-clamps, as in Fig. 16, to hold the laminations in compression until the holding devices are in place.

Long connecting wires are soldered to the leads, Fig. 17. Care must be taken to assure a permanent joint. Larger wires should be lapped and wrapped with fine wire before soldering. The secondary lead marked "B-1 secondary, 30 turns" may be connected with "B-1 start, 3rd layer secondary" and a common lead taken from them. The connecting leads should be about 2 feet long and fitted with lugs soldered in place. These leads may be insulated by wrapping and shellacking or by slipping sections of loom over them. If it is necessary to remove the identification tags when making the soldered joints, they should be immediately replaced to avoid any confusion later.

Build your own

ARC WELDER

Part Two

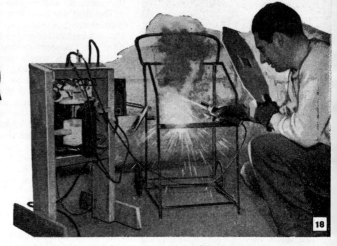

The welder parts are wired temporarily and used to weld the cabinet frame

NO ATTEMPT has been made to rewind the transformer, described, earlier pg., with enough primary resistance to prevent blowing the line fuses when an excessive load is thrown on the secondary. In fact, it is best to have the primary resistance comparatively low to permit a current-controlling device known as a reactor to be introduced in the primary circuit, as shown in the wiring diagram, Fig. 20. Selection of the various welding currents or "heats" is controlled by inserting plugs, connected to a primary loop and two welding cables, into jacks connected to the transformer leads. A jack board, Fig. 21, supports the jacks which are labeled for ease in selecting the different secondary and primary combinations. Further adjustment of the current is made by regulating the reactor.

To make the reactor, cut enough laminations to make a core the size indicated in the upper detail of Fig. 19. Note that the center lamination is slightly longer than the others, and has holes drilled in each end. The laminations are held together by wrapping tightly with tape. A square tube having inside dimensions just large enough to permit easy insertion of the core is glued together as detailed in Fig. 19. One half of the tube is wrapped with 200 turns of wire of the same size used in the transformer primary coil. Each layer of wire should be insulated with cotton cloth and shellac.

To make the jack board, cut out and drill 3 pieces of hard-pressed board to the dimensions given for the cover plate, Fig. 21. The holes should make a snug fit with the 3-in. lengths of

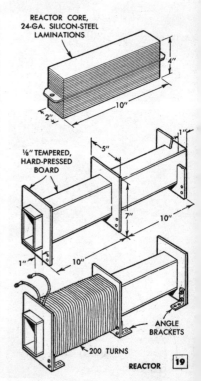

REACTOR CORE, 24-GA. SILICON-STEEL LAMINATIONS

4"

10"

2"

⅛" TEMPERED, HARD-PRESSED BOARD

1"

5"

7"

10"

1"

10"

ANGLE BRACKETS

200 TURNS

REACTOR

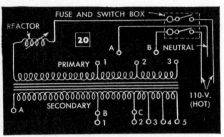

TABLE III — SECONDARY CONNECTIONS

A-1	30 turns	B-1	dead	C-1	15 turns
A-2	45 turns	B-2	15 turns	C-2	dead
A-3	50 turns	B-3	20 turns	C-3	5 turns
A-4	55 turns	B-4	25 turns	C-4	10 turns
A-5	60 turns	B-5	30 turns	C-5	15 turns

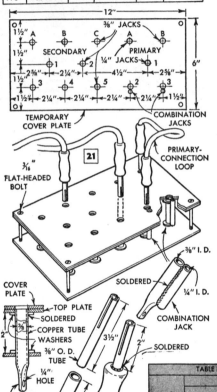

copper tubing used for the jacks. Note that jacks A and 1 for the primary are made of ¼-in. i.d. tubing and that combination jacks 2 and 3 of the primary consist of ¼ and ⅜-in. tubes soldered together so that either of the two loops, described later, can be used. All others are of ⅜-in. i.d. tubing. The jacks are sandwiched between the pieces of board which are spaced by washers soldered to the jacks as indicated in the sectional drawing, Fig. 21. The whole unit is held together by bolts at each corner of the boards. The ends of the jacks that project through the bottom of the jack board are flattened and drilled for connection with the transformer leads.

The primary-connection loop, Fig. 21, is next. Although only one loop is used at a time, two are required, one with ¼-in. plugs, the other with ⅜-in. plugs. These two loops of different sizes are necessary to prevent a connection across B and 1 on the primary, which would give high-voltage currents on the secondary that would be dangerous to handle and unsuitable for arc welding. The plugs, Fig. 22, are made from lengths of ¼ and ⅜-in. copper tubing each of which is split lengthwise with a saw for a distance of 1½ in. from one end to produce a tight fit when inserted into the bore of the jack tubes. The other end is soldered into a 3½-in. length of ¼ or ⅜-in. i.d. copper tubing so split end projects 2 in. A 12-in. length of No. 8 gauge flexible wire is soldered to the ends of the larger tubes. The plugs are then insulated with tricycle handle grips, leaving the split tubing exposed for a distance of 2 in. Plugs for the ground and electrode-holder cables are made in the same manner. These cables are of No. 2 gauge rubber-covered flexible wire each about 20 ft. long. In use, these cables are plugged into the secondary circuit.

The transformer and other electrical parts now can be mounted in a temporary wooden frame as shown in Fig. 18, and used to weld the frame for the welder

TABLE IV — NO-LOAD VOLTAGES AND MAXIMUM AMPERAGES

Secondary Combinations	Primary Combinations									
	110 Volts						220 Volts			
	A-1		A-2		A-3		B-2		B-3	
	Volts	Amps.	Volts	Amps.	Volts	Amps.	Volts	Amps.	Volts	Amps.
A-1	30	110	20	165	15	220	40	165	30	220
A-2	45	73	30	110	23	143	60	110	45	148
A-3	50	66	33	100	25	132	67	98	50	132
A-4	55	60	37	89	28	118	73	90	55	120
A-5	60	55	40	82	30	110	80	83	60	110
B-2	15	220	10	330	8	415	20	330	15	440
B-3	20	165	13	252	10	330	27	244	20	330
B-4	25	132	17	195	13	252	33	200	25	264
B-5	30	110	20	165	15	220	40	165	30	220
C-1	15	220	10	330	8	415	20	330	15	440
C-3	5	660	3	1100	3	1100	7	940	5	1320
C-4	10	330	7	470	5	660	13	508	10	660
C-5	15	220	10	330	8	415	20	330	15	440

cabinet, Fig. 24. The wiring diagram, Fig. 20, indicates how the connections are made to a split 220-volt power line. Use a d.p.s.t. switch and box with two 30-ampere fuses. The transformer leads are connected to the jacks, which are labeled to correspond with the tags on the leads. By making a connection across primary jacks A and 1 with the connection loop, 110 volts are impressed on the 110 turns. The combinations of jacks A-2 and A-3 give 110 volts through 165 and 220 turns respectively. When connections across B-2 and B-3 are used, the voltage is 220 through 165 and 220 turns. Table III gives the number of turns for the various secondary combinations. Table IV gives the approximate no-load voltages with the different combinations of primary and secondary hookups. These voltages can be varied by adjustments of the reactor.

Before starting to weld, several accessories must be purchased. An electrode holder as shown in Fig. 25 is connected to one of the 20-ft. cables and a lug or clamp is connected to the other to serve as a ground cable. A helmet of the type shown in Fig. 25 or a hand-held face shield, shown in Fig. 18, must be used to protect the eyes and face from the rays of the welding arc. Do not attempt to arc weld with dark-colored goggles such as used for oxyacetylene welding. To protect the hands, leather welders' gloves should be used. In addition you will need 5 lbs. each of $\frac{1}{16}$, $\frac{3}{32}$ and

The electrical parts are mounted in a frame having two wheels for ease in moving around the workshop

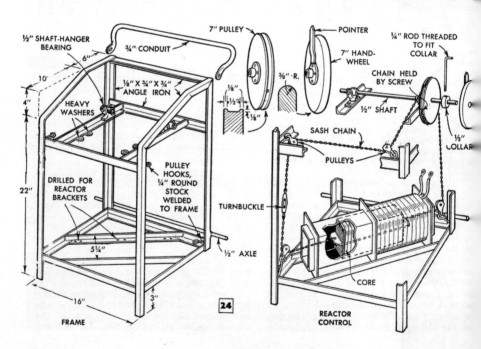

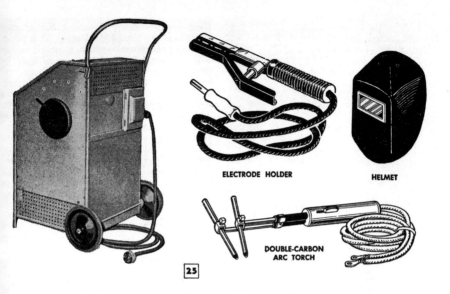

ELECTRODE HOLDER   HELMET

DOUBLE-CARBON ARC TORCH

25

-in. mild-steel electrodes or welding ds. These must be the coated type for se with an a.c. welding machine, because e d.c. type will not work properly.

If you are inexperienced in arc welding, ake some practice welds on scrap iron to t the feel of handling the arc before weld-g the frame. To start welding, clamp the ound-cable lug to the work and then con-ect the cable to jack B on the secondary. onnect the electrode-holder cable to jack on the secondary. Then connect the pri-ary across B and 2 with the connecting op. Adjustment of the reactor, which may laid on the floor, is made by sliding the re in the tube and locking it in place with all wooden wedges. Start with the reac-r wide open and cut down the current by oving the core into the coil until you get e desired current. You may have to use different combination on the jack board. rc welding requires from 30 to 40 volts to aintain an arc manually. The amperage ay vary considerably depending on the e of the electrode used.

With a ⅛-in. electrode in the holder d your eyes protected with the helmet, ratch the tip of the electrode across the rap iron as you would a match, and then ickly lift it about ⅛ in. to form an arc tween the tip and the iron. When a ddle of molten metal forms on the iron, wly move the rod toward the right. Si-ultaneously with this movement feed the d downward as it melts off, thus main-ining a uniform arc length. The melting d will deposit a bead of weld metal on e scrap iron. To break the arc, merely ll the rod away from the weld. After the

weld cools, remove the coating of slag, which covers the surface of the weld, with a cold chisel and wire brush. The surface of a good weld will have uniform ripples in it. If the tip of the rod sticks or "freezes" to the work, move the rod from side to side vigorously while pulling upward. If this does not free the rod it must be immedi-ately released at the jaws of the holder to avoid overheating and injury to the rod coating. Difficulty in starting and main-taining an arc usually can be overcome by increasing the welding current slightly. Practice welding straight, flat beads with various sizes of electrodes, and experiment with the adjustments on the welder until the best current settings have been found. Then butt two pieces of scrap iron together, leaving a gap of 1/16 in. Make a small weld at each end of the scrap-iron pieces to hold them together, and run a continuous weld along the joint. After cooling, break the pieces apart through the center of the weld and examine it for depth of weld penetra-tion. Insufficient penetration is caused by using too low a welding current or too fast a rate of travel. Fillet welds, which are used to join two pieces of metal at right angles, also should be practiced. When welding joints of this type, hold the rod at an angle which bisects the angle between the two plates. If difficulty is encountered in producing a weld that is fused into both pieces uniformly, the work may be tilted at a 45-deg. angle and the rod held vertically.

After satisfying yourself of your ability to make a good weld, start making a cab-inet frame, Fig. 24, which supports all the various parts shown in Fig. 23. All the angle-iron parts for the frame should first be cut, fitted and tack-welded together. Then, after checking for trueness, make continuous welds at all the joints. The entire assembly is mounted on wheels. Dimensions for locating the angle-iron supports for the transformer are not given as they must be determined from the size and type used. Four large washers, welded to the supports to correspond with the bolt holes in the mounting brackets of the transformer, hold it firmly in place. The reactor is set on angle irons welded diagonally across the bottom of the frame and is controlled by a handwheel, as shown in Fig. 24. By turning the handwheel, the position of the core in the tube is adjusted. However, as a strong pull is exerted on the core when the reactor coil is energized, the core must be locked in place after it is adjusted. This is accomplished by turning the 1/4-in. rod, Fig. 24, which is threaded to fit a tapped hole in a 1/2-in. collar on the handwheel shaft. The rod, which extends through the top panel of the cabinet, acts as a setscrew and thus prevents the shaft from turning. The jack board is supported by a panel of hard-pressed board covering the slanted portion at the top of the frame. This panel becomes the permanent jack-board cover. The temporary jack-board cover may be used as a template to drill the holes accurately. The switch box is welded to the rear of the frame and the electrical parts are wired as in Fig. 20. A length of 3-wire (No. 10 gauge) flexible cable and a 3-way plug and receptacle are used for connection between the switch box and power line. The sides of the frame are covered with panels of hard-pressed board and perforated metal, as shown in Fig. 25. All panels are bolted to the inside surface of the angle-iron framework. After painting the entire cabinet, label the jacks and number five equally spaced positions of the reactor handwheel to indicate the position of the core in the reactor coil. A record of best operating current adjustments for various rod sizes should be kept for reference.

The double-carbon arc torch, Fig. 25, is a useful accessory for this welder as it supplies a self-contained arc flame for welding and heating metals.

ARC WELDING for beginners

1

METALWORKING industries have for many years used electric arc welding as a means of fabricating metal parts. Recently this fast and economical method of joining metal has been made available to the home craftsman, job shop, garage owner and farmer in the form of small arc-welding machines, which cost no more than average home-workshop power tools.

Basically, an arc welder is a tool for making things of metal which is used in much the same way as screws, bolts, nails or glue are used when working with wood. A weld properly made is as strong or stronger than the metal which is welded and, in addition, it can be made watertight or airtight. Although welding machines are

Arc welding offers a quick and economical method for making repairs on automobile and truck frames.

used principally for joining metals, the heat of the welding arc often is employed for cutting. Heating small metal parts for bending, forging and heat-treating is another use for the versatile welder. Still another handy use for the arc welder is for cutting holes in metal parts intended for bolted assembly.

Welding machines are of two general types—those that supply an alternating welding current, which are commonly called a.c., and those that supply direct welding current, called d.c. Most a.c. machines have transformers designed and built for a specific current input. For ex-

Above, repairing spring-tooth harrow with 180-amp. a.c. welder. Below, using portable d.c.-type welder for on-the-spot repairing of tandem disc harrow

Small 60-amp. welder is ideal for home craftsmen when repairing or making things of metal around the house

ample, the machine shown in Fig. 6 A will supply a maximum of 60 amp. welding current when connected to a 110-volt power line protected with a 30-amp. fuse. This low current input makes a welder of this size an ideal machine for the home craftsman when repairing such equipment as the lawn mower, shown in Fig. 4, or when building new things of sheet metal, pipe and light structural iron. The garage mechanic or sheet-metal worker will find a welder of this size very useful for repairing damaged car bodies and fenders made of material as thin as 20 gauge. The machine, shown in Fig. 6 B, is also an a.c. transformer type having a rated output of 180 amp. welding current. Since it draws only a maximum of 37.5 amp. from the power line, this welder can be used on most 230-volt rural power lines having a power-line transformer of 3 k.v.a. or larger. A welder of this size is sufficiently large to handle all types of farm welding, Fig. 2, automobile and truck repair work, Fig. 1, and light manufacturing.

A d.c. welder consists of an electric generator, which produces d.c. for arc welding. It is driven either by an electric motor or a gasoline engine as shown in Fig. 6 C. Although higher in initial cost, the engine-driven d.c. welder has a distinct advantage over an a.c. transformer-

type welder in that the d.c. generator is not dependent upon an outside source of electrical energy to produce the welding current. This makes it self-contained and, therefore, portable. When mounted on wheels, Fig. 3, the engine-driven d.c. welder can be towed to the location of the job to be welded. Thus, it is especially useful for farmers and job-shop operators for repairs on large-size machines which

180-amp. welder is sufficiently large to handle all farm welding jobs from the building of a baled-hay loader, above, to making small repairs on a hand rake, below

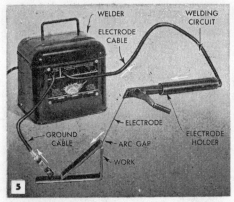

5

White arrows show path of current, or welding circuit. If welder is a.c. type, direction of current alternates or reverses each time current flow makes complete cycle

cannot be moved, or for doing emergency repair work on farm equipment out in the field, as shown in Fig. 11.

Regardless of the type of arc-welding machine used, the metal being welded must become a part of an electric circuit. To do this, the ends of two insulated flexible cables are connected to terminals on the welding machine or, if the machine is the type shown in Fig. 5, the cables are connected with jack and plug fittings on a control panel. The other end of one of these cables is connected to the work to be welded and this is known as the ground cable. The other end of the second cable, known as the electrode cable, is connected to an electrode holder, which is held in the operator's hand. An electrode, or welding rod, which is a metallic rod incased in a flux coating, is clamped in the electrode holder. When

6 TYPES OF WELDERS

A 60-AMP. A.C. TRANSFORMER-TYPE WELDER

B 180-AMP. A.C. TRANSFORMER-TYPE WELDER

C 180-AMP. D.C. ENGINE-DRIVEN WELDER

7 PROTECTIVE CLOTHING

SHIRT-COLLAR BUTTONED

SKULL CAP

WORK SHIRT, LONG SLEEVES BUTTONED AT CUFF

OVERALLS OR WORK PANTS

NO CUFFS

WORK SHOES (NOT OXFORDS)

8 TOOLS AND ACCESSORIES

HELMET

GLOVES

CHIPPING HAMMER

ELECTRODE

WIRE BRUSH

C-CLAMPS

PLIERS

COLD CHISEL

SOAP STONE

6-FT FOLDING RULE (WOODEN)

BLACKSMITHS' HAND HAMMER

2-FT. SQUARE

welding, the electric current flows from the machine to the electrode holder and through the welding rod. As the tip of the rod is brought momentarily in contact with the work and then immediately raised to form a small gap between the work and the rod tip, the current jumps the small gap and the welding arc is created. The current is then carried through the metal of the work and back to the welding machine through the ground cable as shown in Fig. 5. This is called the welding circuit.

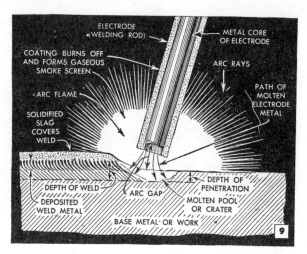

As the heat of the welding arc is very intense and highly concentrated, it is ideally suited for its purpose because the arc can be directed and confined to only that area of the metal being welded.

Fundamentally, arc welding is accomplished by heating the adjoining edges of the workpieces to the melting point and then adding enough molten metal from the electrode to reinforce and fill up any gap or space between the parts being welded, Fig. 10. To learn how to arc-weld, an understanding of what happens within the arc, Fig. 9, is necessary. The moment an arc is struck between the tip of the electrode and the base metal or work, a small pool of molten metal is formed directly beneath the electrode tip. This pool is called the crater, the depth of which is the distance the weld extends into the work and is known as the penetration of the weld. Simultaneously with the formation of the crater, the tip of the electrode is melted and forced across the arc into the crater where it combines with the base metal to form the weld. As the welding rod melts, a portion of the flux coating burns off, forming a gaseous smoke screen which envelops the arc, thereby protecting the molten metal from contamination by the oxygen and nitrogen present in the surrounding atmosphere. The remaining portion of the flux coating melts and is carried to the crater where it combines with any impurities in the molten metal. This action results in a slag which floats to the surface of the molten weld metal and solidifies as the weld cools. The slag coating thus formed covers the deposited weld metal and further protects it from the atmosphere as it cools.

Many different chemicals are used in compounding the flux coatings. Some coatings contain as few as five different chemicals, while others contain as many as thirty-five. The type of flux coating largely determines the operating characteristics of the electrode; for example, its stability, position of the rod in relation to the work, penetration of the weld metal into the work and the shape of the finished weld making it either concave or convex. Another important operating characteristic determined by the rod coating is polarity. When the electrode cable is connected to the negative terminal on a d.c. welder, the polarity is known as "electrode negative." If the electrode cable is connected to the positive terminal, the polarity is said to be "electrode positive." Some electrodes will operate only on one specified polarity, while others will operate on either polarity. Electrodes used with a.c. welding machines must be the type that will operate with either polarity since a.c. alternates from negative to positive each time the flow of current makes a complete cycle. Therefore, a.c. electrodes can be used with d.c. welders on either polarity. However, d.c. electrodes

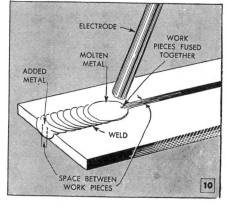

11

Gasoline-engine-driven d.c. welder mounted on auto front-axle assembly can be towed to location of the job

	TYPE OF STEEL			
12 MATERIALS USED TO MANU- FACTURE FARM EQUIPMENT	Low Carbon	Med. Carbon	High Carbon	Cast Iron
SHEET METALS (FENDERS ETC.)	X			
ANGLE IRON	X			
PIPE (PLUMBING)	X			X
MACHINERY FRAMES (AGR'L)		X		
HARROW DISCS			X	
HAYRAKE TEETH			X	
FORGINGS	X	X		
PLOW SHARES			X	X
FILES AND CHISELS			X	
ROUGH GEARS AND SPROCKETS		X		X
MOWER WHEELS				X
ENGINE BLOCKS AND HEADS				X
FURNACE GRATES AND BOWLS				X
I-BEAMS AND CHANNELS		X		
SPLINESHAFTS AND AXLES		X		
SPRINGS			X	
BUMPERS			X	
SHOVELS		X		
BOLTS	X			
RIVETS	X			
MACHINED GEARS (HARDENED)		X		

tant. Many sizes are available, ranging from $\frac{1}{16}$-in.-dia. to $\frac{3}{8}$-in.-dia. core wires. The smaller diameter rods cannot carry as much current as the larger rods and are used for welding thin material where less amperage is needed to melt the metal.

In addition to the welding machine and electrodes, a few other accessories are needed. A helmet or face shield, Fig. 8, should always be used when arc welding. Do not attempt to arc weld with goggles alone. Helmets are made of lightweight, heat-resisting black fiber, and have a fitting to hold an especially colored glass which permits the user to view the arc safely during the welding process. The helmet also has an adjustable headband with a tilting device to allow the face shield to be swung up clear of the face when the actual welding process is stopped momentarily to place a new electrode in the holder. It is advisable to wear a skull cap beneath the helmet. Ordinary work clothing, when worn as shown in Fig. 7, is best for welding, and

designed for one specific polarity cannot be used with a.c. welders. When purchasing electrodes, be sure to specify the type of welder and polarity with which the electrodes are to be used. Specify also the type of material to be welded, because the rod or core metal of the electrode should be of approximately the same chemical analysis as the metal being welded. Thus, a different kind of electrode is used for cast iron than for ordinary steel. The amount of carbon in the steel must also be considered. The table, Fig. 12, shows the carbon content of various metal parts. For bronze, stainless steel or aluminum a still different type of electrode is used. The size of the electrode, or diameter of the core wire, is also impor-

gauntlet-type gloves, Fig. 8, should be worn. For light welding, combination canvas and leather gloves will do. A welder's chipping hammer to remove the slag coating from the welds and a wire brush to clean the welds and material to be welded will be needed. A number of C-clamps of various sizes to hold the work before welding and a pair of pliers or tongs to handle hot pieces of metal after welding are also needed. For measuring, marking and assembling metal parts, a 6-ft. folding rule, some sticks of soap stone and a 2-ft. carpenter's square will come in handy. Other tools in Fig. 8 will also be found useful.

After purchasing or building the type and size of welding machine best suited to

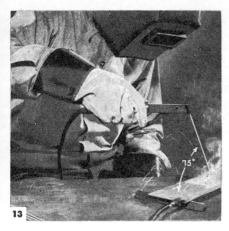

13

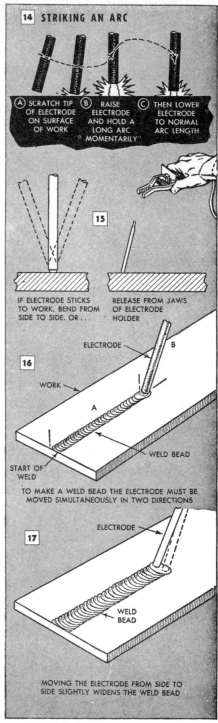

(A) SCRATCH TIP OF ELECTRODE ON SURFACE OF WORK (B) RAISE ELECTRODE AND HOLD A LONG ARC MOMENTARILY° (C) THEN LOWER ELECTRODE TO NORMAL ARC LENGTH

15

IF ELECTRODE STICKS TO WORK, BEND FROM SIDE TO SIDE. OR . . .   RELEASE FROM JAWS OF ELECTRODE HOLDER

16

ELECTRODE

WORK

START OF WELD

WELD BEAD

TO MAKE A WELD BEAD THE ELECTRODE MUST BE MOVED SIMULTANEOUSLY IN TWO DIRECTIONS

17

ELECTRODE

WELD BEAD

MOVING THE ELECTRODE FROM SIDE TO SIDE SLIGHTLY WIDENS THE WELD BEAD

your particular needs, you will be ready to start teaching yourself how to weld. For best results, the welder should be connected to a separate circuit as close as possible to the current entrance switch box. The corner of the farm workshop or basement where welding is to be done should be kept clear of inflammable material and should have a concrete, cinder or crushed-stone floor. A workbench having a steel plate for a top and slightly lower than desk height will be needed, because a comfortable sitting position is important when learning to weld. A strained or awkward body position will result in fatigue and lack of control. All practice welding should be done on low-carbon-steel scrap such as angle iron and sheet metal. High-carbon and alloy steel, cast iron or nonferrous metals should not be used by the beginner until he has mastered the technique of mild-steel welding.

Practice starting or "striking" an arc first. If your welding machine is the small 60-amp. size, use a 1/16-in. electrode and practice on a piece of 16-ga. sheet metal. If your welder is a 180-amp. size, use a 1/8-in. electrode and a piece of 10-ga. sheet metal. First, fasten the ground cable of the welding machine to the steel top of the welding bench. The entire bench top will then be grounded and any work or practice pieces placed on the bench top will also be grounded. If a steel-topped bench is not used, the ground cable must be fastened directly to the metal being welded. Regulate the amperage control on the welding machine to produce the correct amount of current for the size and type of electrode to be used. This information is supplied with each box of electrodes purchased. After regulating the amperage control to the proper setting, place the uncoated portion of the electrode between the jaws of the electrode holder so that the rod is

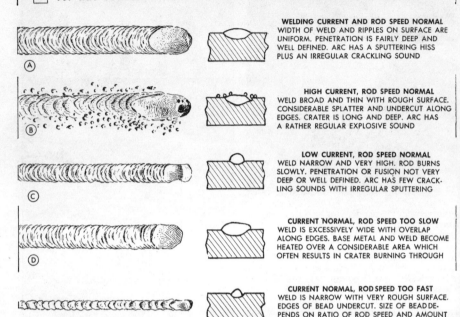

WELDING CURRENT AND ROD SPEED NORMAL
WIDTH OF WELD AND RIPPLES ON SURFACE ARE UNIFORM. PENETRATION IS FAIRLY DEEP AND WELL DEFINED. ARC HAS A SPUTTERING HISS PLUS AN IRREGULAR CRACKLING SOUND

(A)

HIGH CURRENT, ROD SPEED NORMAL
WELD BROAD AND THIN WITH ROUGH SURFACE. CONSIDERABLE SPLATTER AND UNDERCUT ALONG EDGES. CRATER IS LONG AND DEEP. ARC HAS A RATHER REGULAR EXPLOSIVE SOUND

(B)

LOW CURRENT, ROD SPEED NORMAL
WELD NARROW AND VERY HIGH. ROD BURNS SLOWLY. PENETRATION OR FUSION NOT VERY DEEP OR WELL DEFINED. ARC HAS FEW CRACKLING SOUNDS WITH IRREGULAR SPUTTERING

(C)

CURRENT NORMAL, ROD SPEED TOO SLOW
WELD IS EXCESSIVELY WIDE WITH OVERLAP ALONG EDGES. BASE METAL AND WELD BECOME HEATED OVER A CONSIDERABLE AREA WHICH OFTEN RESULTS IN CRATER BURNING THROUGH

(D)

CURRENT NORMAL, ROD SPEED TOO FAST
WELD IS NARROW WITH VERY ROUGH SURFACE. EDGES OF BEAD UNDERCUT. SIZE OF BEAD DEPENDS ON RATIO OF ROD SPEED AND AMOUNT OF CURRENT USED. NORMAL ARC SOUND

(E)

clamped firmly at a 90-deg. angle to the jaws. Then turn on the power switch on the welder and lower the helmet to protect your face and eyes from hot sparks and arc-ray burns.

The welding arc is started by momentarily bringing the tip of the electrode in contact with the work and then raising the electrode slightly to form a gap of approximately ⅛ in. between the tip of the rod and the work. The beginner may encounter some difficulty when starting or striking an arc the first few times due to the tendency of the electrode tip to stick or freeze to the work. To avoid this, gently scratch the tip of the electrode across the surface of the work as if striking a match. The arc will start with a sudden burst of light and sparks. This is startling at first, but do not pull the electrode away suddenly as this will extinguish the arc. Instead, raise the electrode slowly, as in Fig. 14, until the tip is ⅛ to 3/16 in. away from the work. Then slightly lower the electrode until the arc gap is approximately the diameter of the rod. Practice this until you can maintain the arc for a few seconds' duration. After some experience, the correct arc length can 'be controlled by looking at the puddle of molten metal and listening to the regular crackling sound given off by the arc. To stop the arc, simply move the electrode away from the work. If the electrode sticks

to the work, immediately bend it from side to side, Fig. 15, and quickly jerk it away from the work with the holder. If this action does not free the rod, release it from the jaws of the holder. If you find that it is impossible to hold or maintain the arc, increase the welding current slightly. Also, check the ground connection for proper contact with the workpiece.

After becoming proficient in starting and maintaining an arc, try running a weld bead, which is a continuous deposit of weld metal. To lay a bead, two movements indicated by lines A and B, Fig. 16, are used. First, strike an arc and then slowly and uniformly move the electrode to the right in a straight line while maintaining the correct arc length by steadily feeding the electrode down toward the work while the electrode tip melts away. Tilt the electrode toward the direction of travel as shown in Fig. 13. This will enable you to keep your eye on the molten crater and control the rate of travel by observing the width of the weld. The tilt of the electrode also tends to force the molten metal away from the direction of travel and keeps the flux or slag flowing over the deposited weld metal. After laying a weld bead 5 or 6 in. long, allow it to cool slightly, and then remove the slag coating with the chipping hammer and wire brush. Carefully inspect the surface of the weld bead and compare

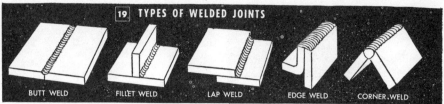

19 TYPES OF WELDED JOINTS

BUTT WELD   FILLET WELD   LAP WELD   EDGE WELD   CORNER WELD

it with those shown in Fig. 18, A to E inclusive. Teaching yourself to weld is simply a process of trial and error. If, for example, the bead appears as in Fig. 18E, the rod speed or rate of travel was too fast. Try laying another bead at a slower speed. If, after cleaning this bead, it appears as shown in Fig. 18B, you will know the rod speed was normal but the current setting on the welding machine was too high. So, reduce the welding current and lay another bead. In other words, eliminate only one condition or variable at a time. Changing more than one variable at a time only results in confusion for the beginner. It is also a good idea for the beginner to deliberately lay a bead with too low or too high a current or too fast or slow a speed. In this way, he will learn to recognize an abnormal condition during the actual welding process. Another condition which must be taken into consideration is heat put into the workpiece due to welding. A piece of hot metal will alter the welding conditions. To avoid this, quench the workpiece in water after each weld bead is laid. Practice running flat beads until a smooth weld of uniform width and height can be laid at will. Also, practice laying beads with all the different rod sizes your welder will handle.

It is often necessary to lay a bead that is somewhat wider than can be accomplished by using the two electrode movements described. To do this, a third movement, weaving the rod from side to side as in Fig. 17, is incorporated. The rate of travel is reduced to compensate for the greater width of the weld.

After becoming proficient at laying a weld bead, practice joining two pieces of sheet metal with a butt weld. First, butt the edges of the sheet metal together and tack-weld with a series of small welds, about ¼ in. long, spaced every 4 in. along the joint as in Fig. 20. Then, turn the sheet metal bottom side up and raise it off the bench top by placing two short pieces of angle iron under it as indicated. Follow the same procedure used in making the practice beads. It may be found that a slightly lower current setting is necessary to prevent the molten crater from burning through in some places. If the sheet metal is fairly thin, a single pass or weld on one

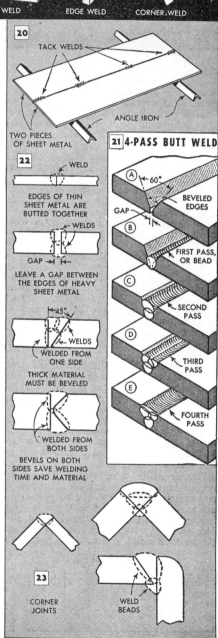

20
TACK WELDS
ANGLE IRON
TWO PIECES OF SHEET METAL

22
WELD
EDGES OF THIN SHEET METAL ARE BUTTED TOGETHER

WELDS
GAP
LEAVE A GAP BETWEEN THE EDGES OF HEAVY SHEET METAL

45°
WELDS
WELDED FROM ONE SIDE
THICK MATERIAL MUST BE BEVELED

WELDED FROM BOTH SIDES
BEVELS ON BOTH SIDES SAVE WELDING TIME AND MATERIAL

21 4-PASS BUTT WELD
(A) 60° BEVELED EDGES
GAP
(B) FIRST PASS, OR BEAD
(C) SECOND PASS
(D) THIRD PASS
(E) FOURTH PASS

23
CORNER JOINTS   WELD BEADS

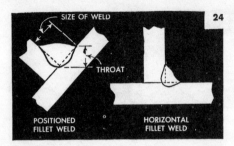

POSITIONED FILLET WELD   HORIZONTAL FILLET WELD

side will give 100 percent penetration. To test for complete penetration, turn the work over and inspect the other side. A good weld should have a small uniform bead here. If the two edges of the metal at the joint can still be seen, a larger electrode with an increase in welding current should be used. However, if this is beyond the limits of the welding machine on hand, a gap may be left between the edges of the workpieces or the edges can be beveled and a number of welds laid in as shown in Fig. 22. The size of the welding machine will determine when a bevel is necessary. Fig. 21 shows the procedure for a weld of 100 percent penetration from one side on heavy material.

Although welding can be done in all positions, the beginner should thoroughly familiarize himself with making various joints in the flat position before attempting position welding. Flat welding includes all types of joints in which the weld can be laid in horizontally. Fig. 19 shows five types of joints that the beginner can very easily learn to weld together in the flat position.

When welding light sheet metal, the most important requirement is good fitup. The two pieces of metal being joined should be held or clamped tightly together and then tack-welded. Also, lap welds, Fig. 19, rather than butt welds should be used wherever possible because proper fitup is much more readily obtained with a lap joint and the chance of burn-through is minimized.

Corner welds on various thicknesses of material are shown in Fig. 23. If the material is light sheet metal, the corner welds are made by running a fast, single-pass bead along the outside of the corner as indicated in the left-hand drawing of Fig. 23. On heavier metal, two or three passes or

beads may be necessary and, when possible, a smaller bead welded along the inside of the corner, as shown in the right-hand drawings of Fig. 23, will greatly strengthen the joint. The corner weld, shown in the lower right-hand illustration in Fig. 23, can also be used on lighter metal by leaving a gap between the pieces instead of beveling as indicated.

When the edge of one piece of metal is joined to the side of another so the two pieces are at right angles to each other, a fillet weld is required as shown in Fig. 19. The size of a fillet weld is determined by the leg length of the largest isosceles right triangle which can be inscribed within its cross-sectional area, as indicated by the dotted lines in Fig. 24. The strength of a fillet weld is determined by the throat dimension multiplied by the length of the weld. The length of a fillet weld should always be at least four times its size. For a weld with strength equal to that of the material being welded, the size of the fillet weld should be equal to the thickness of the material. For maximum strength, both sides of the joint should be welded.

There are two methods of making fillet welds, positioned and horizontal, as shown in Fig. 24. The easiest method for the beginner is positioned fillet welding. To do this, the pieces to be welded must first be fastened together at right angles to one another with tack welds. Both of the pieces are then tilted and propped up so the surfaces of the pieces are at approximately a 45-deg. angle to the horizontal as indicated in Fig. 24. The electrode is held the same as for making a butt weld and is moved at an even pace along the seam without any side-to-side movement. The surface contour of a good fillet weld should be nearly flat and have a slight concavity along the sides where the weld joins the metal pieces. Horizontal fillet welding is used when one member of the joint must remain in the vertical position as in Fig. 24. Hold the electrode at a slight angle as for flat welding and at about 45 to 60 deg. from the horizontal. Move the electrode at a steady, uniform rate of speed and point the rod at the corner of the joint. Use the highest welding current you can handle to assure penetration of the weld into the corner of the joint. Also hold a shorter arc than used when making positioned fillet welds. When fillet welds too large to be made with a single weld are required, several beads, one on top of the other, are built up until the desired size is obtained as shown in Fig. 25. Be sure to remove the slag that covers each bead before laying another.

3-PASS FILLET WELD

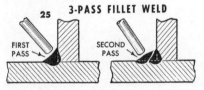

FIRST PASS   SECOND PASS   THIRD PASS

ARC WELDING TORCH

Carbon Electrodes Produce Arc for Soldering, Brazing and Light Welding

HERE'S a tool you'll find handy. It's light and easily made, ready for use on a wide range of small work where it is unnecessary to heat large areas or quantities of metal. Dental laboratories have used it for melting alloys in connection with the casting of bridgework. It has also proved satisfactory on light welding jobs where a ⅟₁₆-in. welding rod can be used.

The complete unit consists of a reactance coil connected in series with a carbon holder. Fig. 1 shows the core dimensions for the coil. A pile of transformer steel or, for that matter, stove-pipe iron will be satisfactory. The iron is piled 2 in. thick from laminations each 2 by 7½ in. as shown. The exact thickness of the steel is of no importance so long as it is no thicker than ordinary stove-pipe iron. When the core has been stacked to a compressed thickness of 2 in. it is bound securely with tape. Upon this core are wound 10 layers of No. 14 double cotton-covered magnet wire. The first layer consists of 72 turns of wire. The starting end of the wire should be left 8 in. long and marked S, as in Fig. 2. When the first layer has been wound in place, the wire is folded out as shown in Fig. 3 to form a tap connection. After this, the second layer is wound on without cutting the wire. A total of 70 turns should be wound in the second layer. When this layer has been finished, it is tapped exactly as previously described and succeeding layers wound on with the number of turns indicated in Fig. 2, tapping at the end of each layer. As the taps are made, they are numbered 1, 2, 3, and so on. Having completed the winding of the coil, a pair of mounting brackets, Fig. 6, is formed from channel iron. The detail shows the dimensions and method of forming these to produce a pair of combination mounting and clamping brackets suitable for preventing hum in the core and for

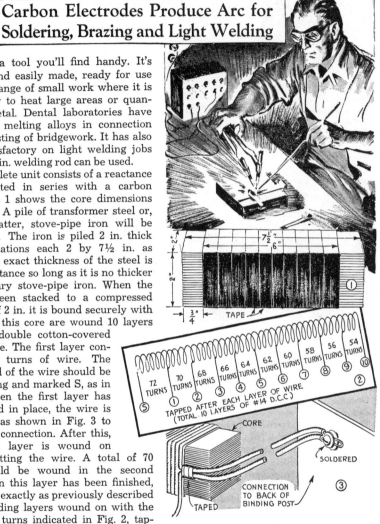

mounting the coil on a base as in Fig. 5. The various tap wires from the coil are connected to binding posts on the terminal board, detailed in Fig. 4. Fig. 8 shows a back view of this terminal board together with all of the connections needed to put the unit into service. It should be noted that the taps from the coil are marked on this detail with the same numbers as were

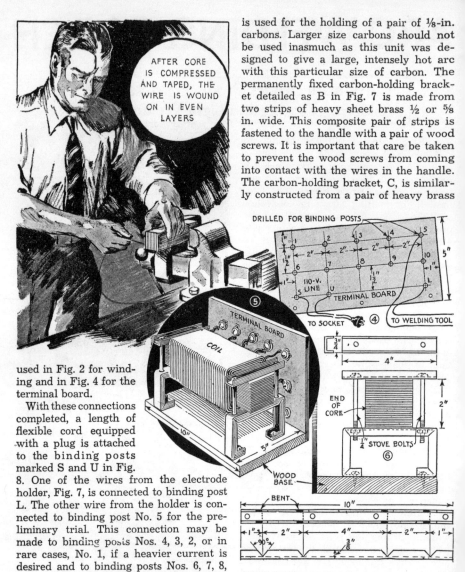

AFTER CORE IS COMPRESSED AND TAPED, THE WIRE IS WOUND ON IN EVEN LAYERS

DRILLED FOR BINDING POSTS

TERMINAL BOARD

110-V. LINE

TO SOCKET   TO WELDING TOOL

END OF CORE

STOVE BOLTS

WOOD BASE

BENT

is used for the holding of a pair of ⅛-in. carbons. Larger size carbons should not be used inasmuch as this unit was designed to give a large, intensely hot arc with this particular size of carbon. The permanently fixed carbon-holding bracket detailed as B in Fig. 7 is made from two strips of heavy sheet brass ½ or ⅝ in. wide. This composite pair of strips is fastened to the handle with a pair of wood screws. It is important that care be taken to prevent the wood screws from coming into contact with the wires in the handle. The carbon-holding bracket, C, is similarly constructed from a pair of heavy brass

used in Fig. 2 for winding and in Fig. 4 for the terminal board.

With these connections completed, a length of flexible cord equipped with a plug is attached to the binding posts marked S and U in Fig. 8. One of the wires from the electrode holder, Fig. 7, is connected to binding post L. The other wire from the holder is connected to binding post No. 5 for the preliminary trial. This connection may be made to binding posts Nos. 4, 3, 2, or in rare cases, No. 1, if a heavier current is desired and to binding posts Nos. 6, 7, 8, 9, or 10 to produce small values of welding current. The binding post to which this connection is made should be determined in each case in accordance with the current requirements for the particular job. This arrangement gives great flexibility to the unit and will enable the user to do many jobs which would not be possible if all work had to be done with a fixed value of welding current.

The electrode holder detailed in Fig. 7

strips and fastened to the angle bracket, E. This bracket as well as a wood or Bakelite thumb control, D, is attached to the U-bracket, which in turn is screwed to the handle. The joint should be just tight enough so that when the handle is gripped you can easily manipulate the thumb control and thus adjust the arc. As indicated, the sections of brass used to make the carbon holders are riveted together 1¾ in. from the ends and twisted just back of the

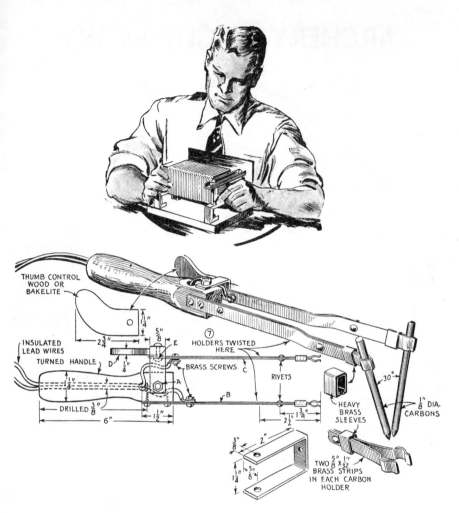

THUMB CONTROL
WOOD OR
BAKELITE

INSULATED
LEAD WIRES

TURNED HANDLE

2¾"

5"/8

E

HOLDERS TWISTED
HERE

⑦

D

¼"

BRASS SCREWS

C

RIVETS

1¼"

A

B

DRILLED ⅜"

1½"

6"

2½"

1¾"

HEAVY
BRASS
SLEEVES

30°

⅛" DIA.
CARBONS

⅜"

2"

¼"

5"/8

TWO ⅝" × 1/32"
BRASS STRIPS
IN EACH CARBON
HOLDER

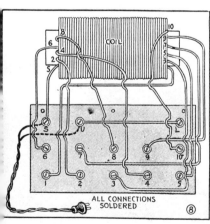

COIL

ALL CONNECTIONS
SOLDERED

⑧

rivet joint so that the carbons will be given a 30° angle. Of course, some experimenting will be necessary to bring the carbons to just the right position.

To use the torch, connect the leads from the carbon nolder to the unit as previously described, plug into the power supply and bring the carbons together by adjusting with the thumb. The arc is easy to pull. For soldering or brazing, the torch is applied to the work and the brazing spelter or solder slowly fed in. The same procedure is used when welding. Welding rods should not be placed in the holder. Use the unit as a torch to supply the heat and feed in the welding or brazing rod.

ARCHERY—FLIGHT BOWS

WOULDN'T YOU like to own a bow that will drive an arrow the length of five football fields? Then, according to expert bowmen R. A. Branaka and Clarence Haugen, you should take up flight archery. One of the first flight bows made by Mr. Branaka won a divisional national championship for Mrs. Branaka with a record shot of 395 yards. Mr. Haugen holds the divisional men's national title with a record shot of 547 yards.

Flight bows differ greatly from

Lower left, wrapping riser with calfskin to form a secure handgrip. Lower right, some archers use a leather "flipper" to release the arrow

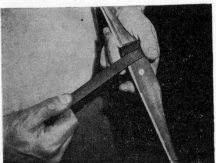

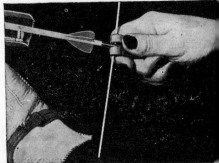

those made for target practice or hunting. They are short and sturdy, and because they are made of special laminated materials including several kinds of tough, springy woods, flight bows have tremendous driving power. Building a flight bow, as in Figs. 1, 2 and 3, is a procedure employing such hand operations as rasping, scraping, sanding and polishing a single piece to several sectional sizes. For this reason it is not possible to detail and describe each step of the process. The first step is to build the two bending forms detailed in Fig. 2, as you will need these as soon as you begin construction of the bow. One form is used for bending the recurve tips, Fig. 1, and the other is specially made for applying the glass-cloth (Conlon) strip to the backing as in the upper detail, Fig. 2. Special clamps are made for use with this form by bending 3/8 x 1-in. flat steel to a U-shape and drilling 5/16-in. holes near the ends for a 1/4-in. pin which is inserted through a hole drilled in the form. The web of the clamp is drilled and tapped for a cap screw. This type of clamp makes it necessary to protect the bow with a strip of sheet metal to prevent damage from the end of the screw as it is turned down. The large form is 42 in. long, which is the finished length of the bow, and the curved ends are cut on a 3½-in. radius.

Bowmakers usually begin construction by making the riser (handle) and the recurve tips. The latter must be steamed for at least 30 minutes before they can be bent over the form. The walnut stock is 3/8 in. thick and 1 in. wide. The tips are cut to 14-in. lengths before bending. The riser, Fig. 3, is cut with a 10-in. radius at each end. It should be noted that in the assembly of the laminations the riser is slightly off-center. Note also that the bow has two parts, the upper half being referred to as the upper limb and the lower half as the lower limb. After the riser has been sawed to the rough

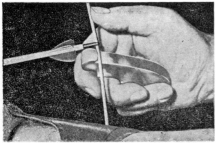

The hook-type release is used by many flight archers

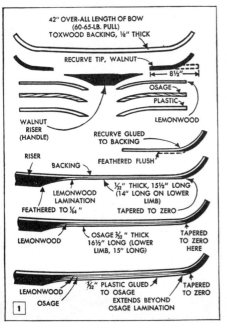

Flight bow being roughed with special scraper made from power-hacksaw blade. Operation is known to archers as tillering. Wood rasps may also be used

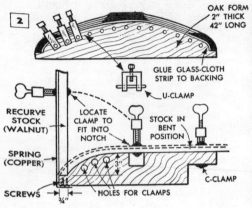

OAK FORM 2" THICK 42" LONG

GLUE GLASS-CLOTH STRIP TO BACKING

U-CLAMP

RECURVE STOCK (WALNUT)

LOCATE CLAMP TO FIT INTO NOTCH

STOCK IN BENT POSITION

SPRING (COPPER)

C-CLAMP

SCREWS → ¾"

HOLES FOR CLAMPS

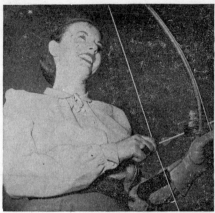

Arrows used in flight archery are made by professional arrow makers because they must be accurate

form and the curved surfaces smoothed by sanding, it is glued to the center of the toxwood backing strip. (Toxwood consists of thin layers of selected maple bonded with a special resin adhesive.) Before the glue dries, wipe off all the excess so that a smooth joint results. Next, the walnut recurve tips are steamed and bent. After drying thoroughly in the forms, they are removed and cut to 8½-in. over-all length and glued to the toxwood backing. The lower ends of the tips are feathered flush before the lemonwood laminations are applied. Note that these are 14 and 15½ in. long, Fig. 1. At the riser ends, the lemonwood laminations are tapered to ¹⁄₆₄ in., but are feathered or tapered to zero at the outer ends where they join the recurves. Apply the Osage laminations in the same manner, but note before cutting stock that one is 15 and the other 16½ in. long. Locate the center of the bow and measure 4½ in. each way. Then bandsaw the riser to the form shown by the dotted lines in Fig. 3. The recurve tips are tapered by hand, the dotted lines serving merely as guides to the rough size. At this stage the bow is ready for nocking and rough shaping, or tillering.

The recurve tips are nocked for the bowstring as in the center photo on the opposite page. Use a ³⁄₁₆-in. round file and file the notch at approximately the angle indicated. The notch should continue around to the opposite side of the tip. Be sure that it is cut to the same depth and at the same angle on both sides of the tip. Brace (string) the bow with a linen bowstring. Then hold it firmly in a padded vise and scrape the limbs to bring the bow to the proper tiller, or bend. This is one of those jobs that must be done by stages with frequent periods of testing with a spring scale. Bowmakers usually use a fish scale for testing. Scraping can be done with a cabinet scraper with fair

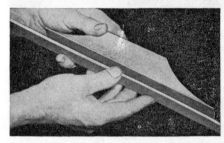

Riser is first glued to toxwood strip, which consists of resin-bonded layers of maple selected for grain

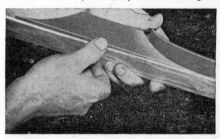

Above, the lemonwood lamination follows curve of the riser and is tapered to 1/64-in. thickness at the end. Below, professional bowmakers use a special bending jig of this type for bending recurve tips

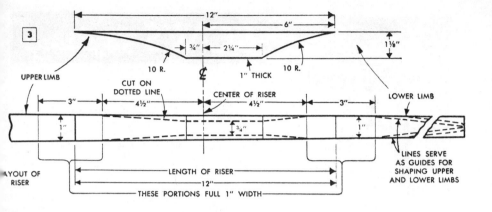

3

12"

6"

¾" 2¼"

1⅛"

UPPER LIMB

10 R.

¢

10 R.

1" THICK

CUT ON
DOTTED LINE

CENTER OF RISER

LOWER LIMB

3"

4½"

4½"

3"

1"

¾"

1"

LAYOUT OF
RISER

LENGTH OF RISER

LINES SERVE
AS GUIDES FOR
SHAPING UPPER
AND LOWER LIMBS

12"

THESE PORTIONS FULL 1" WIDTH

Upper photo, one of several types of plastic over-draw attachments. Center, cutting nocks (notches) in the recurve tips of a flight bow. Below, bowmakers finish the bow by dipping in tank containing varnish.

success but bowmakers prefer a discarded power-hacksaw blade having one side ground to a cutting edge. As the scraping proceeds, check the pull with the spring scale, drawing the bowstring 24 in. from the center of the bow at each trial check. As each check is made, note carefully the arc of each limb of the bow. Both should flex to the same arc during the test. If not, scrape excess stock from the stiffer one until both flex uniformly when the bow is braced.

When tillering and scale checks bring the pull to about half the desired weight of 60 to 65 lbs., the bow is ready for application of the plastic, which is glued and clamped in place in the same manner as the other laminations. Application of the plastic will increase the pull somewhat beyond the 60 to 65-lb. limit and it will be necessary to continue the scrape-and-weight-check procedure until the desired pull is restored.

The final step in building up the laminations is the application of a Conlon (glass cloth) strip to the toxwood backing. A length of glass cloth slightly longer than the bow is placed over the large bending form. Coat the toxwood backing with glue and place the bow on the form over the glass-cloth strip. Then apply U-clamps and allow to dry thoroughly. Once more it will be necessary to scrape the bow to restore the proper pull. Work carefully and check frequently this time or you may exceed the limit. When the pull has been correctly established, sand the bow to a glass-smooth surface and apply two thin coats of varnish.

Now, how about the proper technique of flight-bow archery? You'll have to use the trial-and-error method to discover that. But to get yourself started on the right foot, it would be advisable to contact your local archery club for some pointers. Then keep practicing until you attain a smooth, one-operation maneuver.

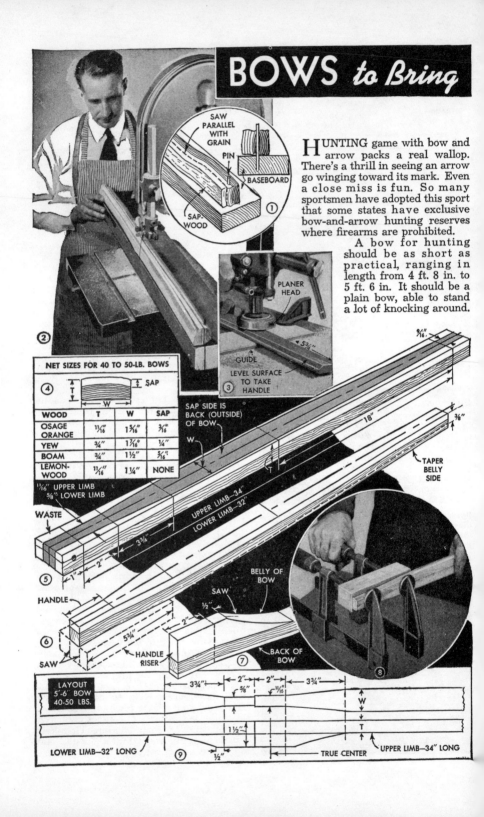

BOWS *to Bring*

HUNTING game with bow and arrow packs a real wallop. There's a thrill in seeing an arrow go winging toward its mark. Even a close miss is fun. So many sportsmen have adopted this sport that some states have exclusive bow-and-arrow hunting reserves where firearms are prohibited.

A bow for hunting should be as short as practical, ranging in length from 4 ft. 8 in. to 5 ft. 6 in. It should be a plain bow, able to stand a lot of knocking around.

NET SIZES FOR 40 TO 50-LB. BOWS			
WOOD	T	W	SAP
OSAGE ORANGE	11/16″	1 3/16″	3/16″
YEW	3/4″	1 1/16″	1/4″
BOAM	3/4″	1 1/2″	5/16″
LEMON-WOOD	11/16″	1 1/4″	NONE

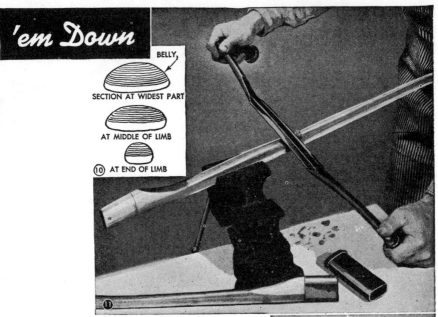

'em Down

BELLY

SECTION AT WIDEST PART

AT MIDDLE OF LIMB

(10) AT END OF LIMB

(11)

The drawing weight need not be excessive; you can bring down the toughest game in the country, including moose, bear and wild boar, with a 45 to 50-lb. bow and a steel broadhead arrow. Most hunters prefer a flat or semiflat bow. The demountable type of semiflat bow described here is popular because of ease of transportation, and the knockdown handle in no way affects smooth, fast shooting. If this is your first bow, by all means make it of lemonwood, as this compact and nearly grainless wood permits mechanical shaping without any regard to grain structure. If you want the best, however, use osage orange or boam. Yew is good, too, although a little too soft for rough usage. All bow woods except lemonwood require careful following of the grain.

Start by roughing out the back of the bow. Osage orange is perfect in this respect; just peel off the bark, and the remaining layer of sapwood, about ³/₁₆ in. thick, is just right. Yew and boam have more sapwood and will require trimming down. This can be done best on a band saw as in Figs. 1 and 2, mounting the stave on a guide board and then saw-

(12) BORING THE HANDLE TUBE

(13) VISE PRESSURE GIVES OVAL SHAPE

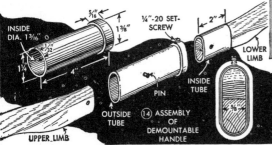

INSIDE DIA. 1³/₁₆"

⁵/₁₆"

¹/₃₂

1³/₈"

1¼"

4"

¼"-20 SET-SCREW

2"

LOWER LIMB

UPPER LIMB

OUTSIDE TUBE

PIN

INSIDE TUBE

(14) ASSEMBLY OF DEMOUNTABLE HANDLE

⁵/₈"

THE HUNTING BOW should be as short as practical, with pulling weight of 40-60 lbs. Style shown is semi-flat, with demountable handle for ease in transportation

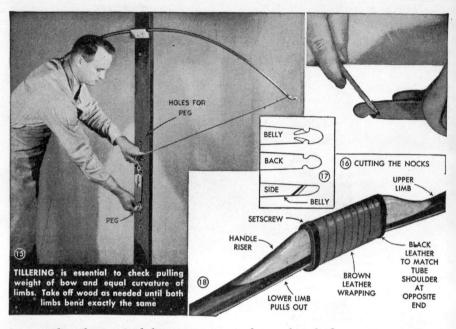

HOLES FOR PEG

PEG

BELLY

BACK

SIDE

⑰

BELLY

⑯ CUTTING THE NOCKS

UPPER LIMB

SETSCREW

HANDLE RISER

⑱

LOWER LIMB PULLS OUT

BROWN LEATHER WRAPPING

BLACK LEATHER TO MATCH TUBE SHOULDER AT OPPOSITE END

ing on a line the required distance away from the heartwood. Pins holding the stave should be a snug drive fit in holes drilled squarely across the chord of the grain, as indicated in Fig. 1. If there is too much heartwood, it can be trimmed down with the same setup. Where there is just a little extra wood on the heart side, a planer head in the drill press will remove it in a jiffy, Fig. 3. In the absence of power tools, the staves can be trimmed with a drawknife. The first stage of cutting gives you a flat stick about ¾ by 1½ in. with a thin layer of white sapwood on the back as shown in Fig. 5. Here you can see why it is easy to work with lemonwood; you have no sapwood to worry about, and the compact grain permits ripping and jointing to straight lines. All the other woods will be crooked, the back of the bow following every dip and curve in the grain. After band-sawing, smooth up the back of the bow with drawknife and scraper, following the grain. Fig. 4 shows table of net sizes for bows of different woods.

On the back of the stave, draw the outline shown in Fig. 5, band-saw to shape and taper the belly side as in Fig. 6. You will cut across the grain to some extent in both operations, but it is only on the back of bow that you positively must follow the grain. Glue the handle riser in place, Fig. 8, and then band-saw it both ways to the shape shown in Fig. 7. Both limbs of the bow are treated in the same way except that the upper limb should be 2

in. longer than the lower one, as in Fig. 9.

The demountable feature is accomplished by fitting the limbs of the bow inside a metal tube. You can buy telescoping tubes for this purpose, or you can make your own. Fig. 14 shows the general nature of the assembly. The short inside tube is pinned to the lower limb and the long outer tube is pinned solidly to the upper limb, the lower limb being a slide fit inside the outer tube, where it is held rigidly by means of a setscrew. Making your own telescoping tube is just a matter of turning and boring, Fig. 12, and then squeezing the assembled tubes in a vise as in Fig. 13, to get the required oval section. It is advisable to heat the work, otherwise the steel may crack at the shoulder portion. The original fit of the round tubes should not be too snug.

Figs. 10 and 11 show the final stage of shaping the bow, rounding off the belly with a drawknife or coarse and fine rasps. Osage orange may be so knotty as to require entire shaping by filing. Whenever you run into a knot, leave a little extra wood to compensate for the natural weakness caused by the defect. Finish off the limbs by scraping with a hook scraper or a piece of broken glass.

As you work down the belly side, tiller the bow frequently as shown in Fig. 15, checking its drawing weight, and more important, the bend of the limbs. Some workers tiller against a wall and use a grid of pencil lines to check for equal bending.

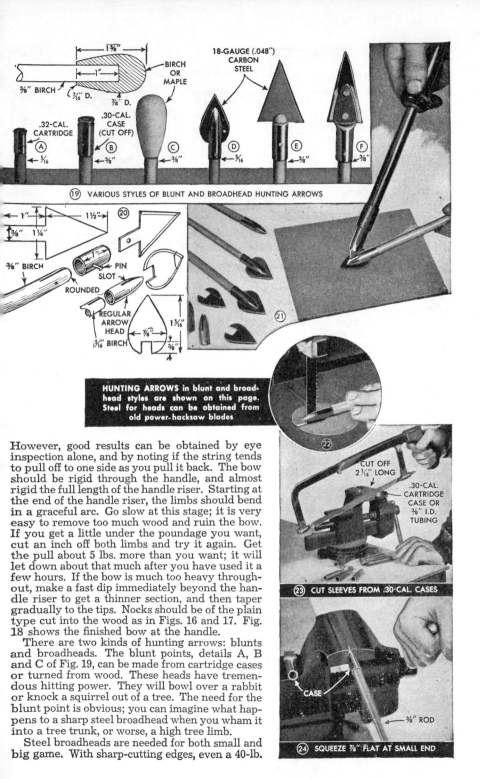

18-GAUGE (.048") CARBON STEEL

BIRCH OR MAPLE

⅜" BIRCH 1⅜" 1" ⁷⁄₁₆" D. ⅞" D.

.32-CAL. CARTRIDGE (A) ←⁵⁄₁₆→

.30-CAL. CASE (CUT OFF) (B) ←⅜"→

(C) ←⅜"→

(D) ←⁵⁄₁₆→

(E) ←⅜"→

(F) ←⅜"→

⑲ VARIOUS STYLES OF BLUNT AND BROADHEAD HUNTING ARROWS

1" 1½" ⑳
⅜" 1¼"

⅜" BIRCH 1" PIN SLOT ROUNDED

REGULAR ARROW HEAD ⅞" 1⁵⁄₁₆"
⁵⁄₁₆" BIRCH ⅜"

㉑

HUNTING ARROWS in blunt and broadhead styles are shown on this page. Steel for heads can be obtained from old power-hacksaw blades

㉒

However, good results can be obtained by eye inspection alone, and by noting if the string tends to pull off to one side as you pull it back. The bow should be rigid through the handle, and almost rigid the full length of the handle riser. Starting at the end of the handle riser, the limbs should bend in a graceful arc. Go slow at this stage; it is very easy to remove too much wood and ruin the bow. If you get a little under the poundage you want, cut an inch off both limbs and try it again. Get the pull about 5 lbs. more than you want; it will let down about that much after you have used it a few hours. If the bow is much too heavy throughout, make a fast dip immediately beyond the handle riser to get a thinner section, and then taper gradually to the tips. Nocks should be of the plain type cut into the wood as in Figs. 16 and 17. Fig. 18 shows the finished bow at the handle.

There are two kinds of hunting arrows: blunts and broadheads. The blunt points, details A, B and C of Fig. 19, can be made from cartridge cases or turned from wood. These heads have tremendous hitting power. They will bowl over a rabbit or knock a squirrel out of a tree. The need for the blunt point is obvious; you can imagine what happens to a sharp steel broadhead when you wham it into a tree trunk, or worse, a high tree limb.

Steel broadheads are needed for both small and big game. With sharp-cutting edges, even a 40-lb.

CUT OFF 2³⁄₁₆" LONG

.30-CAL. CARTRIDGE CASE OR ⅜" I.D. TUBING

㉓ CUT SLEEVES FROM .30-CAL. CASES

CASE

⅜" ROD

㉔ SQUEEZE ⅞" FLAT AT SMALL END

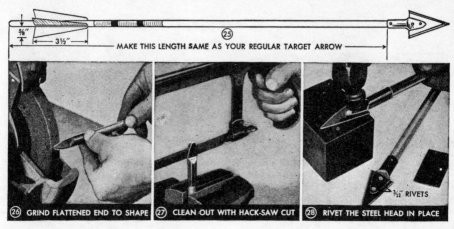

⁵⁄₈" ← 3½" → ——— MAKE THIS LENGTH SAME AS YOUR REGULAR TARGET ARROW ———

②⑤

¾₂" RIVETS

㉖ GRIND FLATTENED END TO SHAPE ㉗ CLEAN OUT WITH HACK-SAW CUT ㉘ RIVET THE STEEL HEAD IN PLACE

bow will send one of these shafts right through a two-point buck. The smallest practical head is the lancet shown at D, Fig. 19. This is made by slotting a regular bullet-type arrow head, and then soldering the notched steel head into the slot as in Figs. 20, 21 and 22. Easiest type to make in any size of broadhead is the tang-and-sleeve style shown at E and explained in Fig. 20. The step-by-step operation in making a broadhead, style F, is shown in Figs. 23 to 28. If you use .30-cal. ball cartridge cases, it will be necessary to have a tang on the broadhead for needed strength. With a sleeve of thicker copper or steel tubing, the split ends of tube alone will hold the head, which can be made a simple,

triangular shape without tang. Old power hacksaw blades furnish good steel for heads. All of the styles shown can be purchased readymade if desired. Fletching of shafts follows standard practice except that the feathers are preferably of the low, long triangular style as shown in Fig. 25. Complete construction kits including heads, cut feathers and birch shafts can be purchased at a nominal cost and provide an ideal method of working. The diameter of shafts will depend somewhat on the pull of your bow. If the pull is 40 lbs. or under, ⁵⁄₁₆ or ¹¹⁄₃₂-in. shafts are plenty heavy. Bows pulling over 45 lbs., especially when big broadheads are used, must have ⅜-in. shafts to stand up under the terrific impact.

ARCHERY KITS

Compact and easy to carry, this archery tackle box has space for almost everything that's needed in the field. Compartments can be arranged to suit your convenience

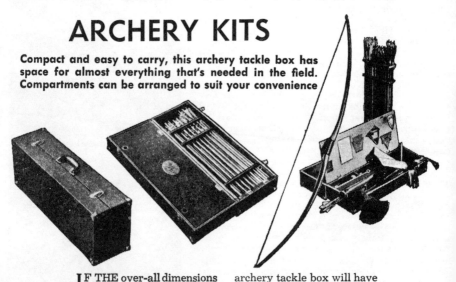

I F THE over-all dimensions shown on the drawing are followed, one half of this archery tackle box will have space enough for 36 arrows and the other half can be

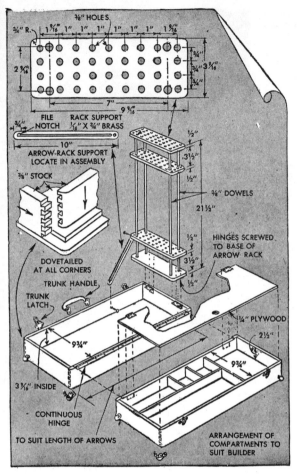

⅜" HOLES

¾" R.

1⁵⁄₁₆" 1" 1" 1" 1" 1" 1" 1⁵⁄₁₆"

2⅜"

¾"
¾" 3⁵⁄₁₆"
¾"

7"

9⁵⁄₁₆"

FILE
NOTCH

RACK SUPPORT
½" X ¾" BRASS

10"
ARROW-RACK SUPPORT
LOCATE IN ASSEMBLY

⅜" STOCK

DOVETAILED
AT ALL CORNERS

TRUNK HANDLE

TRUNK
LATCH

9¾"

3⅞" INSIDE

CONTINUOUS
HINGE
TO SUIT LENGTH OF ARROWS

½"

3½"

½"

⅜" DOWELS

21½"

½"

3½"

½"

HINGES SCREWED
TO BASE OF
ARROW RACK

¼" PLYWOOD

2½"

9¾"

ARRANGEMENT OF
COMPARTMENTS TO
SUIT BUILDER

divided into compartments to carry such necessities as arm guards, gloves, string wax, repair thread and other items that are a part of every archer's kit. The corners are dovetailed and the two sidepieces are rabbeted for a close fit. Arrangement of the compartments is made to suit your own requirements. The dividing section fits into the half that contains the compartments and has a finger hole reinforced with a metal grommet. Construction of the rack for the arrows is shown in the upper and right-center details. Notice that the metal arrow-rack support is fitted after the rack is completed and hinged to the box. After the two halves of the box are joined with a continuous or piano-type hinge, all corners are rounded and fitted with metal reinforcements. The handle and latches are of the type used for trunks.

ARCHERY
TARGET

There will be no possibility of a strong wind blowing your archery target off its tripod and possibly breaking expensive arrows if you attach it to the tripod as shown. Two strong rubber bands cut from an old inner tube are fastened together to make one long band and then fitted with hooks. The band is run through a hole in one leg of the tripod and is hooked into the target as indicated. When not in use, the band is hooked into the hole in the tripod leg to prevent losing it.

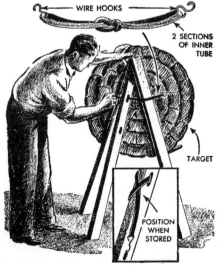

WIRE HOOKS

2 SECTIONS
OF INNER
TUBE

TARGET

POSITION
WHEN
STORED

Protective guard of ¼-in.-mesh hardware cloth is stapled to pulley side of wood box

A. E. Bogg Machine and Tool Co. photo

New do-it-yourself kits permit homeowner to assemble his own

ATTIC FAN

Dayton Electric Mfg. Co. photo (above)

Kloppenborg Aluminum Foundry photo

AMONG THE MANY do-it-yourself products recently offered the homeowner are attic-fan kits which the buyer assembles himself and installs in a simple wooden box at a considerable saving. The kits provide all the necessary parts, namely: Fan blade, pillow-block bearings, shaft, pulleys, collars and belt, and are offered with or without a ¼-hp. motor. The box in which the fan is mounted is assembled of 1 x 12 lumber and ¼-in. plywood and is covered on one side with wire mesh. Some makers offer a fan that does not require a box for certain installations.

The size of your house determines the size of the fan. The fan you select should have a c.f.m. (cubic feet per minute) rating equal to or slightly greater than the gross cubic content of the house. A 36-in. fan will cool the average six-room house 15 to 25 deg. Where it is desired to cool the sleeping rooms only and not the entire house, the fan should have a capacity of 1.2 times the cubic content of the rooms to be cooled. Gross cubic content of your house is found by multiplying its width by its length by the ceiling height.

Suction box partially dismantled shows typical vertical installation of fan over ceiling grille. Pillow-block bearings do not permit horizontal mounting

Suction box of plywood and wallboard provides duct between fan and grille. See drawing below. Fan exhausts air out attic window or louver in gable

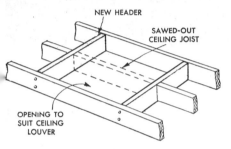

NEW HEADER

SAWED-OUT CEILING JOIST

OPENING TO SUIT CEILING LOUVER

Of the two most common installations, a suction box over a ceiling grille is considered the most efficient as it allows a more even air flow throughout the house, especially when it is possible to place the grille in a hall that is fairly centrally located in the house. The suction box consists of an airtight duct or hood that connects the fan to the ceiling grille. Where the attic is prac-

tically airtight, the fan can be set in front of a gable or dormer window fitted with a louver, or shutter. Here, the entire attic acts as a suction chamber to pull the hot air up out of the house through a stairway or ceiling grille. As the stored-up heat in the attic and living quarters is discharged out through the attic louver, cool night air is drawn into the house through open windows. In this installation, a shelf or other means is used to support the fan vertically, and a canvas duct, or sleeve, is used to connect the fan box to the outer wall. It is recommended that the distance between the fan blade and the window louver should not be less than 6 in. Such an installation, being semipermanent, allows the fan to be used elsewhere in the house as a window fan or circulating room fan. Fitted with a handle, the fan becomes a portable unit.

Fan kits are available in 20, 24, 30 and 36-in. sizes. In installing one of these fans in my home, I selected a 30-in. Dayton fan

Standard ceiling louver, or shutter, in hallway opens quietly when fan starts, closes automatically when fan stops. Louvers are available in various sizes

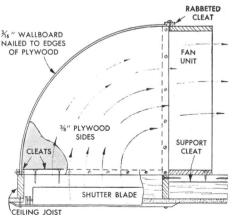

RABBETED CLEAT

3/16" WALLBOARD NAILED TO EDGES OF PLYWOOD

FAN UNIT

3/8" PLYWOOD SIDES

CLEATS

SUPPORT CLEAT

SHUTTER BLADE

CEILING JOIST

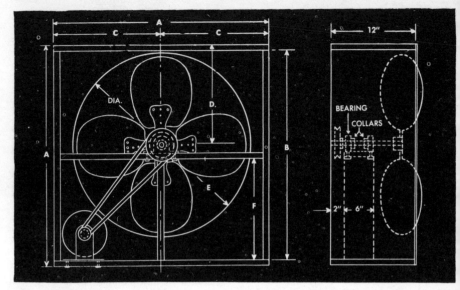

kit and installed it in a suction box over a ceiling grille which I placed in a hall between the bedrooms. My first job was to cut the opening for the grille. Here again, the size of the grille is determined by the size of the fan. Generally speaking, the grille area should be 25 percent greater than the fan area. I used a commercial shutter-type metal grille, but a wooden "egg crate"—type grille, made of half-lapped slats, will do. During winter, a piece of blanket insulation can be placed over it. In cutting the opening for the grille, I had to cut out a section of only one ceiling joist as shown in the detail on the opposite page. You may find it necessary to cut through a second joist, depending on the size of the grille. In either case, the severed joists are bridged across with headers to box-in the opening. The drawing shows how I made the suction box of plywood and wallboard. Rigid insulation board is good, too. You'll notice that I mounted the fan at the edge of the opening. Some recommend placing the fan one fan diameter from the edge of the opening. The suction box should be made as airtight as possible. I nailed cleats to the top edges of the headers and screwed the plywood sides to the cleats and to the fan box. Sheet wallboard conformed nicely to the curved sides by first slipping it under a rabbeted cleat across the top of the fan box. If the attic is insulated with loose fill, the joists should be floored in front of the fan. The drawing and chart at the top of the page give box dimensions for three different-size Dayton fans. The exhaust side of the box is faced with ¼-in. plywood, cut out to suit the blade diameter.   ★ ★ ★

BLADE DIA.	CFM CAP.	HP REQD.	DIMENSIONS (Inches)					
			A	B	C	D	E	F
20″	4840	¼	27	25½	13½	11⅝	21	12¾
24″	5900	¼	30	28½	15	13⅝	25	13¾
30″	6700	¼	34	32½	17	16⅝	31	14¾

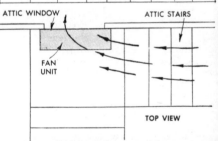

Below, where there are stairs to the attic, fan can be mounted directly in attic window and stair door left open. Such installation allows fan to be removed and used elsewhere in house as circulating fan

FIG. 1

FIG. 2

Photo courtesy Insulite Division, Minnesota & Ontario Paper Co.

Conversion of waste attic space into comfortable rooms like this one economically solves the problem of providing more living room for the growing family. Often two rooms are possible over the average, one-story house

Attic Space

YOUR ATTIC, if large enough, is the best place for an extra bedroom or two, a sewing room, den or study, and perhaps also an extra bathroom. A recreation room of the kind where activities will not be disturbing to other members of the household can be located here. Attic rooms that are properly designed can be just as livable and attractive as any other rooms in the house. Often they can be rented and then provide an extra source of income.

Examples of attic conversions: Figs. 1 to 4 show a few examples of how wasted attic space can be transformed into attractive and comfortable rooms. Fig. 1 shows one end of an attic before building two large bedrooms as shown in Fig. 2. In this case the stairway was located crosswise and near the center of the house. Such a stairway arrangement is a "natural" for two attic rooms as it can open into a short hallway between them. A shed-type dormer extends along one side to accommodate four windows These and others at the gables provide adequate cross ventilation. One of the finished rooms is shown in Fig. 3.

FIG. 3

Photos courtesy Insulite Division, Minnesota & Ontario Paper Co

Large, single room, a spacious hallway for children's play space on rainy days, and lots of extra closet space are possible where a stairway is located at the rear of a house between two lower rooms as shown abov

Because of the stairway position at one end of the house, the unfinished attic shown in Fig. 4 was planned for only one bedroom and a hallway, as shown in Figs. 5 and 6. However, full advantage was taken of low storage space on one side of the hallway for extra closets. The wide hall offers extra play area. Cross ventilation is obtained between the windows at the gable ends.

Another rather small attic, shown unfinished in Fig. 8, was transformed into a small but complete "one-room" kitchenette apartment as shown in Figs. 7 to 11. Alcoves were built to accommodate the combination davenport and double bed, the dressing table and desk, the kitchen cabinets, range and refrigerator. Cove lighting provided pleasant all-over illumination.

Figs. 12 to 14 show how wasted space in an attic was transformed into a family and guest fun room. Note the music-bar motif in decoration, which concealed cove lighting. Acoustical-correction wall covering was used to minimize the transfer of noise to other parts of the house.

Taking inventory of attic space: You can determine the conversion possibilities of your attic space quickly by measuring its width, length and rise — vertical distance between the floor and roof ridge, as in Fig. 15. The relation between the rise and width

gives you the slope or "pitch" of the roof When the rise (R) is ¼, ⅓ or ½ of the width or span (S), the roof has a ¼, ⅓ or ½ pitch respectively. A roof having ¼ pitch doe not provide enough headroom for atti rooms. If your roof has a ⅓ or ½ pitch there is plenty of headroom as you can see by referring to Fig. 16. This gives figure on the usable floor width between side wall of various heights, and also the width o horizontal parts of ceilings at 7 and 8-ft heights. Unless an attic has a rise of at leas 8 ft., it will not have enough headroom to be satisfactory for living quarters. If you house has a hip roof—one that slopes at th ends as well as at the sides—the space fo room conversion also will be reduce considerably.

Checking joist strength: Assuming tha you have enough space in your attic for on or more rooms, the next step is to obtain th advice of a competent architect or contrac tor regarding the strength of the joists. Fin out whether they are capable of adequatel supporting the weight of floors, walls an furnishings of the added rooms, especiall where a bathroom is to be located. Don neglect this important check unless th house was originally designed and built fo the addition of attic rooms.

The reason for this check is that joist

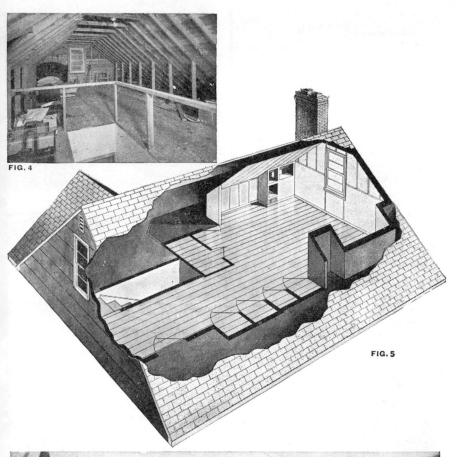

FIG. 4

FIG. 5

FIG. 6

Photos courtesy Insulite Division. Minnesota & Ontario Paper Co.

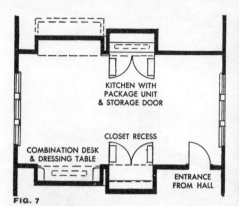

KITCHEN WITH
PACKAGE UNIT
& STORAGE DOOR

CLOSET RECESS

COMBINATION DESK
& DRESSING TABLE

ENTRANCE
FROM HALL

FIG. 7

FIG. 8

FIG. 9
One-room, kitchenette apartment created from a narrow attic—an ideal place for a young couple having limited income, and a profitable investment for the home owner. Photos show vanity nook and kitchen alcove, complete with every needed facility, all instantly available, yet all entirely out of the way when not in use

FIG. 10

FIG. 11

FIG. 12

IG. 13

Photos courtesy Wood Conversion Co.

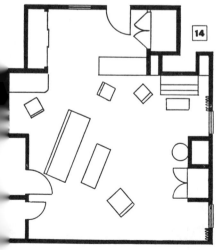

14

in an attic often are only ceiling joists, perhaps of 2 by 6-in. stock, and in some cases even of 2 by 4-in. stock. Ceiling joists need only be strong enough to carry ceiling weight. Usually 2 by 6-in. joists are not strong enough for the 40-lb. minimum load in residential structures, unless their span is only 7 ft. For longer spans heavier joists are needed, which then are known as floor joists. Excessive weight on joists will cause them to sag and vibrate noticeably; may even cause plaster to crack and loosen. Therefore, don't attempt to build rooms on joists of insufficient strength. If it is necessary to install wider joists in your attic, these will raise the floor level and make it necessary to revise your original inventory of attic space.

The floor joists of a bathroom should be capable of supporting a load of 60 or 70 lbs. per sq. ft. of floor area, because of added weight of plumbing fixtures and possibly a tile floor. Extra strength also is needed to compensate for the weakening of some joists that must be cut to accommodate pipes. Locating a second-floor bathroom directly over a bathroom or over closets on the first floor, assures much more support than locating it over a large room where the joist span is considerably greater.

Room planning: Before beginning with the work, accurate planning is essential. A little foresight may avoid costly mistakes of construction and unsatisfactory results. After taking complete measurements of your attic, you first plan the room arrangement on paper to scale. This can be done easily on cross-ruled paper as discussed in

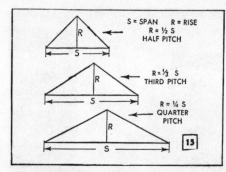

S = SPAN R = RISE
R = ½ S
HALF PITCH

R = ⅓ S
THIRD PITCH

R = ¼ S
QUARTER
PITCH

15

16	USABLE ATTIC SPACE					
One-Third Pitch Roof						
Width of attic in feet	Usable floor space when vertical side wall is:			Horizontal ceiling when ceiling height is:		
	4 ft.	5 ft.	6 ft.	7 ft.	8 ft.	9 ft.
24 ft.	12 ft.	9 ft.	0 ft.	3 ft.	0 ft.	0 ft.
26 ft.	14 ft.	11 ft.	8 ft.	5 ft.	2 ft.	0 ft.
28 ft.	16 ft.	13 ft.	10 ft.	7 ft.	4 ft.	1 ft.
30 ft.	18 ft.	15 ft.	12 ft.	9 ft.	6 ft.	3 ft.
One-Half Pitch Roof						
20 ft.	12 ft.	10 ft.	8 ft.	6 ft.	4 ft.	2 ft.
22 ft.	14 ft.	12 ft.	10 ft.	8 ft.	6 ft.	4 ft.
24 ft.	16 ft.	14 ft.	12 ft.	10 ft.	8 ft.	6 ft.
26 ft.	18 ft.	16 ft.	14 ft.	12 ft.	10 ft.	8 ft.
28 ft.	20 ft.	18 ft.	16 ft.	14 ft.	12 ft.	10 ft.

Section 1. Include in your plan the position of all partitions, the location of doors and windows, stairway, chimney, soil stack as well as other constructional details. If you want an estimate on the cost of your attic conversion, take the detailed plan to your lumber dealer and also to heating, plumbing and electrical contractors.

The exact size of the rooms and their arrangement depends on the type of house, the location or absence of a stairway, the chimney, soil stack and vent pipes, windows and dormers, as well as the available headroom. Each house presents its own individual problems but in most cases satisfactory solutions can be worked out to obtain well-arranged and comfortable rooms.

Bathroom location: If your attic is of average size you can probably include a hall-way between two bedrooms, and perhaps also a bathroom. The best location for a bathroom is directly over one below, or close to this position. From the angle of plumbing, this arrangement makes possible shorter pipe lengths at less cost, and more efficient operation of the plumbing system. A bathroom between two rooms must have adequate light and ventilation, besides headroom. If the bathroom is to be located on one side of an attic as shown in Fig. 17 a dormer will be needed to provide sufficient headroom. A gable-type dormer will serve to house a small bathroom, but a shed-type dormer such as shown in Fig. 19 can extend over the adjoining bedroom as indicated in Fig. 17. An interior view of the finished bedroom is shown in Fig. 18 and the bathroom is shown in Fig. 20.

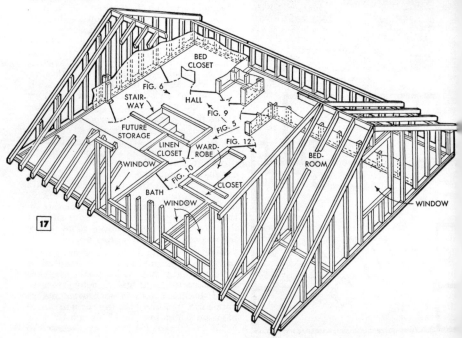

17

FIG. 18

FIG. 19 Photos courtesy Douglas Fir Plywood Assn.

Closet space: Most attics offer storage possibilities in the space between the low, "knee" partitions between the rooms and the eaves. Instead of closing off this space and wasting it, plan on installing built-in cabinets, wardrobes, shelves and drawers. Sliding doors permit full access to such spaces and have advantages over hinged doors that swing out into the rooms, often interfering with the best utilization of floor space.

Stairway location: Many houses already have a stairway leading to the attic. This, unless its location is entirely unsatisfactory, provides a starting point for attic planning. Other houses merely have a trap door for access to the attic. Often it is possible to install a suitable stairway. This may or may not be at the location of the existing trap door.

Building a permanent stairway: The opening in an attic floor to accommodate a stairway is a stairwell. It may be made for a straight flight as in Fig. 21-A, or two flights with a landing between them, details B and C. Where a turn is necessary, a landing between two flights is much better than winding steps, which are more difficult to build and are dangerous to use. The width of a stairwell and steps should not be less than 3 ft. Detail D shows a stairwell opening framed with double headers and trimmers. Double headers support cutoff joists. Trimmers, which may have to be doubled for added strength, are actually extra joists installed at the limits of the opening, and run parallel to other joists. It is important that sufficient headroom be provided under the ceiling adjoining a stairwell.

You can determine the proper length of a stairwell for a single flight of stairs to an attic as follows: Stretch a chalk line tautly from the head of the stairs—at the height of the finish attic floor—to the finish floor below, at any angle from 30 to 36 deg. from horizontal. A slightly steeper angle may be necessary, but it should never exceed 50 deg. Drop a plumb-bob line so that it will intersect the diagonal line 7 in. above the floor as shown in detail E, and not less than 7 ft. below the ceiling line. The intersection represents a point on the first tread directly over the riser.

Treads and risers: Most satisfactory tread

FIG. 20 Photo courtesy Douglas Fir Plywood Assn.

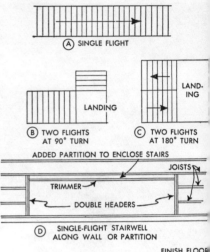

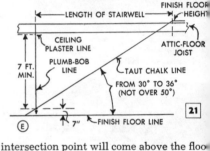

width is 10 to 10¾ in., which does not include the "nosing," which may project from 1 to 1¾ in. beyond the riser. The best riser height is 6¾ or 7 in. See Fig. 22-A. Some variation from these dimensions may be necessary, but the sum of the tread width and riser height should be about 17½ in.

The number of risers in a stair flight can be found by dividing the vertical distance between the two finish floors by 7—the preferred riser height. The result is usually a whole number plus a decimal part of a riser. Where the decimal stands for less than one half of a riser, you disregard the decimal and divide the whole number into the vertical distance, to get the exact height of each riser. Should the decimal represent more than one half of a riser, you use the next higher whole number. For example, dividing a vertical distance of 107.5 by 7 gives you 15.36. Then you divide 15 into 107.5, giving 7.166 for the exact riser height in inches. The number of treads in a flight is always one less than the number of risers. Tread run, Fig. 22-A, is found by dividing the length of the stairwell in inches by the number of treads.

Stair stringers: Stair stringers, usually cut from 2 by 10-in. stock, are the framing members that support the steps. Usually three are required. Their center-to-center spacing should not exceed 24 in. Open stringers, detail B, are easier to install than closed stringers, which are dadoed to take the treads and risers.

Stringers may be marked for cutting the step notches as follows: Readjust the diagonal chalk line at its lower end so that the

intersection point will come above the floor a distance equal to the exact riser height minus the tread thickness. Then carefully measure the angle X at the intersection as shown in detail C, using a protractor. Use the same angle to mark the first riser cut at the foot of the stairs, detail D. The length of this mark should equal the riser height minus tread thickness. From the lower end of this mark, run a line at right angles to it and also lay off a notch to fit over a kick plate, details B, D and E. Measure the length of the taut diagonal line accurately from the intersection to the top end. Transfer the measurement to the edge of the stringer, starting from the first riser mark already made. Then divide this distance equally by the number of treads, marking these points on the edge of the stringer, detail D. With these points as a guide, and holding a square as in detail E, mark off the notches to be cut. The top riser line goes entirely across the stringer as in detail F, as this end of the stringer comes against the head end of the stairwell as shown in detail G. The other stringers are marked by using the first as a template.

In a closed stairwell, the outside stringers are nailed to studs, spaced from them a distance equal to the thickness of the plaster

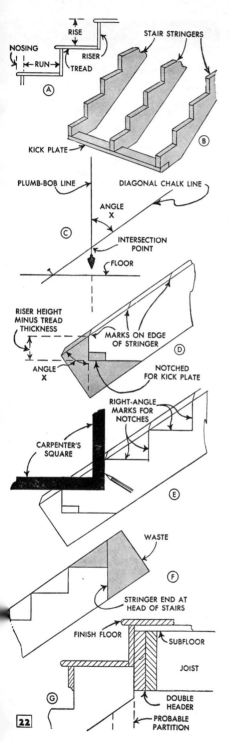

NOSING
RISE
RISER
RUN
TREAD
STAIR STRINGERS
RISER
(A)
KICK PLATE
(B)
PLUMB-BOB LINE
DIAGONAL CHALK LINE
ANGLE X
(C)
INTERSECTION POINT
FLOOR
RISER HEIGHT MINUS TREAD THICKNESS
MARKS ON EDGE OF STRINGER
(D)
ANGLE X
NOTCHED FOR KICK PLATE
RIGHT-ANGLE MARKS FOR NOTCHES
CARPENTER'S SQUARE
(E)
WASTE
(F)
STRINGER END AT HEAD OF STAIRS
FINISH FLOOR
SUBFLOOR
JOIST
(G)
DOUBLE HEADER
PROBABLE PARTITION

22

or other wall covering, by means of blocking. If a wall is already plastered, a stringer may be placed over the plaster and then nailed to studs, using 20-d. nails. The top ends of the stringers are nailed to the stairwell framing, and the lower end to the kick plate, which is nailed to the floor. After covering the walls of a stairway, you nail on the risers first, then the treads. The top riser, which comes to the underside of the extending attic finish floor, detail G, must be a little wider than the other risers, as the flooring is not as thick as a tread. The amount of rise will still be the same.

From behind the stairway, you edge-nail or screw the risers to the treads for added rigidity. Where a landing and two flights of stairs are required, you frame the landing first at a height so that both flights will have the same riser heights. There should be no variation either in tread width or riser height in any flight of steps.

Disappearing stairs: If the building of a regular stairway involves too many constructional changes, or if there is not sufficient space, a glide-away stairway of the kind shown in Fig. 23 is easy to install. Stairways of this type, with variations in mechanical features, are prefabricated by a number of manufacturers. Disappearing stairs are counterbalanced so that practically no effort is required to push them up into the attic. Some types combine both folding and sliding features. After selecting the kind of disappearing stairs you desire, get information concerning the space required for its installation before you plan the position of attic partitions.

Chimney concealment: Plan room arrangement so that the chimney will be concealed or made as inconspicuous as possible. This may be done in a number of ways, such as enclosing it in a closet, letting it serve as a corner where two partitions join at right angles, or letting three sides project beyond a wall and adding closets or shelves on either side. Plan on a 2-in. clearance between the brickwork and the framing around a chimney, Fig. 46, which is required by most building codes.

Daylight and ventilation: If the roof is already provided with one or more dormers, and there are windows in the gable ends of the house, your planning will be influenced by these to a great extent. Windows in gables may have to be enlarged for better appearance and greater utility. Dormers may have to be built in the roof to get enough window space and headroom. The addition of dormers will be necessary in case the attic is completely closed and has only louvers for ventilation.

Removing insulation from floor: The insulation, if any, that lies between the floor joists and on the ceiling below, will not be needed here after the attic rooms are insulated. Therefore you can remove it and re-use it elsewhere. Store it on some boards laid across joists. If the attic is already floored you may find it economical to lift some of the flooring in order to get at the insulation.

Installing floor joists: If the existing joists in your attic are only ceiling joists, and are not strong enough to take the weight of added rooms as already discussed, floor joists of proper width must be installed. This is done without removing the existing ceiling joists. The new joists are placed alongside and nailed to the ends of rafters as shown in Fig. 24, assuming the rafters are spaced 16 in. on centers. The joists should extend on the plates of supporting walls a distance of not less than 3 in. and they should be spaced on 16-in. centers.

Where the plaster of a ceiling is keyed to wood or metal lath, it is not always possible to place the added joists directly on the plates since the plaster extends slightly above them. To overcome this trouble you can nail spacing blocks of 1-in. stock to the edges of the joists wherever they rest on partitions and walls, or you can nail blocks to the plates before placing the joists on them as shown in Fig. 25. All the blocks must be of uniform thickness. It is likely that you will have to cut the ends of joists at an angle to permit fitting them under the roof boards as indicated by the dotted lines. Usually only a small corner at the end of the joists need be removed for this purpose. Reducing their width at their bearing ends for a greater distance than necessary tends to weaken them.

Where joists have a span greater than 10 ft., it is advisable to install bridging of 2 by 2-in. stock at the center of the span, or at intervals as explained in other part. At both ends of an attic where the end joists are often nailed to studs, the existing joists should be brought up to the level of the new floor joists by nailing on lengths of 2-in. stock of sufficient width as shown in Fig. 26.

Wiring, heating and plumbing: Before laying the subfloor, the underfloor work should be completed. This includes the installation of electric cable or conduit, plumbing pipes and heating pipes or ducts. The location of electrical and heating outlets, as well as the arrangement of bathroom fixtures should be indicated on your plan. The average home owner generally finds it best to have the electrical, heating and plumbing work done by professional workmen.

Electrical cable or conduit is installed between or across joists as may be necessary. Where conduit crosses joists they are

FIG. 23   Photo courtesy Farley & Loetscher Mfg. Co.

notched so that it will come flush with the upper edges. The joists are bored to accommodate flexible cable at points far enough below the top edges so that flooring nails will not penetrate the cable. As the wiring in partitions is done after framing them, the underfloor cables are cut long enough to permit the ends to be extended through the subfloor and sole plates to outlet boxes.

Where only a few outlets are to be installed in an attic, connection can be made to the lines of an existing circuit, at a junction or outlet box. In many cases however, the wiring for attic rooms should be a separate circuit. Then it will be necessary to make a connection directly at the distribution box where service lines enter. Extensions on a circuit, or a new circuit, should not be connected to "live" lines until the wiring has been inspected and approved. Tapping to live wires then is done while the main house switch is turned off.

Underfloor heating and plumbing pipes are also installed between or across joists before a subfloor is laid. Vertical ducts to registers in partitions or pipes to heating units or to bathroom fixtures can be located accurately and extended upward above the floor line.

Opening a subfloor: In homes designed for the addition of second-floor rooms where the attic already has a subfloor, it is

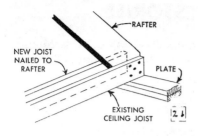

NEW JOIST NAILED TO RAFTER

RAFTER

PLATE

EXISTING CEILING JOIST

[2]

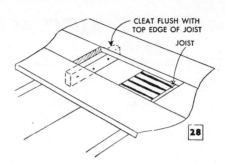

CLEAT FLUSH WITH TOP EDGE OF JOIST

JOIST

[28]

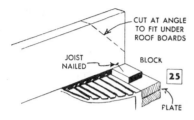

CUT AT ANGLE TO FIT UNDER ROOF BOARDS

JOIST NAILED

BLOCK

[25]

PLATE

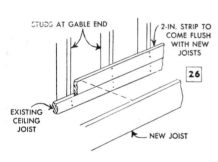

STUDS AT GABLE END

2-IN. STRIP TO COME FLUSH WITH NEW JOISTS

[26]

EXISTING CEILING JOIST

NEW JOIST

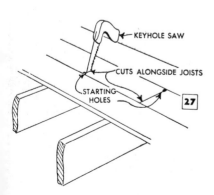

KEYHOLE SAW

CUTS ALONGSIDE JOISTS

STARTING HOLES

[27]

possible that the wiring terminals, and the pipe or duct stubs for heating and plumbing connections are provided. Then it is only necessary to extend these to the desired locations. This may require removing portions of a subfloor. To do this you saw along the sides of two joists as shown in Fig. 27, so that the piece of floor board can be lifted out. After the openings have served their purpose, you replace the pieces, nailing them to cleats, which in turn are nailed to joists, flush with their upper edges as in Fig. 28. Flexible electric cable can be "fished" from one opening to another between two joists. When cable or pipe must be installed across joists, you remove one or more lengths of subfloor boards, which cross the joists, in order to notch or bore the joists and install the cable or pipe. After this is done the floor boards are simply replaced.

Laying attic subfloors: Generally it is not necessary to run a subfloor entirely to the side walls of the house, but only a short distance beyond the short "knee" partitions of an attic, or as far as storage space is desired. For the subfloor you can use 1-in. boards, either plain or tongue-and-groove type, as covered in other part. The boards are usually laid at right angles to joists in an existing attic. Laying them diagonally involves difficulties when attempted under an existing roof.

To assure laying the boards straight across the joists, you mark the center of joists with a chalk line snapped from the ends of the attic. If the attic already has a "catwalk" of boards that are the same thickness as the subfloor, you can start laying the subfloor alongside this. The subfloor should not be butted against a chimney. Saw the boards to a length that will assure a 2-in. clearance from the brickwork. After the subfloor has been laid so that you will have a good surface to work on, any structural alterations on the roof or wall of the house, such as adding a dormer, are undertaken.

AUTO ACCESSORIES

Tissue Dispenser in Automobile Is Handy for Passengers

Conveniently mounted on the side panel of a car underneath the dashboard, a cleansing tissue dispenser will be handy for all passengers in the car. Any metal dispenser will do as long as it has some provision for mounting with screws. Or, if necessary, flanges for the screws can be

TISSUE HOLDER

soldered to the ends of the container. Best location for the dispenser is, as shown, on the right-hand side of the car. In this position it will not interfere with the driver.

Rear-View Mirror Aids Motorist When Parking Automobile

If it's difficult to avoid scraping the sidewalls of your tires when parking a car, a rear-view truck mirror may be the solution to the problem. The mirror should have an arm that is long enough to extend beyond the running board so that it can be adjusted properly. Before mounting the mirror, try it in several positions to see which one is the most satisfactory.

AUTO–AIRFILTERS

Since neglect of the air-filter screen on an automobile will eventually affect the engine's performance, care should be taken to assure periodic cleaning of the unit. According to most car manuals, this should take place about every 1000 miles. The job of cleaning the screen may be simplified to a great extent by washing it in a container, similar to the one shown, which has been partly filled with kerosene. Sides of the container are semicircular in shape and, together with a center strip, are cut from large tin cans to form the container itself. Another strip is bent to form a base and is soldered in place. One end of the container is flared slightly and fitted with a ¼-in.

Air-Filter Screen of Car Washed Easily In Container Assembled From Sheet Tin

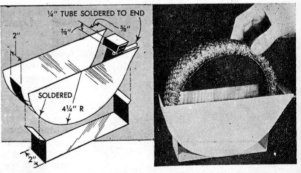

tube to facilitate emptying when finished. After the screen has been washed thoroughly, it should be drained and oiled before installing it again.

AWNINGS

CANVAS AWNINGS can inexpensively turn hot summer days into cool, comfortable ones.

Keeping cool is simplified once we understand that it isn't the air temperature that makes us hot, but the direct rays of the sun.

Orienting your home to the summer heat takes planning, even with canvas, so it's a good idea to take stock of which windows invite the solar rays.

Protection will be needed on the east, south and west exposures some time between dawn and dusk, since the sun rises in the east, follows a southerly path and sets in the west.

The wonderful thing about window and patio awnings of canvas is that they can be designed to meet the changing path of the sun's rays. They can be easily erected and just as easily furled, or dismantled, to give shade where and when you want it.

Structural support is usually provided by metal and rope, also flexible and easily handled materials.

If you have built or remodeled recently it's likely that the windows of your house are higher, wider and more handsome than ever. Soft-looking, colorful canvas provides an excellent companion to glass. This heavy fabric effectively screens 75 percent of the sun's rays. Colors of interior fur-

Sliding canvas panels offer colorful window-wall protection while canvas umbrella shades eating area

It's hard to tell if this dining area is indoors or out, as lightweight canvas roof gives feeling of spaciousness and openness. Matching roll-down shade is doubly decorative in dining area and kitchen

nishings can be kept fresh and unfaded on even the sunniest days, while also keeping the rooms cool.

Vertical shields, pivotable screens, fences, portable shelters, outdoor curtains, sliding panels and giant umbrellas are a few of the many fascinating uses for canvas. Stretched overhead, it shades and protects yet still allows you to enjoy that wonderful out-of-doors feeling.

If you live where summers are hot or moist, a sliding canvas roof will give you real control of your patio's climate. When opened to the night air immediately after sundown, an area protected during the day from the heat of the sun will cool off rapidly. Sprinkling a stationary canvas roof with water will give you further cooling by evaporation.

Your sun stoppers can be as gay and

colorful as you like, since canvas comes in a variety of solid hues, multicolored stripes and floral-backed patterns. Don't be afraid of bold, vivid hues in your awnings, particularly where they cover small areas and serve as accessories. An accent of color at windows and doorways is the finishing touch needed by many nondescript brick, stucco or frame walls.

As a guide in choosing canvas for your awnings or patio cover, you may possibly want to use the color of your exterior walls or roof. In this way the awnings will not only reflect the sun's rays but also your good taste.

By matching or coordinating the colors of your outdoor and indoor furnishings, you can create harmony between areas separated by window walls.

Certain photos and information courtesy of National Cotton Council of America

A canvas sunshade adds color and design to entrance of home and offers cool, inviting welcome on hot summer days. The iron-frame lacing provides varied and unusual patterns of shade and sunlight

A New Role For Awnings

WHETHER YOU are the proud owner of a new five-room house in a treeless subdivision or you live in the home your grandparents built, canvas or wood awnings can offer practical *and* attractive solutions to your sun problems.

Canvas is available in almost any color under the sun, from kelly green to chartreuse, electric blue to gray, maroon to coral, and chocolate to beige. The choice depends upon you and your home, and you can have fun exploring the hundreds of decorative possibilities.

For instance, by choosing awnings to compliment exterior walls, you can actually give your house a new look during the summer months. Sun shades in clear yellow will highlight gray stone, while rich chocolate canvas will increase the eye appeal of white stucco. Repeating the color of the roof in your awnings will create harmony between the top of your house and

its body. You will want bold stripes on wide windows and solid colors on narrow openings.

If your house is extremely modern, canvas awnings can be shaped into interesting contours to match its structural personality. You can extend an inviting welcome to summer-tired guests with a brilliantly colored canopy over an entrance bared to the blazing sun. With a canvas roof and pivotable sun screens, you can reclaim a terrace taken over by the midsummer heat and make your outdoor living an enjoyable all-day affair. You can have for your home any awning to blend with any style of architecture, to fit any window, protect any entrance, cover any terrace.

You can have a man called in to make your awnings, or better still, you'll be surprised at the wonders that you can construct easily and inexpensively with little more than a saw and hammer. Depending on what type of awning you prefer, cedar strips, bamboo strips or plain ordinary wood lying around the basement or back yard idle may be used.

Wooden awnings, in many ways far superior to the common variety of cloth window awnings, will last indefinitely. Even though they cover two thirds of the window to provide maximum protection against sun and rain, your view is not obstructed because you still can look through them as you would a Venetian blind.

These wooden awnings are designed for free passage of air and strong winds will not damage them. They also are designed to drop flat against the window, a desirable protective feature in the case of a summer home which is closed for the winter season.

Using lengths of standard 4-in. beveled siding for the slats and following along on the detailed drawing seen first, the work requires merely nailing the proper slats to "saw tooth" stringers, adding simple stand-off curtain-rod braces and hanging them with screw eyes.

The width of the awning for any particular window is determined by the width of the sash, plus 24 in. The dimensions given in the drawing are for a 28 x 60-in. sash, 15 slats being cut 52 in. long. Where a span of several windows is to be fitted, the complete awning can be made in several sections with false stringers added for additional support.

If you have a table saw, a wooden jig may be used to cut the saw-tooth member uniformly. Here, of course, the depth of

You can make your home cooler and more attractive with a colorful awning, or, as shown below, use a canvas screen to keep out the sun and let in the breeze

Awnings at windows mean comfort inside, while inviting terrace roof adds to your outdoor enjoyment

the notches is cut in the edge of the pieces first. The stringers are laid out for 4-in. notches, the lines being extended across the full width of the piece. These serve later as index marks in positioning the work on the jig.

As shown in the drawing, the jig is tapered 11 deg. and correspondingly spaced index marks are made along the tapered edge. After all notch cuts are made, a chisel is used to break out the waste blocks quickly.

Canopies are made similarly and supported with the same kind of standoff braces. A choice of two

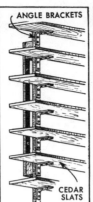

Year-round awnings of cedar slats control sun's rays

styles of canopy front is given in the drawing. Likewise it is optional whether the scalloped edging is to be added to the awnings. The standoff braces are of ¼-in. cold-rolled rod, the ends being flattened.

Bamboo: A second type of awning suggestion is easily constructed from bamboo. Lengths of bamboo nailed to a wooden frame provide a window awning that not only allows sufficient air circulation to prevent the forming of a hot-air pocket under the awning, but also permits more light to filter through than the conventional fabric awning.

In addition to these advantages, the bamboo awning is inexpensive and especially attractive on a summer cottage where an informal effect is desired.

Nail a wooden frame to the outside window casing so that the bamboo is supported at a 45-deg. angle. Then paint the frame and allow it to dry before covering with

Awnings can be made from lengths of bamboo

the bamboo. To prevent splitting of the bamboo slats, nail holes should be drilled through them before fastening to the frame.

Solar awnings: To keep the radiant heat of the sun out of your house during the summer but still take full advantage of its warmth during the winter months, use windows fitted with solar awnings.

Even on cold overcast days, these awnings reflect a maximum amount of light into the room. Covering only the top halves of the windows, they are an especially attractive fixture on a large or small home of modern design.

The awnings consist of a series of ¼ x 6-in. cedar slats long enough to extend 4 in. beyond the sides of the windows. The slats are mounted on strips of wood with angle brackets, and wooden blocks, along with another set of wooden strips, bring the awnings flush with the wall of the homeowner's house.

The spacing, of course, is determined by the latitude in which the awnings are to be used and, once this is done, further adjustment is unnecessary. For instance, if your home is located at 43-deg. north latitude, spacing the slats 5 in. apart keeps out the sun's rays from the middle of April to the latter part of August.

However, if desired, the awnings can be attached with storm-sash hangers and removed for the winter.

A useful hint for any kind of awnings that you may plan to construct or already have picked out for your home is this easy-to-renovate formula. Awnings that have faded, but are otherwise in good condition, may be freshened in appearance by painting them with a solution of raw linseed oil, 2 parts, and turpentine, 1 part.

Certain photos and information courtesy of National Cotton Council

In addition to their usefulness as awnings, these two before and after shots show what a decorative touch these smart slatted awnings lend to a plain-looking house, especially when painted a complementary bright color

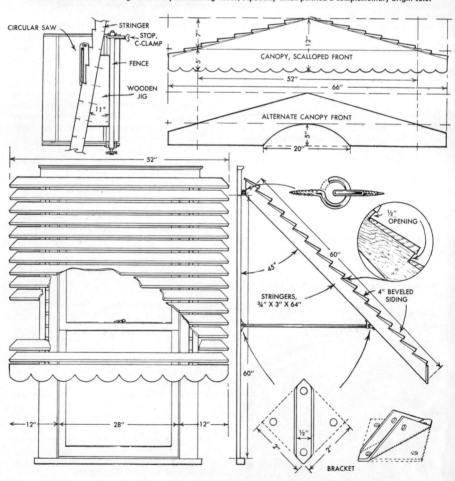

CIRCULAR SAW
STRINGER
STOP, C-CLAMP
FENCE
WOODEN JIG
11°

7"
5"
12"
CANOPY, SCALLOPED FRONT
52"
66"

ALTERNATE CANOPY FRONT
5"
20"

52"

12" 28" 12"

½" OPENING
60"
45°
STRINGERS, ¾" X 3" X 64"
4" BEVELED SIDING

60"

BRACKET
2" ½" 2"

BABY CAR–CRIBS

BUSY MOTHERS with daily shopping and visiting schedules will appreciate the convenience of this dual-purpose car crib because it doubles as crib and sidewalk stroller without any alteration or adjustment. The sturdy frame is made from stock sizes of aluminum, ¼ x ¾ in. in sectional size, and is joined with aluminum rivets where indicated in the details below. Note, in detail A, that an opening is allowed between the frame members to take short axles, which can be lengths of threaded ⅜-in. rod or common machine bolts. Two nuts, one on each side of the frame, lock the axles in place. If bolts are used as axles, the wheels are mounted beforehand. After riveting together the parts which form the basket frame, seat hooks and front rests, the handle is bent from thin-walled conduit and attached to the spacer and to the basket frame as in the assembly details. Although not shown, a rubber handle-bar grip of the type used on bicycles can be fitted over the upper end of the handle. The semi-pneumatic wheels are held on the axles with cotter pins and washers. Care should be taken in the assembly to make sure that the wheels track straight ahead, as otherwise the cart may not roll freely. The basket is made from heavy muslin or light canvas with four buttoned flaps which loop over the basket frame as shown. Note that the flaps are cut away and hemmed separately to clear the corners and handle.

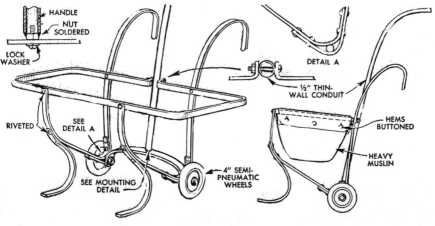

HANDLE
NUT SOLDERED
LOCK WASHER
RIVETED
SEE DETAIL A
SEE MOUNTING DETAIL
4" SEMI-PNEUMATIC WHEELS
DETAIL A
½" THIN-WALL CONDUIT
HEMS BUTTONED
HEAVY MUSLIN

BABY CRADLES

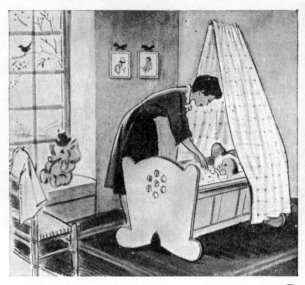

PATTERNED after an original in Holland, this reproduction of an old Dutch cradle offers something unusual in a baby's bed. Its quaintness is typified by a curtain hood, originally provided to protect the baby from drafts. The sides are attached to the head and foot like the rails of a bed, using fasteners taken from an old bed, or purchased. Plywood, ¾ in. thick, will save gluing up solid stock for the head and foot pieces. The pattern for these, Fig. 1, can be enlarged to suit; 4-in. squares will increase the pattern to the size of the original, but 3-in. squares will make it somewhat smaller and less difficult to handle when sawing. While a bandsaw is the tool to use, the work can be cut by hand with a keyhole saw.

Assembly of the bed is detailed in Fig. 2. Note that the sideboards are paneled and fitted with cleats on the inside to support slats or a spring. The cutout design in the head and foot can be simplified by boring seven holes in a circular pattern. Use an expansive bit and make clean-cut holes by backing the work with a scrap block or boring from each side. The bracket that supports the curtain is screwed to the head.

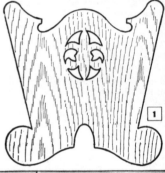

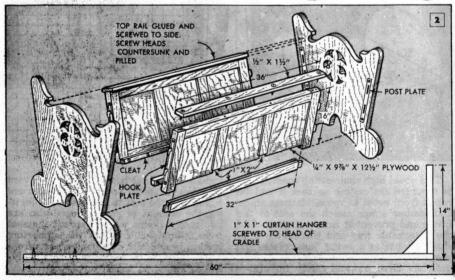

TOP RAIL GLUED AND SCREWED TO SIDE. SCREW HEADS COUNTERSUNK AND FILLED

½" X 1½"

36"

POST PLATE

16"

CLEAT

¼" X 9⅞" X 12½" PLYWOOD

HOOK PLATE

1" X 2"

32"

1" X 1" CURTAIN HANGER SCREWED TO HEAD OF CRADLE

14"

60"

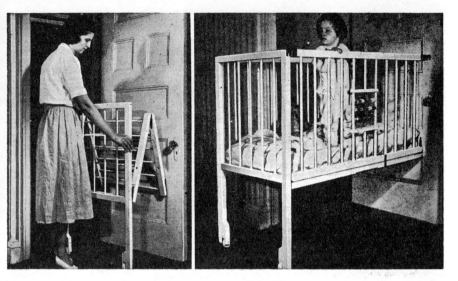

BABY CRIB

A TAKE-OFF on the space-saving idea of the in-a-door bed, this on-a-door crib will appeal to young parents living in limited quarters. Attached to the inside of a closet door, the crib, minus the sides, is designed to fold flat and to swing with the door. The closet, of course, provides convenient storage for the standard mattress and sides of the crib. The bottom of the crib consists of two hinged sections which are locked in the open position by the side panels. Holes for the side-panel dowels are aligned by clamp-ing top and bottom rails together and bor-ing at one time, drilling only about ½ in. deep into the top rail. Glue, plus wedges driven in saw cuts made in the ends of the dowels, anchor the latter in the rails. Pro-jecting dowel pins in the lower rails of the side panels fit registering holes in the bot-tom assembly and a pivoted metal fixture clamps the two together. Slotted flat-steel plates engage round-headed screws to at-tach the side panels to the end panel and closet door.

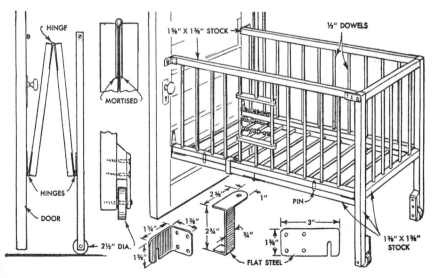

BABY CRIB

**When baby naps outdoors or on the
porch, screen wire keeps insects out
and the baby in. Crib is collapsible**

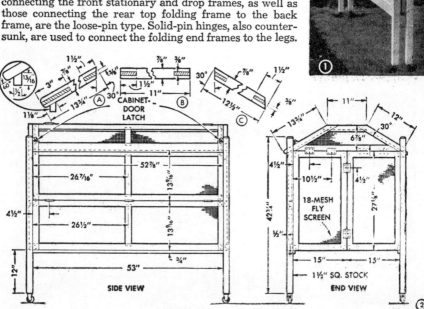

YOU won't have to worry about flies and
other insects bothering your baby if
you keep it in a screened crib like this one,
which is covered with fine-mesh screen
wire. Since it can be folded as in Fig. 1, you
can move the crib to the most pleasant
spot in the yard or pack it in the car for picnics. An added
advantage of the bed is that there are no sliding parts or bars
to catch and pinch small fingers and toes.

Overall dimensions of the crib are given in Fig. 2, and the
dimensions for the three hinged top pieces are shown in details A, B and C. Tongue-and-groove construction is used
in assembling the various panels, and most of the panels are
hinged to the other members. Fig. 3 shows in cross section
how the screen is fitted in all frames, and details A and C of
Fig. 4 illustrate the method of joining frame members. As
each frame is cut, the pieces should be fitted for a trial assembly to check and determine that they are square.

Hinges which are countersunk should be fitted next. Those
connecting the front stationary and drop frames, as well as
those connecting the rear top folding frame to the back
frame, are the loose-pin type. Solid-pin hinges, also countersunk, are used to connect the folding end frames to the legs.

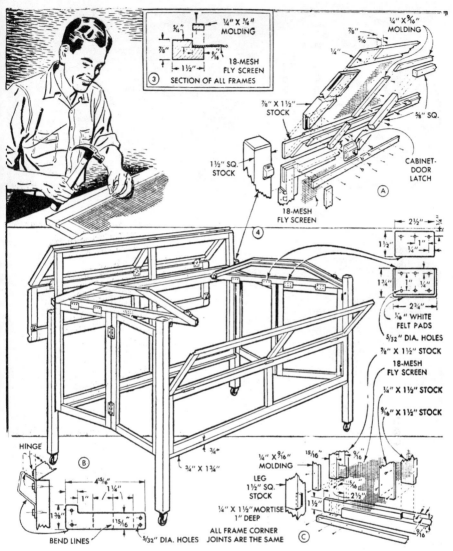

SECTION OF ALL FRAMES

All other hinges are screwed on the surface of the frame pieces and are the loose-pin type. The manner in which the bed folds is indicated in Fig. 4, and the location of the hinges can be determined by reference to this illustration. Before final assembly, the frames should be painted, applying first an undercoat followed by two coats of enamel. Sand lightly after each coat has dried. Then a coat of wax should be applied to protect the surface during assembly.

The bumper and mending plates, Fig. 4, and the top rest bumper, detail B, should be made next. If desired, white felt pads are fitted beneath the plates where they may strike and mar the wood. Note in Fig. 4 that some of the plates attach to the top and bottom members of the end frames, and some are fastened to the top members only. Small cupboard catches are installed as shown in Fig. 4 and detail A which serve to lock the crib in the open position and keep the child from pushing up the top.

To protect the parts of the crib where the members are not hinged, felt strips can be glued to the edges, and as a protection for the top when it is folded back, rubber bumpers can be installed. The casters, which should be installed last, are preferably a type that is relatively free wheeling so the crib can be moved easily.

Wooden **BAIT BOX** *has cantilever action trays*

WIRES GO THROUGH LID

½" SQUARES

GLUED AND TACKED

THIS PIN IS ⅞" LONG

PIN

You Will Be Proud Of This Bait Box

You'll never regret being unable to obtain a metal bait box if you make this fine wooden one, which also affords a very interesting woodworking project. The original box was made of ½-in. walnut, but any available hardwood will do. A careful study of the drawings will show you how the box is assembled. The upper and lower halves are identical in size and shape, the top of the box being rabbeted into the upper half and the bottom dadoed into the lower half. Notice in one of the lower left-hand details how the abutting edges, when the box is closed, are rabbeted on opposite edges to form an interlocking joint that excludes water and dirt. The box is put together with simple glued miter corners. When the glue has dried, the corners are slotted horizontally and reinforcing splines are glued in place, after which all corners and top edges are carefully rounded. Two five-compartment trays of ¼-in. stock are made as shown and pivoted to the box with cantilever arms of hard maple. The attaching or pivoting pins are simply pieces of ⁵⁄₁₆-in. dowel having narrow shoulders or heads turned on the ends as shown in one of the lower details. The pins are inserted through the levers and then glued into holes in the trays, the heads on the pins keeping the levers from slipping off. Hinges and snap locks taken from an old suitcase may be used on the box. A handle is jigsawed from matching wood and is attached by means of wire "hinges" as shown in the lower left-hand detail. After a careful and thorough sanding, the box is given a weatherproof finish by applying three coats of spar varnish inside and outside.

Bait Carrier Fastened to Shirt Keeps Tackle at Hand

When wading in midstream or fishing along the shore, it's difficult to carry a tackle box with a supply of extra baits. However, with this canvas carrier, three or four lures can be carried with no inconvenience. The carrier is made of light khaki cloth and each pocket is about 2 by 4 in., the number of pockets being determined by the number of lures you wish to carry.

Bait Net Made From Umbrella

UMBRELLA FRAME COVERED WITH BOBBINET

An easily carried minnow net that will fit into a small space can be made from a discarded umbrella frame. Cut fine-meshed bobbinette to fit the ribs of the frame, using linen fish line as thread to sew the net to the frame. The handle is removed and a fairly heavy cord is tied to the shaft of the umbrella when seining for minnows.

BALL

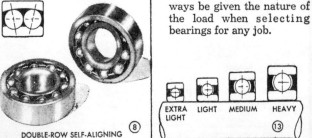

RADIAL LOAD   THRUST LOAD

③

THRUST LOAD   RADIAL LOAD

KINDS OF LOADS
NORMAL LOADS ARE USUALLY A COMBINATION OF THRUST AND RADIAL LOADS

LOADING GROOVE

④ **SINGLE-ROW RADIAL WITH LOADING GROOVE**

⑤ **SINGLE-ROW RADIAL WITHOUT LOADING GROOVE**

⑥ **SINGLE-ROW ANGULAR CONTACT**

⑦ **DOUBLE-ROW ANGULAR CONTACT**

⑧ **DOUBLE-ROW SELF-ALIGNING**

BEARING TYPES
FIVE OF THE MOST POPULAR TYPES ARE SHOWN ABOVE

EXTRA LIGHT   LIGHT   MEDIUM   HEAVY

⑬

B ECAUSE of excellent manufacturing methods, servicing of ball bearings usually is negligible, but the time does come when a bearing may need replacement or, more often, adjustment. Also, if interested in building your own power tools, ball bearing "know how" is essential for best results.

Kinds of loads: Any bearing is subject to two kinds of loads: thrust and radial. The thrust load is a push or pull parallel with the spindle, Fig. 2; the radial load is across the spindle, Fig. 1; both types of loads are diagrammed in Fig. 3. In most power tools, the load is a combination of the two. The load in a wood lathe, for example, is primarily radial, but it can be seen that in certain operations such as boring and faceplate turning there is a thrust load as well. Some consideration must always be given the nature of the load when selecting bearings for any job.

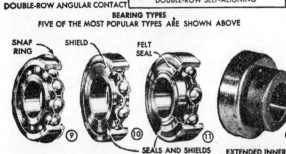

SNAP RING   SHIELD   FELT SEAL

⑨   ⑩   ⑪   ⑫

SPECIAL FEATURES

SEALS AND SHIELDS CAN BE ON ONE OR BOTH SIDES

EXTENDED INNER RING WITH SETSCREW

BORE SIZES		
Bore No.	Bore Size in Inches	Average Load*
0	.3937	¼ HP.
1	.4724	¼ or ⅓ HP.
2	.5906	¼ or ⅓ HP.
3	.6693	⅓ or ½ HP.
4	.7874	½ or ¾ HP.
5	.9843	¾ or 1 HP.
6	1.1811	¾ or 1 HP.
7	1.3780	1 or 1½ HP.
8	1.5748	1 or 1½ HP.

*HP. rating is for light series.

BEARINGS

Bearing types: Although there are hundreds of bearing types, selection for typical power tools usually is confined to three or four popular styles, as shown in Figs. 4 to 8. The single-row radial with loading groove or a similar device, Fig. 4, contains the maximum number of balls which can be introduced into a bearing. It is the strongest type of bearing for a pure radial load, and will also stand up under all average thrust loads. It is never used for thrust alone. The single-row radial, Fig. 5, has fewer balls, but because the outer and inner rings are continuous this bearing has higher thrust capacity. The angular-contact type, Fig. 6, is preferred for jobs where end play must be restricted. This bearing will take a maximum thrust load, but from one direction only unless it is of the type manufactured to take thrust from either direction. The double-row angular contact, Fig. 7, is used where maximum rigidity is desired. The latter is seldom used in pairs because it has practically no "give," indicating that two in tandem would re-

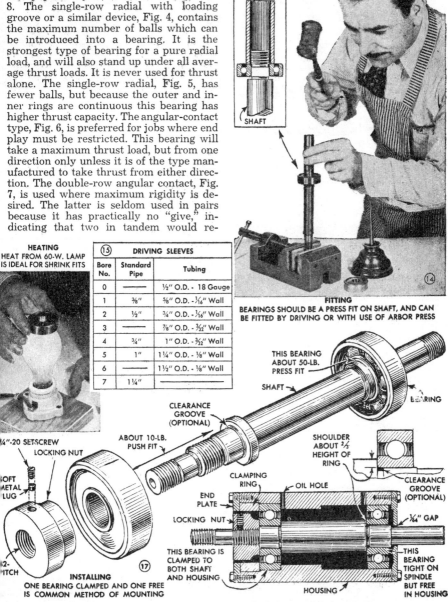

PIPE
SHAFT

⑭

FITTING
BEARINGS SHOULD BE A PRESS FIT ON SHAFT, AND CAN BE FITTED BY DRIVING OR WITH USE OF ARBOR PRESS

HEATING
HEAT FROM 60-W. LAMP IS IDEAL FOR SHRINK FITS

⑮		DRIVING SLEEVES	
Bore No.	Standard Pipe	Tubing	
0	———	½" O.D. - 18 Gauge	
1	⅜"	⅝" O.D. - 1⁄16" Wall	
2	½"	¾" O.D. - 1⁄16" Wall	
3	———	⅞" O.D. - 3⁄32" Wall	
4	¾"	1" O.D. - 3⁄32" Wall	
5	1"	1¼" O.D. - ⅛" Wall	
6	———	1½" O.D. - ⅛" Wall	
7	1¼"		

THIS BEARING ABOUT 50-LB. PRESS FIT

SHAFT

BEARING

CLEARANCE GROOVE (OPTIONAL)

ABOUT 10-LB. PUSH FIT

SHOULDER ABOUT ⅔ HEIGHT OF RING

CLEARANCE GROOVE (OPTIONAL)

¼"-20 SET-SCREW
LOCKING NUT

SOFT METAL LUG

CLAMPING RING

OIL HOLE

END PLATE

LOCKING NUT

1⁄64" GAP

THIS BEARING IS CLAMPED TO BOTH SHAFT AND HOUSING

THIS BEARING TIGHT ON SPINDLE BUT FREE IN HOUSING

2-PITCH

⑰

INSTALLING
ONE BEARING CLAMPED AND ONE FREE IS COMMON METHOD OF MOUNTING

HOUSING

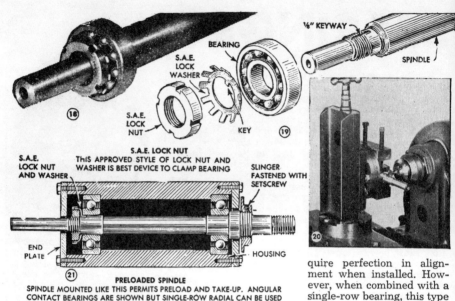

⅛" KEYWAY

SPINDLE

BEARING

S.A.E. LOCK WASHER

S.A.E. LOCK NUT

KEY

(18)

(19)

(20)

S.A.E. LOCK NUT AND WASHER

S.A.E. LOCK NUT
ThIS APPROVED STYLE OF LOCK NUT AND WASHER IS BEST DEVICE TO CLAMP BEARING

SLINGER FASTENED WITH SETSCREW

END PLATE

HOUSING

(21) **PRELOADED SPINDLE**
SPINDLE MOUNTED LIKE THIS PERMITS PRELOAD AND TAKE-UP. ANGULAR CONTACT BEARINGS ARE SHOWN BUT SINGLE-ROW RADIAL CAN BE USED

ABOUT .015" END PLAY CLEARANCE

END PLATE

(22) **FLOATING SPINDLE**
BOTH BEARINGS ARE PRESS FIT ON SPINDLE AND PUSH FIT IN HOUSING

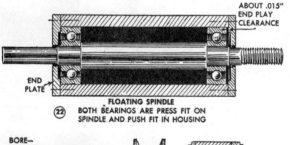

BORE— ONE SIZE SMALLER THAN FRONT

CLAMP RING

FELT RING

REAR BEARING IS FREE IN HOUSING

S.A.E. LOCK NUT

(23) **CENTER DRIVE**
A STANDARD FORM OF INSTALLATION FOR LATHES, GRINDERS, BUFFERS, ETC.

SPRING LOADING RING (OPTIONAL)

SLINGER (PRESS FIT)

EXTENDED INNER RING

(24) **SELF-ALIGNING SPINDLE**
USES SELF-ALIGNING BEARINGS WITH EXTENDED INNER RING

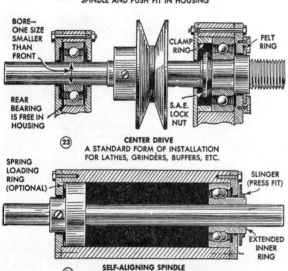

quire perfection in alignment when installed. However, when combined with a single-row bearing, this type makes an excellent installation for certain tools. Fig. 8 shows the double-row self-aligning type. Although rated somewhat lower than the single-row radial for any kind of load, the self-aligning feature makes it very popular with the home mechanic.

Special features: Most bearings can be obtained with a metal shield or felt seal on one or both sides, Figs. 10 and 11, the latter, the "sealed for life" type. A snap or retaining ring, Fig. 9, is sometimes useful when there is no shoulder against which the bearing can be located. An extended inner ring, Fig. 12, is a favorite with home workshoppers because it provides an easy way to clamp the bearing to the shaft.

Sizes and numbering of bearings: The most-used bearing sizes for home-workshop power tools are those having bores of about ⅜ in. and up. These sizes are standardized with a system of bore numbers, of which sizes 0 to 8 are given in Fig. 13. Each bore number is made in four outer ring sizes, Fig. 13, the light and me-

HAMMER OR PRESS HERE

PRESSURE IS ON OUTER RING

Wrong!

INNER RING SUPPORTED

VISE JAWS

BEARING REMOVAL
ALWAYS APPLY PRESSURE THROUGH INNER RING

Right!

Wrong!

PRESSURE IS ON OUTER RING

GEAR PULLER

Right!

LATHE DOG

dium series being the most popular for all small power tools. Most manufacturers designate the light series as "200 series" and medium as "300 series." A No. 304 bearing is medium series, No. 4 bore. In practically all numbering codes, the two right-hand figures give the bore number or the bore size in millimeters. L or 1 in the third digit from the right indicates extra light series; 2 is light series; 3 is medium series; 4 is heavy series; 5 is nonloading groove light series, and 6 is nonloading groove medium series. Other numbers to the left indicate type or extra features. Small power-tool construction is mainly of the light series type. This is sturdy enough for all average loads and does not require a bulky housing. A fair guide to the selection of a suitable bore size for any power tool is the motor rating given in Fig. 13. For example, if you are making a lathe to be driven with a ⅓-hp. motor, you would use No. 2 or 3 bore light series bearings. Of course, if you wanted a hollow spindle, you would have to take a bigger bore to accommodate the Morse taper.

Installation: In the basic installation, Fig. 17, both bearings are a press fit on the spindle and a push fit in the housing. The press fit should require about 50 lbs. pressure with an arbor press, or equivalent hammer taps, Fig. 14. The turning allowance for press fitting should be about .0002 or .0003 over the bore size, Fig. 13. If the bearing is held with a lock nut, as shown in Fig. 17, a press fit of about 10 lbs. is sufficient. Both bearings are a push fit in the housing, which means that they can be pushed in by hand but there should be no looseness. A study of Fig. 17 will show that one bearing is clamped to the spindle and in the housing. This bearing fixes the spindle and takes up the thrust load. The other bearing, as stated before, is a press fit on the spindle and is a push, floating fit in the housing, which allows for shaft expansion. Press-fit bearings are commonly driven on with a piece of pipe, Fig. 14. Fig. 15 suggests suitable pipe sizes for the bores of various bearings. Heat often is used to expand the bearing so that it can be pushed on by hand for a shrink fit. A 60-watt bulb, Fig. 16, gives off about 240 deg. F. heat and can be used in some cases. Immersion in an oil bath is sometimes used to heat bearings but care should be taken in either case not to use too high a heat.

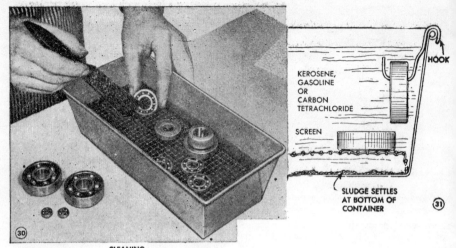

KEROSENE, GASOLINE OR CARBON TETRACHLORIDE

SCREEN

HOOK

SLUDGE SETTLES AT BOTTOM OF CONTAINER

CLEANING
BEARINGS SHOULD BE WELL BRUSHED WITH SOL-
VENT AND THEN BLOWN OUT WITH COMPRESSED AIR

The approved method of locking the fixed bearing to the spindle is the S.A.E. lock nut and washer, illustrated in Figs. 18 to 20. However, this requires a keyway, Fig. 20, which makes more work than the plain lock nut shown in Fig. 17. The S.A.E. lock nut and washer are so arranged that a ¼₄ turn of the lock nut will permit engaging one of the washer prongs.

Fig. 21 shows the S.A.E. lock nut used as the take-up nut on a preloaded spindle to align the inner and outer races. In this installation, the outer rings of both bearings butt against shoulders in the housing. The lock nut is then used to squeeze the inner rings into alignment, creating a preload on the bearings. This kind of installation is particularly recommended for lathes, grinders and other tools where end play must be restricted and a rigid spindle is essential. Fig. 22 is just the opposite. Here, both bearings float in the housing, with about .015 in. end play. This installation is suitable for buffers, countershafts, motors and other jobs where end play need not be controlled exactly. Fig. 23 is a standard installation for center drive and features one bearing locked and the other floating, as previously described. Fig. 24 is a typical installation of the self-aligning bearing. A stiff circular spring is indicated as a means of taking up end play. This is optional and can be eliminated, in which case the left end plate would butt against the bearing, as does the right end. Slingers and felt rings shown in some of the installations are used to keep out dirt.

Bearing removal: Two rules govern bearing removal: keep the bearings clean, and always drive against the inner ring. It can be seen that pressure against the outer ring, Figs. 25 and 28, puts the load through the balls and may damage the bearing. Figs. 26, 27 and 29 show the right way—the inner ring is supported and takes the full force applied.

Cleaning: Surplus grease should be wiped from bearings, after which they are soaked and brushed with suitable solvent. The cleaning pan should have a wire rack, as shown in Figs. 30 and 31, to keep the bearing above the sludge. After cleaning, the bearing should be blown dry with compressed air, Fig. 32. Bearings should not be spun without lubricant since the dry condition makes them liable to scratching. Oil immediately after cleaning, especially if a drying solvent like carbon tetrachloride or alcohol is used.

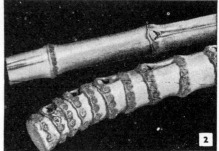

BAMBOO PROJECTS

A cavity can be made for paper-clip tray by turning bamboo parquet paneling on a wood or metal lathe, as above. To split bamboo stem, start it with knife and hammer as below left. Then use two screwdrivers (below right) to make split progress to second saw cut

BAMBOO is one of the most widely used craft materials in the world, yet is rarely seen in American workshops. Most craftsmen, having seen bamboo only in fishing poles, do not know there are more than 1000 varieties of the plant, which is really a grass. Bamboo is enjoying a vogue, however, among handicrafters who appreciate the beauty, durability and utility of this ancient material.

Bamboo for craft purposes is obtainable at most hobby shops in stems (called culms) 6 in. or more in diameter; in roots or root stems (called rhizomes) used for handles and carvings, and in husklike sheaths suitable for weaving. Bamboo also comes in plywood and parquet panels.

In using bamboo, craftsmen should learn to exploit fully its natural shape, color and texture. The tubular stems, however, may be split, sawed, turned or otherwise worked. The pronounced one-way grain

After two saw cuts have been made, split bamboo by driving knife blade into each edge of the lid section

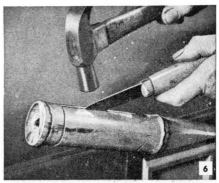

which makes bamboo stems so easy to split also poses some problems in fastening. It is advisable, therefore, to drill holes for all screws, bolts and other fasteners used.

Bamboo stem has a hard, smooth outer cuticle that forms a natural protective finish. Often it is desirable to remove this cuticle so that stain or dye used in coloring the bamboo can penetrate. Many adhesives will not stick to the stem surface until the cuticle has been removed. Also, scraping off the cuticle is an easy way to get rid of stains, shallow scratches and other marks that are unsightly. And it is said that bamboo from which the cuticle has been removed is less likely to split than that in its natural state. If a shiny finish is desired, the "decuticled" bamboo can be given a coat of clear lacquer, shellac or other similar protective material.

Bamboo materials are easily cut with ordinary woodworking tools, can be drilled and threaded like hardwood or metal and respond nicely to rasp (photo 9) and sandpaper. Tools should be sharp to minimize splitting and the formation of "whiskers," particularly in sawing. If a lathe is available, ends of stem sections can be squared accurately by chucking them and taking a facing cut (photo 10) with a keen-edged tool having considerable rake—like a tool used for aluminum turning. Bamboo stems, particularly the thinner ones, are readily bent to permanent curves by heating them with a torch, (as in photo 11) or over a gas burner. Care should be taken not to overheat or scorch them.

The projects described here show but a few of the endless ways in which bamboo can be used in making decorative and useful articles. In some cases, ordinary fishing poles supplied the raw material. Forms such as the root stems and large culms are obtainable from dealers. Although bamboo is a well-known product of the Orient, it is

Lid for rod case is being cut out below. Cut is made 1 in. from end of each side, halfway through bamboo

Procedure in drilling bolt holes in bamboo is shown above. Holes will receive brass bolts and wood screws

Bamboo can be faced either with a half-round rasp as shown above or with a lathe in manner shown below

Bamboo stem can be bent by heating it, as below, and applying the needed force. Then when bamboo cools, it stays put. Take precaution not to burn the material

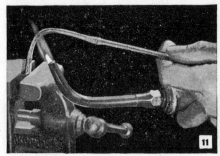

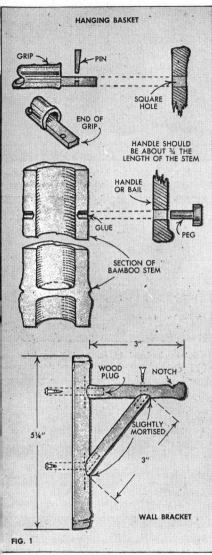

HANGING BASKET

GRIP

PIN

SQUARE HOLE

END OF GRIP

HANDLE SHOULD BE ABOUT ¾ THE LENGTH OF THE STEM

HANDLE OR BAIL

GLUE

PEG

SECTION OF BAMBOO STEM

3"

WOOD PLUG

NOTCH

5¼"

SLIGHTLY MORTISED

3"

WALL BRACKET

FIG. 1

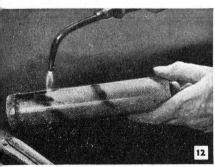

12

13

grown in such near-by places as the southern states and in Puerto Rico.

Hanging basket or vase: The body of this basket is a bamboo stem 1½ in. or more in diameter, and the three-section handle or bail is made from pieces split from stem material 1 in. or so in diameter. Drill ³⁄₁₆-in. holes near each end of the two longer bail sections. With a file, convert one hole in each piece into a square hole, to receive the squared ends of the grip, which are held in position with pins whittled from the same material. The bail is fastened to the body with bamboo pegs held in the body holes with glue. Complete instruction details are given in Fig. 1.

The outside of the basket and bail can be left in its natural condition or may be decorated by scorching lightly with a torch flame. The scorching can be in the form of a decorative pattern suggesting a vine, as shown in photo 12. If cut flowers are kept in the basket, make a sheet-metal lining to hold the water. Although the bamboo itself might be a fair container for water or may be treated with a waterproofing material, the use of a metal liner is advisable in all vases where cut flowers or living plants are to be placed. Photo 13 shows the completed hanging basket.

Wall bracket: For suspending the hanging basket or other object from a wall, a figure-four bracket like that shown in Fig. 1 is strong as well as decorative. The shallow mortised joints add to the strength. Screws used to reinforce the joints engage wooden plugs glued in the ends of the bamboo pieces. The plug at the rear of the horizontal section should, in particular, be

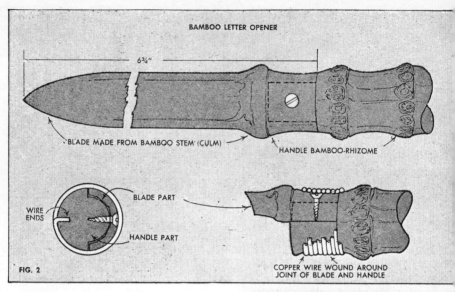

BAMBOO LETTER OPENER

6¾"

BLADE MADE FROM BAMBOO STEM (CULM)

HANDLE BAMBOO-RHIZOME

WIRE ENDS

BLADE PART

HANDLE PART

FIG. 2

COPPER WIRE WOUND AROUND
JOINT OF BLADE AND HANDLE

firmly fastened; a slender crosspin or peg is recommended for the purpose. This use of wooden plugs in ends of bamboo-stem sections is a common means of fastening. The plugs form a firm seating for screws, nails and dowels.

Letter opener or knife: A bamboo letter opener (photo 14) is a useful and durable desk accessory. The one shown has a blade fashioned from a piece of bamboo stem, while the handle is made from a slightly curved section of root stem, or rhizome. This rhizome, or runner, is an underground connection for bamboo plants and numerous roots extend from it. When these roots are trimmed off, decorative rings are left, each consisting of a row of little round spots composed of concentric circles. The root-stem handle can be used also for a knife or other tool, or for an umbrella handle or cane. Although the root stem looks like an ordinary bamboo stem at first glance, it has a solid core, while the aboveground stem is hollow and the joints are usually much closer together.

Cut the handle section to the desired length, about 5½ in. for a letter opener. With a fine rasp, smooth the rings formed by the root scars and finish with a fine sandpaper. With a small brush (photo 15), apply light oak or a similar oil stain to these rings, but do not stain the intervening portions of the root stem. Then give the entire handle a coat of clear lacquer. You can do this finishing either before or after the handle and blade are joined.

A half-round section of culm of the same diameter as the handle forms the blade blank. Shape the blade with a sharp knife

14

Letter opener, paper-clip tray and stamp box, above are but few attractive objects that can be made from bamboo. Below, root scars on handle are brought out by staining. Then finish the handle with clear lacquer

15

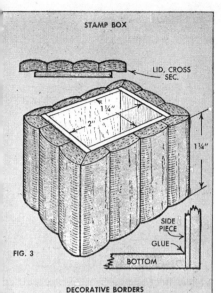

STAMP BOX

LID, CROSS SEC.

1¼"

2"

1¼"

SIDE PIECE

GLUE

FIG. 3

BOTTOM

DECORATIVE BORDERS

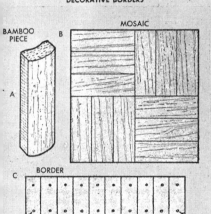

BAMBOO PIECE

MOSAIC

B

A

C

BORDER

SMALL NAILS OR BRASS ESCUTCHEON PINS

16

and sandpaper. Near the blade base there should be a joint, with a ¾-in. extension beyond. Mortise this into the handle as shown in Fig. 2. Use glue and a brass wood screw to fasten the parts, and finish with a winding of copper wire or something similar. Lacquer the wire and blade.

Stamp or trinket box: By splitting a bamboo stem to yield two, three or four sections of equal width, you obtain pieces with one rounded surface, which can be used in making stamp and trinket boxes, decorative borders, mosaic patterns for wall panels and similar arrangements.

The stamp box is assembled by gluing such strips to a rectangular plywood bottom as in photo 16, sanding top and bottom ends of the bamboo pieces after the adhesive has set. Line the interior with colored paper. Each bamboo piece is planed on the flat side and edges to make it uniform and true. Such planing is easiest done on long pieces before they are cut into short sections. The box lid consists of three bamboo strips (see Fig. 3) glued to a rectangular piece of ⅛-in. composition wood that fits inside the box opening. By varying the widths of the bamboo strips, various patterns can be worked out. When an interior lining is to be used in such a box, the shallow grooves resulting from the interior bore of the bamboo stem are not objectionable in appearance.

Bamboo pieces of similar shape can be used to make borders and mosaic patterns, as shown in Fig. 3, B and C. Fig. 3A shows the general shape of such a piece. A simple border, at C, is formed by gluing or nailing strips side by side and can be used to decorate shelf edges, picture frames and so on. A checkerboard mosaic pattern, B, is easy to assemble. When used on a wall, it could have a border like that shown at C.

Parquet paneling: This unusual craft material is made by gluing together short pieces of bamboo stem to form a solid panel, the end grain being arranged to produce a checkerboard pattern (photo 1). Parquet paneling is imported, a typical size measuring ½ x 1 x 1 in. It has a lacquer finish and can be used without further manipulation for wall paneling, table tops, hot-dish pads and many other articles. Because of its interesting structure and pattern, this paneling is an interesting material for making ash trays, trinket trays, coasters, vanity cases, powder boxes and other things involving either turning or carving.

Perhaps the simplest useful object is made by mounting a square or rectangle of the material on a lathe faceplate or in a chuck and turning a cavity that extends to within ⅛ in. or so of the opposite surface. Polish with fine sandpaper and apply lacquer or other protective finish. The delicate coloring of the material is preserved by a clear finish coat. However, you can use oil stain, thinned colored lacquer or various other colored protective materials to add variety. As the piece comes straight from the lathe, it makes a useful trinket tray or coaster. A set of bamboo coasters makes a novel gift which almost anyone would appreciate. Add a half-round piece of bamboo stem 1 in. or so long, and you have an attractive ash tray. The finish for the ash tray should be of a type that will not scorch or burn readily. A lining of thin metal or a glass tray of a suitable shape may also be installed in the bamboo tray.

Stem vase: The parquet material makes an attractive base for a stem vase formed by grouping three or four stem sections of different lengths and diameters (Fig. 4). The stems can be fastened to the base by slipping their lower ends over glue-coated wooden plugs secured to the parquet paneling with wood screws. Each stem should be whittled or filed so it touches at least one of its neighbors, and the areas of contact should be scraped to remove the cuticle so glue will stick to them. The finished vase is shown in photo 17. If the vase is to be used for artificial flowers, no interior work need be done other than drilling through any joint diaphragms that might be present. If cut flowers are to be displayed in the vase, install waterproof metal tubes inside the stems.

Large-diameter stems: Simply by sawing large stems (photo 18) to various lengths, with joints near one end to form bottoms, you produce attractive containers (in background of photo 17) for pencils, brushes, cigars, cigarettes, flowers and stick candy. No special finish is required, other than smoothing the sawed edge. In the Orient, such stem sections are used for vases and brush holders and often are decorated by elaborate carving. Some such examples are very old and are almost black in color. You could imitate such aging by using a dark brown or black stain after the cuticle has been removed.

Modern bamboo candleholder: A graceful holder (photo 19) suitable for a table centerpiece or as a decoration anywhere else is assembled mostly from bamboo stems about ¾ in. in diameter. For the upright portions, stems should be selected for uniformity of diameter and for straightness. The base consists of five half-round pieces split from similar material, although uniformity is not so important. Uprights are fastened to the center base strip by screws engaging wooden plugs. Ends of the uprights should be made concave (photo 20) with a rasp, to fit around the base strip. Glue and nail this strip to a ⅛-in. rectangular panel of plywood or composition ma-

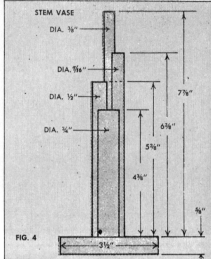

FIG. 4

STEM VASE

DIA. ⅜"
DIA. ⁷⁄₁₆"
DIA. ½"
DIA. ¾"

7⅞"
6⅜"
5⅜"
4⅜"
⅝"

3½"

17

To cut bamboo stem, pencil in line for guide, clamp stem in vise with pads between it and jaws, then cut with ordinary handsaw or hacksaw, as is shown below

18

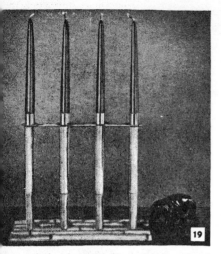

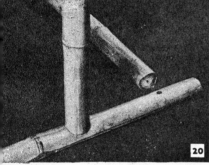

Lower end of each candleholder upright is equipped with wooden plug and filed concave to fit base strip as shown below. A wood screw unites pieces. Hole in base strips should be oversize to permit alignment

terial, and glue the other base strips alongside it.

Upper ends of the uprights are joined by lengths of ¼-in. bamboo stems secured with glue and are capped with metal rings and metal or fiber collars (washers) as shown in Fig. 5. The rings on the model were machined from scrap aluminum tubing, but can be made by bending and soldering sheet metal. Proportions of the holder shown were calculated for best appearance, even to the positions of the stem joints in the uprights. Dimensions are shown in Fig. 5.

Bamboo rod case: An Oriental fishing-rod case was the inspiration for the gun-cleaning rod case shown in photo 21. Such a case is excellent for holding either fishing or gun rods, or slender objects of any kind.

A piece of bamboo stem 1¾ in. or greater in outside diameter and of whatever length required is the starting point. Whenever possible, cut the piece so joints form natural end closures. Otherwise, install wooden plugs. For fishing-rod handles, you may have to hollow out a spot here and there. Sometimes the partitions formed by joint diaphragms can be left in place; at other times you will have to glue in plywood partitions where required. The lid is formed by making two saw cuts part way through the stem and carefully splitting out the section between them. See Fig. 6 for construction details.

Lawn-chair seat and back: Bamboo is considered a very durable material and is able to withstand rain and sun well. Therefore, it seems to be an ideal material for outdoor furniture. Bamboo obtained from cheap fishing poles was used in making the seat and back for the steel-framed lawn chair shown in photo 22. The seat consists

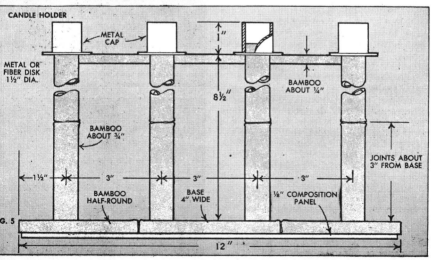

CANDLE HOLDER

METAL CAP

1"

METAL OR FIBER DISK 1½" DIA.

BAMBOO ABOUT ¼"

8½"

BAMBOO ABOUT ¾"

JOINTS ABOUT 3" FROM BASE

1½"   3"   3"   3"

BAMBOO HALF-ROUND

BASE 4" WIDE

⅛" COMPOSITION PANEL

FIG. 5

12"

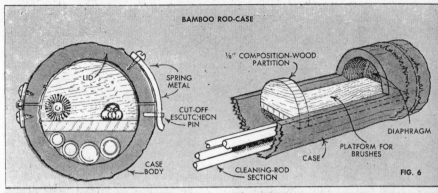

BAMBOO ROD-CASE

LID

SPRING METAL

CUT-OFF ESCUTCHEON PIN

CASE BODY

⅛" COMPOSITION-WOOD PARTITION

DIAPHRAGM

PLATFORM FOR BRUSHES

CASE

CLEANING-ROD SECTION

FIG. 6

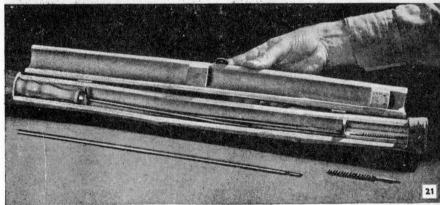

21

of parallel pieces of whole stems, attached with nonrusting bolts to crosspieces. It is used with a cushion, so springiness and smoothness are secondary. Although the back panel of the sample chair was made from bamboo splits fastened with brass nails to oak crosspieces, it was found that the nails had a tendency to loosen. Therefore, screws should be used instead of nails, and the hole at one end of each strip should be oversize or oval so the strip can move with respect to the crosspiece without loosening the screw.

Bamboo is one of the most durable materials the craftsman can use. The people of Malaya, India, China, Japan and the Philippines use bamboo sections for posts and rafters of houses. Bamboo, either whole or split lengthwise into strips, also provides material for walls, floors and roofs. Some homes are finished entirely in bamboo. Because of its wide use, bamboo is cultivated in groves by the people of the Far East. In some localities, bamboo articles are subject to damage by powder-post beetles, which bore holes and hollow out spaces, producing a fine powder as a by-product. Other than these beetles, bamboo has few enemies.

Gun-cleaning rod case above is made from piece of 1¾-in. bamboo stem. Similar case can hold fishing rod, arrows or other slender items. Seat and back of chair below are made from old bamboo fishing rods

22

BAMBOO RODS

WHEN fighting trout or bass take the fly, or when the deep-sea heavyweights it the lure, from there on out everything epends on your skill as a fisherman and on he strength and reliability of your tackle.

After several seasons of hard usage a amboo rod may appear rather shabby and nkempt. Perhaps the tip section has taken "set" or bend; likely the varnish is hipped or cracked badly, and probably the uides are worn and the windings are beinning to fray at the edges. If allowed to o without repair these defects will affect he efficiency of the rod.

The first thing to do in refinishing a rod to make detailed notes of the position of he windings and guides as in Fig. 1. Note lso the width and color of the windings. hen cut through the thread with a sharp azor blade as in Fig. 2. Usually the old arnish can be removed quite easily by craping with either a razor blade or a harp knife as in Fig. 3 but be careful not round the corners of the hexagon secon or to cut any deeper than the varnish oating. Don't use a varnish remover; owever, nail-polish remover can be used

very sparingly to clean off what remains of the varnish, after a thorough, careful scraping. If the ferrules are loose, remove them as in Fig. 6. Then scrape off the old cement, melt new cement, which comes in stick form, and apply in an even coating. Force the ferrule back in place, Fig. 9, and give it a quarter turn to spread the adhesive uniformly. Wipe off all surplus which may be forced out. Sometimes on old rods the bamboo segments will be separated at places along the length, especially near the ferrules. Treat this condition as in Figs. 7 and 8, and be sure to allow plenty of time

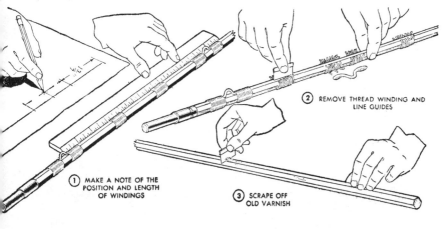

1. MAKE A NOTE OF THE POSITION AND LENGTH OF WINDINGS

2. REMOVE THREAD WINDING AND LINE GUIDES

3. SCRAPE OFF OLD VARNISH

(A) TEMPORARY THREADS HOLD SNAKE GUI

(5)

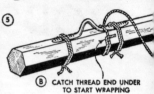

(B) CATCH THREAD END UNDER
TO START WRAPPING

(4) A MUSIC CLIP PERMITS THE USE OF BOTH HANDS TO TURN THE
ROD AND OBTAIN A STEADY TENSION ON THE THREAD

for the glue to dry before unwinding the "clamping" thread. Wipe off surplus glue with a damp cloth before it dries. In this operation, it's important that the segments fit true, otherwise that section of the rod may show up a bend or "kink" which will affect its usefulness.

Now's the time to make sure that the ferrules fit properly. Often old ferrules tend to stick due to accumulated dirt and corrosion of the sliding surfaces. A buffing wheel will polish the parts to a velvety fit, but you have to be careful that the metal is not heated to the point where the cement will be softened. Badly roughened or corroded ferrules will have to be smoothed with very fine emery or "crocus" cloth, Fig. 11, before buffing. It's necessary to be careful that you don't polish away the metal to the point where the parts fit loosely. With the work completed to this stage, check the location of the guides from the reference sketch previously made as in Fig. 1, and mark lightly on the rod the position of each. If there is a set or bend in either or both of the rod tips—most fly rods are provided with two

tips—the bend can be worked out by gentl straightening the tip against the origina set, using both hands. This takes a bit o patience, but the method is effective. An other way is to hang the tip from the ceilin with a weight attached to the lower end Guides should be replaced on the undersid of the bend. Many rods are fitted with th so-called "snake" guides, and any of thes that show undue wear or other damag should be replaced with new parts. Thi also is particularly true of the reel guid and the tip-top guide. If these are worn o grooved they will damage the line.

Fig. 5, details A to D inclusive, shows ho to tie an invisible knot when making th new windings. First give the rod a thinne coat of special rod varnish and allow this t dry thoroughly. You'll note in Fig. 4 a arrangement for maintaining a unifor tension on the thread when making th windings, the thread being pulled throug a music clip attached to a standard. Jaw of the clip should be smoothed so that the do not tear the strands of the silk threa Use the same color and size of thread as th

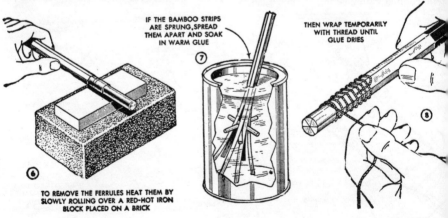

IF THE BAMBOO STRIPS
ARE SPRUNG, SPREAD
THEM APART AND SOAK
IN WARM GLUE

(7)

THEN WRAP TEMPORARILY
WITH THREAD UNTIL
GLUE DRIES

(8)

(6) TO REMOVE THE FERRULES HEAT THEM BY
SLOWLY ROLLING OVER A RED-HOT IRON
BLOCK PLACED ON A BRICK

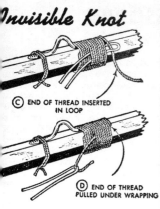

Invisible Knot

(C) END OF THREAD INSERTED IN LOOP

(D) END OF THREAD PULLED UNDER WRAPPING

original windings. It should be remembered that the windings add "tension" to the rod and that's why it's important to duplicate the position of the originals. Although the number of turns may vary, 25 turns per winding is a good average. Some refinishers space in an extra winding to stiffen an old rod, but usually this is not necessary.

Apply thinned white shellac to the windings and when dry follow with several coats of clear collodion or a special silk-thread color preservative. Use your finger for these applications as a brush picks up too much of the finishing material. Follow with three to five coats of rod varnish applied with a small brush as in Fig. 10. Hang the sections of the rod by fitting a wood plug and screw eye in the ferrules. Allow the varnish to dry several days between coats. Rub down the last coat with fine pumice stone and water and finish with dry rottenstone rubbed with chamois. If you wish to

produce an exceptionally fine finish rub down each coat after a thorough drying, using pumice stone only. This leaves the surface slightly rough so that succeeding coats will bond properly. However, the principal purpose of rubbing down each coat is to level the varnish to a film of uniform thickness. After each rubbing clean the rod thoroughly with a damp rag and allow to dry before applying fresh varnish. When not in use the rod should be kept in a case to protect it from breakage, scratches or other damage. A tubular metal case is generally preferable to a cloth one.

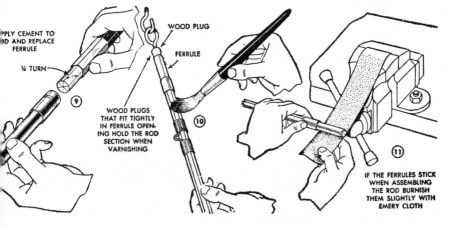

APPLY CEMENT TO ROD AND REPLACE FERRULE

¼ TURN

9

WOOD PLUG

FERRULE

WOOD PLUGS THAT FIT TIGHTLY IN FERRULE OPENING HOLD THE ROD SECTION WHEN VARNISHING

10

11

IF THE FERRULES STICK WHEN ASSEMBLING THE ROD BURNISH THEM SLIGHTLY WITH EMERY CLOTH

BANDSAW ACCESSORIES

The photos above and below show the bandsaw-table extension being used for straight and bevel cuts

An enlarged working area and provision for a long rip fence are advantages of this bandsaw-table extension. The fence is shown in use in Fig. 1, and Fig. 2 shows the table tilted for a bevel cut. Because sizes of bandsaw tables and throats vary, no overall dimensions are given as the extension must be made to suit the saw being used. Fig. 3 shows how the parts are cut and assembled. The table extension consists of a piece of plywood having edges faced with solid stock. These are tongue-and-groove joints glued flush with the surface of the plywood. The opening for the bandsaw table is jigsawed for a snug fit. Four cleats are screwed around the opening on the underside and holes are drilled in them for ¼-in. bolts. Matching holes are drilled and tapped in the sides of the bandsaw table, and the extension is attached to the table with bolts through these holes. Next, add the beveled guide rails for the rip fence and cut the slot for the saw blade, being sure that it is aligned with the slot in the metal table. The rip fence is detailed in Fig. 3. Note that the guide blocks are grooved to fit the guide rails and attached to the end pieces by half-lapped joints. Then one end piece is screwed to the fence and the other is hinged and drilled for a hanger bolt and wing nut for clamping the fence in place. The lower right-hand detail shows how the fence is assembled.

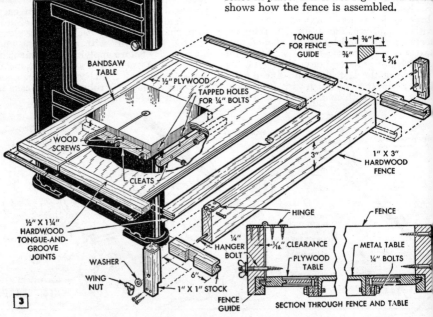

BANDSAW CONSTRUCTION

THIS BANDSAW for cutting wood and metal is a home-built unit throughout, yet it has every essential feature of the average dual-purpose-type machine. The frame is assembled from pipe and fittings, band wheels are made from hardboard for lightness and strength and are mounted on ball bearings. The table tilts on double trunnions, Fig. 1, and the upper wheel-bearing assembly is fitted with a spring-loaded blade-tensioning-and-tracking device. The necessary speed reduction for metal cutting is made through

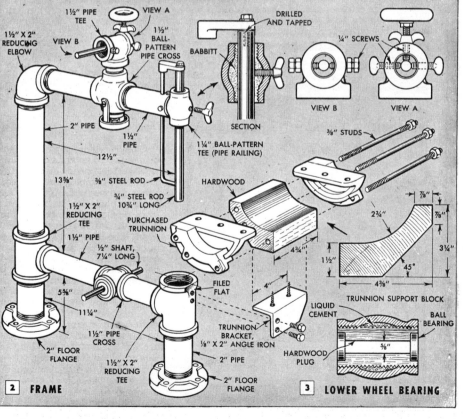

1

1½" PIPE TEE

VIEW A

1½" BALL-PATTERN PIPE CROSS

VIEW B

1½" X 2" REDUCING ELBOW

DRILLED AND TAPPED

BABBITT

¼" SCREWS

BALL-PATTERN PIPE CROSS

VIEW B   VIEW A

2" PIPE

1½" PIPE

12½"

SECTION

1¼" BALL-PATTERN TEE (PIPE RAILING)

⅜" STUDS

13⅜"   ⅜" STEEL ROD

HARDWOOD

1½" X 2" REDUCING TEE

¾" STEEL ROD 10¾" LONG

PURCHASED TRUNNION

⅞"
⅞"
2¾"
3¼"

1½" PIPE

½" SHAFT, 7¼" LONG

4¾"

1½"

45°

4⅜"

5⅜"

FILED FLAT

TRUNNION SUPPORT BLOCK

11¼"

4"

LIQUID CEMENT

BALL BEARING

1½" PIPE CROSS

TRUNNION BRACKET, ⅛" X 2" ANGLE IRON

⅝"

2" FLOOR FLANGE

1½" X 2" REDUCING TEE

2" PIPE

HARDWOOD PLUG

2" FLOOR FLANGE

2 FRAME

3 LOWER WHEEL BEARING

two step pulleys on a jackshaft mounted in a base which has been especially designed and built to reduce vibration to the minimum. A simple belt shift to direct drive provides the higher speeds necessary for cutting wood. Note the trim, neat design of the machine in Fig. 4.

Fig. 2 details the frame and Fig. 3 the lower wheel-bearing and the trunnion assembly. Long and short pipe nipples, reducing elbows, tees and floor flanges are assembled to form the frame shown in Fig. 2. One thing to note especially at the outset: You will see in Fig. 2 that the over-all dimensions are given from side to side and not from center to center. In detailing an assembly of this type made from pipe fittings it is not possible to give precise center to center dimensions. Those given represent the distances on the original assembly with the threaded joints drawn moderately

4

tight. Because of slight allowable variations in threading and tapping pipes and fittings, frames built up in this way from a number of fitting may vary somewhat in over-all size Probably the best procedure is to make a trial assembly, drawing each of the joints as nearly as possible to the same tension. Then check th dimensions. If actual measurement are slightly over or under, it usually is possible to correct the error by tightening or loosening several joints

Note in the frame assembly, Fig. 2 that the blade-tension unit is fitted into a ball-pattern pipe cross, and also that the steel rod, which support the upper blade guide, slides in bearing formed by pouring molten babbitt into a ball-pattern pipe tee Views A and B, Fig. 2, show opposite ends of the pipe tee which house the wheel-tilting mechanism. At th inner end, next to the wheel hub, th spindle pivots on two pointed set screws provided with jam nuts. At the opposite end two horizontal set screws bear against the spindle to prevent lateral movement. The spindle is tilted by a vertical screw fitted with a small handwheel and provided with a wing nut for locking the adjustment. This assembly is supported on a short length of steel tubing threaded at one end and turned, c ground, to a sliding fit in the pip

UPPER SHAFT

1" HARDWOOD PLUG

1 T-COIL ¾" X 2⅛" AUTO VALVE SPRING, 3/32" WIRE

5/32" X 3" SLOT

YOKE, ⅛" X ½" FLAT IRON

½"

HANDWHEEL FOR ADJUSTING BLADE TENSION

7/16" X 6¾" ROD THREADED TO WITHIN 2" OF TOP

STEEL TUBING

RUNNING NUT DRILLED AND TAPPED FOR ¼" STUD (SEE NOTE BELOW)

BALL-PATTERN PIPE CROSS

YOKE ATTACHED TO PIPE CROSS WITH SCREWS

NUT PINNED TO SHAFT

LOCKNUTS

NOTE: ¼" STUD FILED TO ⅛" THICKNESS TO RUN IN 5/32" SLOT

5 UPPER WHEEL TENSION SCREW

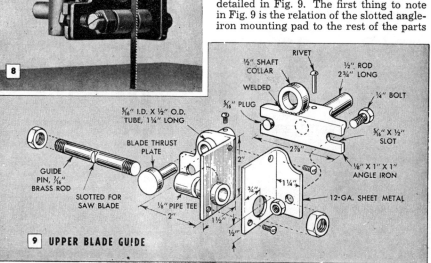

6

Table trunnions and lower guide in place on the band-saw frame. Note that table is recessed for clearance

7

8

Above and below are views of the upper blade guide completely assembled and with the blade in position

cross. The threads in the pipe cross are reamed out as in Fig. 5. A hardwood plug, forced into the upper end of the tube and fastened with three wood screws, forms a bearing for the upper end of the tension spring. The running nut which bears against the lower end of the spring is prevented from turning by a short stud which turns into a tapped hole in the nut. Flats are filed on the opposite end of the stud permitting it to enter a $\frac{5}{32}$-in. slot cut in the wall of the tubing. The stud is provided with a jam nut to hold the adjustment securely. The lower end of the tension screw is fitted with a handwheel and is supported by a flat-iron yoke bent to a U-shape and attached to the pipe cross with short cap screws. To give ample range of adjustment of the upper wheel, the $\frac{7}{16}$ x $6\frac{3}{4}$-in. tension screw is threaded to within 2 in. of the top end as in Fig. 5.

Construction of the lower wheel bearing is easily worked out from the detail in Fig. 3. The double trunnion, which is purchased, is quite simple to assemble by following the upper details in Fig. 3. Note that a flat is filed on one side of the reducing tee at the front of the frame and that two holes are drilled and tapped for cap screws which hold the trunnion bracket. The trunnion must be assembled completely before attaching to the frame. An underside view of the trunnion is given in Fig. 6. The locking handwheel has a threaded sleeve that is turned onto a stud which passes through a hole drilled through the two halves of the outer trunnion. One of the halves of this trunnion is slotted to permit the table to tilt 45 deg. forward.

Two views of the upper blade guide are shown in Figs. 7 and 8, and the assembly is detailed in Fig. 9. The first thing to note in Fig. 9 is the relation of the slotted angle-iron mounting pad to the rest of the parts

9 UPPER BLADE GUIDE

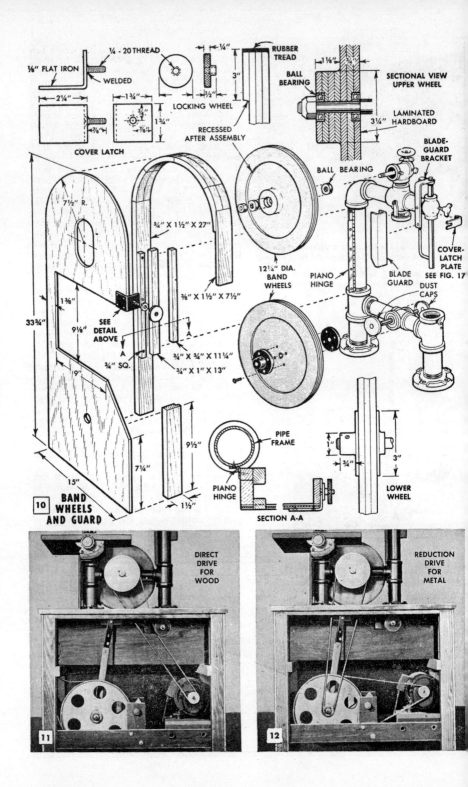

1/8" FLAT IRON

1/4 - 20 THREAD

WELDED

2 1/4"

7/8"

COVER LATCH

1 3/4"

3/4"
7/8"
1 3/4"

LOCKING WHEEL

1/4"

1/2"

3"

RUBBER TREAD

RECESSED AFTER ASSEMBLY

BALL BEARING

1 1/8"   3/4"

SECTIONAL VIEW UPPER WHEEL

LAMINATED HARDBOARD

3 1/4"

BALL BEARING

BLADE-GUARD BRACKET

7 1/2" R.

3/4" X 1 1/2" X 27"

12 1/4" DIA. BAND WHEELS

PIANO HINGE

BLADE GUARD

COVER-LATCH PLATE SEE FIG. 17

DUST CAPS

1 3/8"

9 1/8"

SEE DETAIL ABOVE

A

3/8" X 1 1/2" X 7 1/2"

A

3/4" X 3/4" X 11 1/4"

33 3/4"

9"

3/4" SQ.

3/4" X 1" X 13"

15"

9 1/2"

7 1/4"

1 1/2"

PIPE FRAME

PIANO HINGE

SECTION A-A

1"

3/4"

3"

LOWER WHEEL

10 BAND WHEELS AND GUARD

DIRECT DRIVE FOR WOOD

REDUCTION DRIVE FOR METAL

11

12

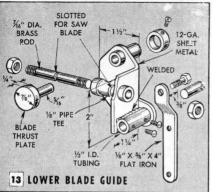

7/16" DIA. BRASS ROD
SLOTTED FOR SAW BLADE
12-GA. SHEET METAL
WELDED
1 1/2"
1/4"
7/8"
5/16"
1/8" PIPE TEE
2"
1/8" PIPE TEE
BLADE THRUST PLATE
3/8"
1 1/4"
1/2" I.D. TUBING
1/8" X 5/8" X 4" FLAT IRON

which make up the complete guide. The short length of tubing which forms a bearing for the blade thrust plate fits into a collar welded to the top of the pad. The latter is welded to a short support rod which passes through a hole drilled transversely at the lower end of the sliding guide rod, Fig. 2, and also Figs. 7 and 8. When the assembly is made, a second rod, 3/8 in. in diameter, is attached to the sliding guide rod with a bracket arm at the upper end. The smaller rod is passed through a hole drilled in the upper arm and the lower end is then bent at a right angle and inserted in a hole drilled part way through the sliding rod, Figs. 8 and 14. This rod, sliding parallel with the support rod, serves to hold the blade guide in the same position relative to the saw blade when the guide is raised or lowered.

The two angles, Fig. 9, are bent to shape from 24-ga. sheet steel and are drilled and

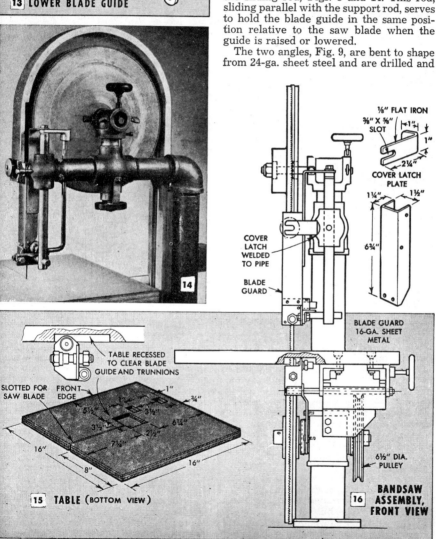

1/8" FLAT IRON
3/8" X 5/8" SLOT
1"
1"
2 1/4"
COVER LATCH PLATE

COVER LATCH WELDED TO PIPE

BLADE GUARD

1 1/4"
1 1/2"
6 3/4"

14

BLADE GUARD 16-GA. SHEET METAL

TABLE RECESSED TO CLEAR BLADE GUIDE AND TRUNNIONS

SLOTTED FOR SAW BLADE
FRONT EDGE
1"
3/4"
5 1/2"
3 1/2"
3 1/2"
6 1/4"
2 1/2"
7 1/4"
16"
8"
16"

15 TABLE (BOTTOM VIEW)

6 1/2" DIA. PULLEY

16 BANDSAW ASSEMBLY, FRONT VIEW

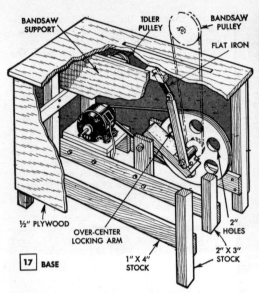

BANDSAW SUPPORT | IDLER PULLEY | BANDSAW PULLEY
FLAT IRON

½" PLYWOOD

OVER-CENTER LOCKING ARM

2" HOLES

17 BASE

1" X 4" STOCK

2" X 3" STOCK

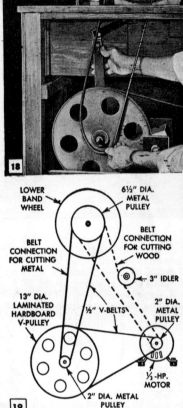

18

LOWER BAND WHEEL

6½" DIA. METAL PULLEY

BELT CONNECTION FOR CUTTING METAL

BELT CONNECTION FOR CUTTING WOOD

3" IDLER

13" DIA. LAMINATED HARDBOARD V-PULLEY

½" V-BELTS

2" DIA. METAL PULLEY

⅓-HP. MOTOR

2" DIA. METAL PULLEY

19 DRIVE FOR METAL AND WOOD

tapped as indicated. The brass guide pin is threaded at each end and slotted at the center for the saw blade. The guide pin is an easy, sliding fit in the reamed pipe tee and a nut on each end permits a lateral adjustment to position the blade in the center of the wide slot in the tee. The thrust plate and the assembled guide pin are shown in position in Fig. 8. Fig. 9 shows a 5⁄16-in. dowel pin, or plug, in the left-hand slot of the mounting pad. The projecting end of the pin enters a hole drilled and reamed through the left-hand angle bracket of the guide and serves to hold the parts in alignment. However, if desired, the hole can be tapped and a cap screw used as in Fig. 8.

The lower blade guide, Fig. 13, is quite similar to the upper guide except that it is supported by a horizontal rod and a flat-iron bracket, which is bolted to the angle bracket and to the side of the lower pipe tee. The horizontal rod enters a hole drilled in the outer half of the trunnion which is next to the guide. The opposite end is inserted in a bushing welded to the side of the angle bracket. Parts of this guide can be made at the present stage of the construction, but do not attach it to the frame until the table has been made and fitted in place and the wheels completed and mounted on the spindles. Then, with a blade in place on the band wheels, it is an easy matter to locate the lower guide in the correct position.

After making the frame guides and table trunnions, the two-speed bandsaw is completed by making the band wheels, table, guard and floor stand which houses the drive. The finished job is shown in Fig. 20. The band wheels are made of ¼-in. hardboard, three disks and one ring of this material being laminated to give a 1-in. tread width, Fig. 10. The hub of the upper wheel is built out with four additional disks of hardboard to provide a bearing mounting as in the sectional

view, Fig. 10, while the lower wheel hub is made from two ½-in. pipe flanges as indicated. Before mounting, the wheel treads are trued in a lathe and fitted with 1-in. rubber tires. The hub of one lower-wheel flange is drilled and tapped for a setscrew which is tightened onto a flat filed on the shaft. The table, Fig. 15, is made from ¾-in. birch plywood and is recessed on the bottom side to fit over the trunnions and blade guide. It also is slotted from one edge to the center to permit insertion and removal of the blade. Fit the table to the trunnions before cutting the slot so that the location of the latter can be determined. The ¼-in. plywood wheel guard, or cover, detailed in Fig. 10 is not essential, although you can include it if desired. However, the blade guard, Figs. 10 and 16, is a necessary

Band-Saw Table Pin
Removed With
a Claw Hammer

safety feature and should not be omitted. Figs. 11, 12, 18 and 19 show how the drive is assembled for cutting wood and metal. Fig. 17 details the closed stand and pivoted jack-shaft. Of course, an open stand, 30 in. high, will serve equally well. The jackshaft is raised for changing belts by a special lever, pivoted at the ends and center as in Fig. 18. The lower end is provided with a bushing to fit the jackshaft. Two pillow-block bearings placed side by side can be used as a jack-shaft bearing in place of the single bearing. A 12-in. metal V-pulley may be substituted for the 13-in. laminated pulley. Before op-erating the machine be sure the blade is centered on the band wheels and is bearing lightly against the blade guides.

The next time you change band-saw blades, try the simple claw hammer-and-block method of removing the table pin. As shown in the photo, the pin can be pulled straight out. This method elimi-nates ugly scratch marks which invariably result when pliers are used.

Simple Ripping Fence for Band Saw

If you need a ripping fence to use on a band saw, one can be made very easily from a strip of hardwood of suitable size and two slender bolts fitted with wing nuts. Holes spaced equal to the width of the band-saw table are bored in the wood strip. Then the bolts are bent at right angles near the head to hook un-derneath the table flange. In use, the bent ends of the bolts are slipped under the edge of the saw table, after which the fence is adjusted to suit and the wing nuts tightened to hold it in place.

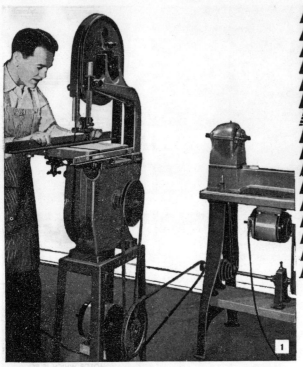

$$\frac{650 \times 2 \times \overset{.55}{2.75}}{\underset{1.7}{8.5} \times \underset{4}{8}} = \frac{357.5}{6.8} = 52.5$$

52 R.P.M.

8"

2"

650 R.P.M. AT COUNTER-SHAFT

8½" PULLEY
2¾" PULLEY

2

BAND SAW

METAL CUTTING

$$\frac{340 \times \overset{2}{12}}{\underset{6}{12}} = \frac{340}{6} = 56.6)$$

57 R.P.M.

340 R.P.M. AT SPINDLE

2"

12"

3

WITH METAL-CUTTING blades now available in sizes and gauges suitable for use on small bandsaws, home craftsmen having metal to cut into lengths or shapes can convert these small machines into power-driven band hacksaws. Any wood-cutting bandsaw having band wheels 9 in. or more in diameter can be used for cutting metal. Of course, the smaller machines are suitable only for light work on small pieces of metal. The metal-cutting bandsaw blade makes a square, smooth cut with no ripples or ridges and it does the job in a fraction of the time required in hand hacksawing.

Reducing blade speeds: Average blade speeds for wood-cutting bandsaws range from 2000 to 3000 f.p.m. (feet per minute) although some later-model machines operate with blade speeds up to 4500 f.p.m. In cutting metal, especially when cutting steel and other hard materials, it is necessary to reduce the blade speed to an average of 200 f.p.m. to avoid undue heating and clogging of the blade. Fig. 1 shows one way to do this by utilizing the lathe countershaft for the first reduction. The pulley hookup and the ratio of pulley sizes is detailed in Fig. 2. The second reduction is made through a 2-in. pulley on the outer end of the lathe countershaft driving an 8½-in. pulley on the bandsaw motor which serves as a second jackshaft. The third reduction, as you can see, is made through a 2¾-in. pulley on the motor shaft driving an 8-in. pulley on the bandsaw. This reduces the band-wheel speed to 52 r.p.m. In this speed-reduction arrangement, the lathe motor is used to drive the setup. Fig. 3 details an alternate hookup giving 57 r.p.m. at the bandsaw pulley. In

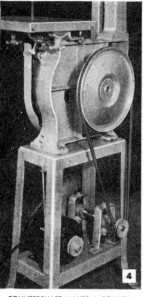

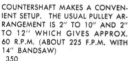
either arrangement, you have the advantage of the speed reductions available through the lathe countershaft. Referring to Table II you will see that the 52-r.p.m. speed of the bandsaw pulley, Fig. 2, gives the desired 200-f.p.m. blade speed on 14-in. band wheels. Although not indicated, the installation shown in Fig. 3 should either be bolted to the floor or to a spreader board for best results. This is not necessary with the type of arrangement shown in Fig. 2. Other speed-reducing drives are shown in Figs. 4, 5 and 6. The drive shown in Fig. 5 is the regular speed-reducing unit supplied with a well-known make of metal-cutting bandsaw. Others shown in Figs. 4 and 6 are improvised from standard machine parts.

The metal-cutting blade: Select the blade for the work according to the data given in Table I. This table is merely representative. It does not include the recommendations of all manufacturers of metal-cutting band-saw blades. Of course, you can do a lot of ordinary work with just one blade, about 18-pitch with a raker set. The main thing to keep in mind in blade selection is the thickness of the work in relation to the number of teeth per inch. There must be at least two teeth in contact with the work

at all times, otherwise you will have trouble with blade breakage If fast cutting is required, use the coarsest pitch and the widest blade the work will permit. For a smooth finish and slower cutting, use a medium or fine-pitch blade. Use the standard-tooth blade on steel and other hard materials and the buttress, or skip-tooth, blade on soft, nonferrous metals and wood. Note the details at the left of Table I. A good all-around blade combination for home-shop work consists of a ¾6 or ¼-in., 6-pitch buttress blade for wood and soft metals and an 18-pitch standard-tooth blade of the same width for steel. Where possible, use wood and metal-cutting blades of the same gauge and width.

Cutting tubing and bar stock: One of the principal uses of the bandsaw fitted for cutting metal is cutoff work on metal tubing and also round and square stock. To prevent round stock from turning while being cut, it is necessary to provide some means of holding the stock securely. Suitable clamping arrangements can be improvised easily as in Figs. 10, 11 and 12. The hardwood V-block, Fig. 12, is the easiest to set up and is, in some respects, the best for average work. It is guided by a wood or

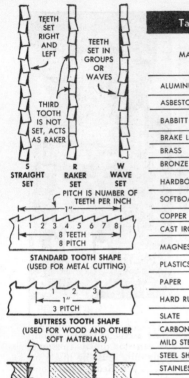

TEETH SET RIGHT AND LEFT

TEETH SET IN GROUPS OR WAVES

THIRD TOOTH IS NOT SET, ACTS AS RAKER

S STRAIGHT SET   R RAKER SET   W WAVE SET

PITCH IS NUMBER OF TEETH PER INCH

1 2 3 4 5 6 7 8 — 8 TEETH — 8 PITCH

STANDARD TOOTH SHAPE
(USED FOR METAL CUTTING)

1 2 3 — 1" — 3 PITCH

BUTTRESS TOOTH SHAPE
(USED FOR WOOD AND OTHER SOFT MATERIALS)

RIGHT! AT LEAST TWO TEETH SHOULD CONTACT THE WORK

WRONG! TEETH TOO FINE; CUTS SLOWLY AND TENDS TO CLOG

WRONG! LESS THAN TWO TEETH IN CONTACT; TEETH MAY BREAK OFF

RIGHT! AT LEAST TWO TEETH IN CONTACT PREVENTS BREAKAGE

5½ R.   3" R.   1½" R.   1" R.   ⅝" R.   ⅜" R.   ¼" R.

CURVES SHOW MINIMUM RADIUS

¾" ½" ⅜" ⁵⁄₁₆" ¼" ³⁄₁₆" ⅛"
WIDTH OF BLADE

USE THE WIDEST BLADE WHICH WILL MAKE THE CUT

Table I — BLADE SELECTOR FOR ALL MATERIALS (1)

MATERIAL	SAW PITCH AND SET (2) — WORK THICKNESS				SAW SPEED IN F.P.M. (3) — WORK THICKNESS			
	¹⁄₁₆"	¼"	1"	3"	¹⁄₁₆"	¼"	1"	3"
ALUMINUM	18S	10S	8S 4B	6S 4B	2400	2400	2000	1500
ASBESTOS SHEETS	24R	14R	8R	4B	2000	1800	1500	1200
BABBITT OR LEAD	14R	10R	8R 4B	6R 4B	2400	2400	1800	1500
BRAKE LINING	10R	10R	6R	4B	2000	1500	1000	1000
BRASS	18S	14S	10S	8S	2400	2000	1500	1200
BRONZE	18R	14R	10R	8R	500	300	200	140
HARDBOARD	10S	8S	6S 4B	6S 4B	3000	2400	2400	2400
SOFTBOARD	10S	8S	6S 4B	6S 4B	3000	3000	2400	2400
COPPER	18S	14S	10S	8S	1200	800	500	300
CAST IRON	18R	14R	10R	8R	200	160	100	75
MAGNESIUM	14S 8B	10S 6B	10S 4B	8S 4B	3000	2400	2400	2400
PLASTICS	18S	14S	8S	6S 4B	2400	2400	2400	2400
PAPER	10S	10S	8S	6S 4B	1500	1000	1000	1000
HARD RUBBER	24S	18S	10S	6S 4B	3000	2400	2400	2400
SLATE	24R	18R	14R	10R	300	200	160	100
CARBON STEEL	24R	18R	10R	8R	250	200	180	140
MILD STEEL	18R	14R	10R	8R	250	200	180	140
STEEL SHAPES	24R	18R	10R	8R	180	140	120	100
STAINLESS STEEL	24R	18R	10R	8R	100	75	50	50
STEEL TUBING	32W	24W			180	140		
WOOD	14S	10S	8S 6B	6S 4B	3000	3000	3000	2400

(1) ADAPTED FROM TABLES BY DOALL AND OTHERS
(2) CAN BE VARIED WIDELY. 18-PITCH, RAKER-SET METAL-CUTTING BLADE IS BEST FOR GENERAL USE.
(3) SPEEDS LISTED ARE NEAR MAXIMUM — LESS SPEED IS SATISFACTORY AND SIMPLY MEANS LOWER CUTTING RATE.

Table II — BANDSAW SPEEDS—F.P.M. TO R.P.M.

WHEEL DIAMETER IN INCHES	FEET PER MINUTE										
	100	120	140	160	180	200	250	300	400	2400	3000
	REVOLUTIONS PER MINUTE										
9	42	51	59	68	76	85	106	127	170	1015	1270
10	38	46	54	61	69	76	95	115	152	920	1150
11	35	42	49	55	62	69	87	104	138	832	1040
12	32	38	45	51	57	64	80	95	128	764	955
13	29	35	41	47	53	59	73	88	118	706	883
14	27	33	38	44	49	54	68	82	108	695	819
15	25	31	36	41	46	51	64	76	102	611	764
16	24	29	33	38	43	48	60	72	96	573	716
18	21	26	30	34	38	42	53	64	84	510	637
20	19	23	27	31	34	38	48	57	76	459	574

EXAMPLE SHOWING USE OF TABLES: 14" BANDSAW CUTTING MILD STEEL ½" TO 1" THICK

FROM TABLE I { BLADE SHOULD BE 10R (10 TEETH PER INCH, RAKER SET). SPEED SHOULD BE 180 F.P.M.

FROM TABLE II { 14" BANDSAW TO RUN AT 180 F.P.M. MUST ROTATE AT 49 R.P.M.

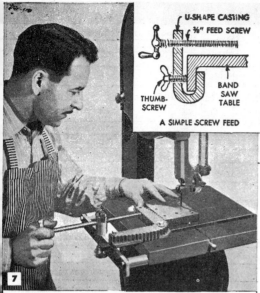

U-SHAPE CASTING

⅜" FEED SCREW

THUMB-SCREW

BAND SAW TABLE

A SIMPLE SCREW FEED

7 A SCREW FEED SAVES EFFORT WHEN SAWING THICK METAL

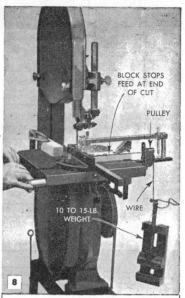

BLOCK STOPS FEED AT END OF CUT

PULLEY

10 TO 15-LB. WEIGHT

WIRE

8 WEIGHT PROVIDES STEADY, UNIFORM FEED

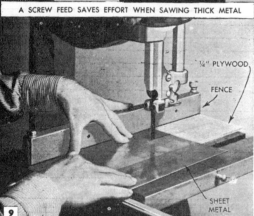

¼" PLYWOOD

FENCE

SHEET METAL

9 USE WOOD UNDER SHEET METAL TO PREVENT BURRING UNDERSIDE

metal bar which fits in the miter-gauge groove milled in the saw table. Another similar device which is quite convenient on small work is pictured in Fig. 10. This also is controlled by a guide bar. On tables not milled for the miter-gauge guide, an ordinary drill-press vise can be used with the guide setup shown in Fig. 11. The vise holds the work and slides against a wooden guide clamped to the machine table. Note that the wooden guide also supports the work to prevent it from tipping under the stress of sawing. Of course, the drill vise must be of the type having both sides milled flat, without any projections.

Mechanical feed: When cutting round stock, the feed usually is freehand, but this can get pretty tiresome when long cuts must be made in heavy, flat stock. Ready-made mechanical feeding devices are available for most small machines and it also is possible to improvise several that work very well. One type of standard attachment for metal-cutting bandsaws is pictured in use in Fig. 7. The feed is controlled by a hand-actuated screw and the unit can be adjusted to make either straight or curved cuts. The V-shaped jaw, shown bolted to a guide bar in the setup in Fig. 7, also can be used free on small pieces which the "V" will span. In this application, the work is set with its corners in corresponding notches on the edges of the "V" and the feed screw is run up until it bears against the back of the jaw. Turning the screw in forces the work against the blade. By placing the point of the screw successively in adjacent notches as the cut progresses, it is possible to produce cuts of a regular curve. The inset detail in Fig. 7 shows how a similar feeding device may be improvised. A small U-shaped casting is drilled and tapped for a ⅜-in. feed screw and a small thumbscrew as shown. This unit is clamped to the lip at the edge of the machine table. For light work the device serves the purpose very well, but it is not suitable for heavy work where the feeding pressures

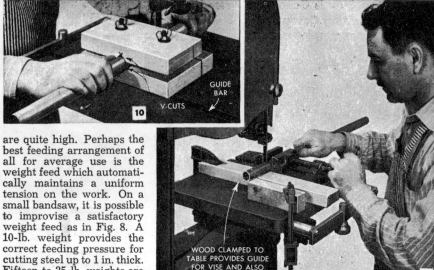

V-CUTS   GUIDE BAR   **10**

WOOD CLAMPED TO TABLE PROVIDES GUIDE FOR VISE AND ALSO A LEVEL SURFACE   **11**

TUBING SHOULD ALWAYS BE SECURELY CLAMPED TO AVOID ROTATION

V-BLOCK 1¾" X 4" X 7"   C-CLAMP SCREW   MITER GAUGE, CLAMP ATTACHMENT SCREW

¼" X ¾" FLAT IRON

WORK

⅜" X ¾" GUIDE BAR   V-CUTS   **12**

are quite high. Perhaps the best feeding arrangement of all for average use is the weight feed which automatically maintains a uniform tension on the work. On a small bandsaw, it is possible to improvise a satisfactory weight feed as in Fig. 8. A 10-lb. weight provides the correct feeding pressure for cutting steel up to 1 in. thick. Fifteen to 25-lb. weights are about the limit on small bandsaws as heavier weights will cause rapid wear and possibly breakage of the blade guides. As you can see, the setup is simple. A pulley (a window-weight pulley will do) is bolted to a corner of the machine table. A cord or wire is attached to the miter gauge and passed through the pulley to support the weight, which can be anything available that weighs the correct number of pounds. The miter-gauge clamp locks the work in place and stop blocks are clamped to the machine table as indicated. In use, the work is located and clamped in place and the machine is started. No further attention will be necessary until the cut is completed.

Sawing thin stock: Thin sheet metal cut by bandsawing has a tendency to form high burrs on the underside. This can be minimized by placing the work on a piece of plywood as in Fig. 9. On thin sheet metal a fine-pitch blade (24 or 32) with a wave set gives the best results. However, for an occasional job in sheet-metal cutting, you can use a coarser blade by feeding slowly with a very light pressure. As a rule, sheet metal is cut by friction sawing but, of course, this method requires a machine capable of very high wheel speeds. The minimum blade speed required in friction sawing ranges from 3000 f.p.m. upward. Best results will be had with blade speeds ranging between 4000 and 5000 f.p.m. This

would mean that a 14-in. bandsaw would have to be run at wheel speeds up to 1200 r.p.m. Many small machines are not designed to withstand the required wheel speed with a sufficient margin of safety For this reason, it is recommended that if friction sawing is done on the small machines the drive be arranged so that blade speeds do not exceed 3000 f.p.m.

General sawing technique: If you are accustomed to operating a bandsaw, you will have no difficulty in cutting metal with the same machine. About the only difference is that in metal cutting the machine operates at a greatly reduced speed and more pressure is required to keep the blade cutting uniformly. Start the cut slowly with light pressure. After the blade is "bedded" in the stock to its full width, the feeding pressure can be gradually increased. It is important to keep the blade cutting uniformly as otherwise it will tend to heat and clog.

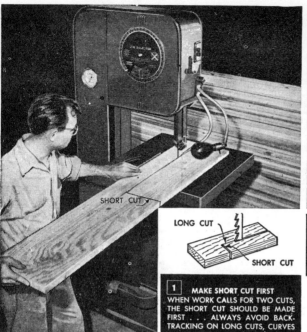

LONG CUT

SHORT CUT

SHORT CUT

| 4 PICKUP ×CUTS× | 2nd CUT |
| POOR - 4 PICKUPS | BETTER - 2 PICKUPS |

1 MAKE SHORT CUT FIRST
WHEN WORK CALLS FOR TWO CUTS, THE SHORT CUT SHOULD BE MADE FIRST . . . ALWAYS AVOID BACK-TRACKING ON LONG CUTS, CURVES

2 BACKTRACK ON U-TURNS
CUT TO THE CORNER AND THEN BACKTRACK ENOUGH TO LEAD THE BLADE INTO THE 2nd CUT. AVOID PICKUP CUTS WHEN POSSIBLE

BANDSAW TECHNIQUES

OPERATING a bandsaw is not difficult and anyone can do it with a little practice, but the difference between merely operating a saw and really doing expert work with it lies in the ability of the operator to do intricate cutting without running into numerous "booby traps." This article is intended to acquaint the beginner with the "tricks of the trade" and help him produce expert work.

Adjustments: After the blade is put on the bandsaw, it must be tensioned. Although some saws have a scale to simplify tensioning, it is merely a matter of drawing up the blade until it "feels" about right, Fig. 10. Note that the blade should not be set too tightly. A ¼-in. blade should have about ¼-in. side play. By means of the tilting screw, the blade is tracked to run in the center of the wheels, left-hand detail, Fig. 7. Turn the drive pulley by hand, as in Fig. 6, to check the adjustment. Then, the guides, which have been completely backed off up to this point, are adjusted. The blade support should be slightly clear of the blade, Fig. 7, right-hand detail, and the guide pins set to align with the bottom of the teeth, Figs. 8 and 9. If the pins are set forward of this point, they will cause the teeth to wear. The guides must also be ad-

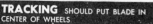

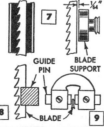

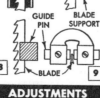

7

¼"

GUIDE PIN

BLADE SUPPORT

8 BLADE **9**

6 **10**

TRACKING SHOULD PUT BLADE IN CENTER OF WHEELS

ADJUSTMENTS

BLADE TENSION MUST BE SET BY FEEL. BLADE SHOULDN'T BE TOO TIGHT

1st CUT   CRISSCROSS   NIBBLE

3   "NIBBLE" NARROW CUTS
SHORT SIDE OF NARROW GROOVES
MUST BE NIBBLED. TECHNIQUE IS
USEFUL ON MANY JOBS. IT WORKS
BEST WITH A HEAVILY SET BLADE

4   "PIVOT" RIPPING CUTS
ON STRAIGHT RIPPING CUTS, THE LEFT
HAND IS HELD ALONGSIDE THE WORK
AND ACTS AS A PIVOT. RIGHT HAND
SWINGS THE WORK TO FOLLOW LINE

DRILLED TURNING HOLE

1st CUT

5   USE TURNING HOLES
BACKTRACKING AND PICKUP CUTS
OFTEN CAN BE AVOIDED BY BORING
HOLES IN THE WORK TO ALLOW FOR
SHIFTING OF THE BLADE POSITION

justed close enough to the blade to keep it from twisting, but they should not come in actual contact with it. They can be set properly by placing a strip of paper between each pin and the blade and pressing the pins together. However, when doing this, be careful not to push the blade out of the vertical position.

Cutting technique: Fundamental bandsawing techniques are described in Figs. 1 to 5 inclusive. The general idea is to do the job with a minimum number of backtracking and pickup cuts. The left-hand diagram in Fig. 2 shows a U-cut made without backtracking, but this method leaves four pickup cuts. When a pickup cut is made

in this manner, the result is never quite as smooth as a cut made in one pass. Therefore, the method shown in the right-hand diagram is better as a little backtracking eliminates two of the pickup cuts.

The blade: For use on smaller bandsaws, blades range from 1/8 to 3/4 in. wide. The best practice, of course, is to use a narrow blade for light sawing, such as cutouts, and a heavier blade for other work. However, to avoid constantly changing blades, the 1/4-in. blade will be found best for all-purpose use. Important considerations in blade selection are the type of tooth and the amount of set. Fig. 13 pictures the standard blade; Fig. 14 shows the buttress

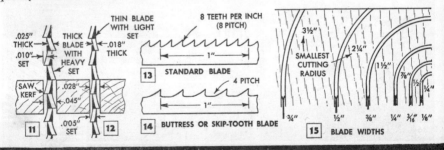

.025" THICK — THICK BLADE WITH HEAVY SET — .010" SET   THIN BLADE WITH LIGHT SET — .018" THICK   8 TEETH PER INCH (8 PITCH)   3½" SMALLEST CUTTING RADIUS   2¼"

SAW KERF   .028"   .045"

13 STANDARD BLADE   4 PITCH   1½"   ⅞"   ½"   ¼"

.005" SET

11   **12**   **14** BUTTRESS OR SKIP-TOOTH BLADE   ¾"   ½"   ⅜"   ¼"   3/16"   ⅛"   **15** BLADE WIDTHS

THE BLADE USE A SAW BLADE TO SUIT THE JOB. A ⅛" BLADE IS EXCELLENT FOR CUTOUTS BUT USELESS FOR RESAWING. A ¼" WIDTH IS BEST ONE-BLADE CHOICE

THE BANDSAW CUT ALWAYS SHOWS SOME WASHBOARDING, DEPENDING ON SAW SET. LEAD IS USUALLY TO OUTER EDGE OF THE TABLE

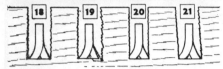

| NORMAL WASHBOARD-ING CAUSED BY TEETH | ONE LONG TOOTH CAN DO A LOT OF DAMAGE | HONED TEETH CUT SMOOTHER BUT WORK HARDER | BLADE LEADS TOWARD SHARP SIDE |

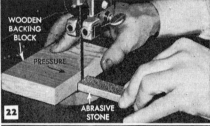

SMOOTHER CUTS CAN BE OBTAINED WITH HONED TEETH

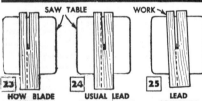

| HOW BLADE SHOULD CUT | USUAL LEAD IS TO OUTSIDE | LEAD CORRECTED |

or skip-tooth type blade. The latter is preferred by many craftsmen for sawing wood and plastics. Standard blades are available in a number of thicknesses from 20 to 28 ga., but a thin blade with a light set, Fig. 12, is commonly used on small bandsaws. The buttress blade in Fig. 11 is thicker and carries more set. Although the teeth of this blade are usually hardened and cannot be filed, the extra hardness retains both sharpness and set about twice as long as a blade of filing temper. The radius limitations of the various blade widths, Fig. 15, must also be considered when choosing a saw blade.

The bandsaw cut: Every tool makes a mark on the work, and the marks of a bandsaw blade resemble a washboard, Figs. 17 and 18. A blade having a heavy set "washboards" more than one with a light set, and a poorly made blade with a few long, snaggle teeth, as in Fig. 19, makes an exceptionally rough cut. Smoother cutting is attained by honing the teeth lightly as shown in Figs. 20 and 22. However, if the honing is overdone, it dulls the blade. If one side of the blade is dull and the other side sharp, the blade leads off toward the sharp side, Fig. 21. A perfect blade cuts straight, as in Fig. 23. Because the inside surface of the blade is in constant contact with the wheels, it dulls faster than the other side, and the blade tends to lead to the outside, Fig. 24. This lead is corrected by feeding the work at a slight angle as shown in Fig. 25.

Resawing: The job of making thin boards out of thick ones, or resawing, is the kind of work the bandsaw does better than any other type of saw. The simple resawing setup shown in Figs. 26 and 28 functions

RESAWING IS A JOB BANDSAW DOES BETTER THAN ANY OTHER SAW. WORK UP TO 6" THICK CAN BE CUT WITH 1/3-HP. MOTOR.

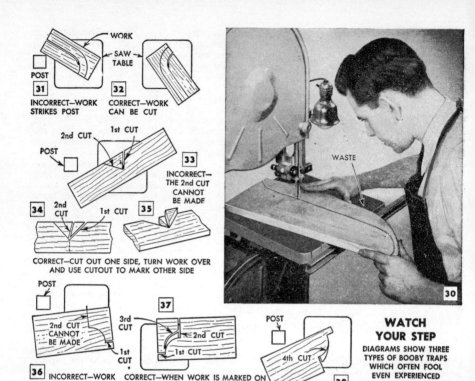

WORK

SAW TABLE

POST

31 INCORRECT—WORK STRIKES POST

32 CORRECT—WORK CAN BE CUT

POST

2nd CUT

1st CUT

33 INCORRECT—THE 2nd CUT CANNOT BE MADE

34 2nd CUT **35** 1st CUT

CORRECT—CUT OUT ONE SIDE, TURN WORK OVER AND USE CUTOUT TO MARK OTHER SIDE

POST

2nd CUT CANNOT BE MADE

1st CUT

36 INCORRECT—WORK MARKED ON WRONG SIDE

37 3rd CUT 2nd CUT 1st CUT

CORRECT—WHEN WORK IS MARKED ON OPPOSITE SIDE, ALL CUTS CAN BE MADE

POST

4th CUT

38

WASTE

30

WATCH YOUR STEP

DIAGRAMS SHOW THREE TYPES OF BOOBY TRAPS WHICH OFTEN FOOL EVEN EXPERIENCED SAWYERS

just as well as more elaborate fences. Fig. 27 shows the same job being done with a standard bandsaw fence and a wooden spring. Sometimes it is advisable to make circular-saw cuts on both edges of the work, as in Fig. 29, to serve as guidelines and also to reduce the cutting load. The blade used for resawing should be as wide as the bandsaw will carry, although good work can be done with the ¼-in. blade. The buttress blade, with its hard temper and heavy set, is ideal for this work and does not clog with sawdust.

Booby traps: Certain bandsaw jobs can be cut in only one way, which is peculiar to that particular job. An example is shown in Fig. 30. Note that if the cut is made as in Fig. 31, the swing at the end of the cut will cause the work to strike the bandsaw frame and the cut cannot be completed. The right way to do this is to begin sawing at the opposite end as in Fig. 32. Most center cuts in long work must be completed by turning over the work as in Figs. 33 to 35.

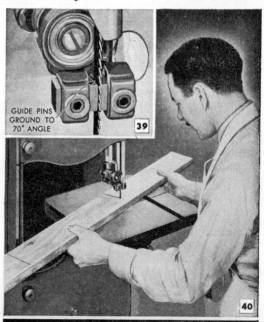

GUIDE PINS GROUND TO 70° ANGLE

39

40

ANGLE GUIDES ARE USEFUL FOR INTRICATE SAWING AND SQUARE CUTOFFS IN LONG WORK

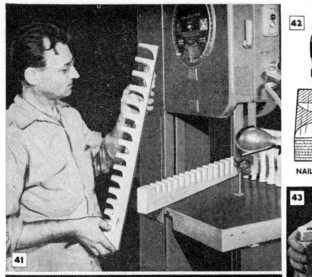

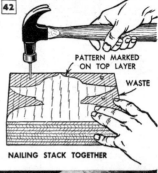

PATTERN MARKED ON TOP LAYER

WASTE

NAILING STACK TOGETHER

STACK HELD IN FORM

STACK SAWING IS USEFUL IN MAKING DUPLICATE PARTS. SIX LAYERS OF ¾" STOCK OR 15 LAYERS OF ¼" PLYWOOD ARE EASILY CUT IN ONE OPERATION

It also will be found that many booby traps are due to marking the work on the wrong side. The job shown in Fig. 36 cannot be continued, but if the work is marked on the other side, all cuts are easily made, Figs. 37 and 38. As bandsawing experience is acquired, each job is automatically visualized before it is started, thus eliminating "blind alleys" and excessive backtracking.

Angle guides: If the outer ends of the guide pins are ground to a 70-deg. angle and inserted end-for-end as in Fig. 39, long work can be cut off squarely as shown in Fig. 40. This setting also will be found useful for intricate cutting jobs. If the angle guides are used only occasionally for such a special job, it is not necessary to

grind the lower guide pins at an angle. Merely back them off until the blade is again set square.

Stack sawing: The tremendous cutting capacity of the bandsaw makes it practical for sawing several pieces in one operation, Fig. 41. Usually, the work is nailed together as in Fig. 42, but it may be held by a form similar to that shown in Fig. 43. The pattern, of course, is marked on the top layer and the stack is sawed just about as easily as a single piece of work.

Pattern sawing: A typical setup for using a master pattern as a guide to bandsaw duplicate parts is explained in Figs. 44 and 45. Although work of this kind is easy to do and accurate, a blade with a fairly heavy

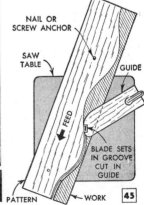

NAIL OR SCREW ANCHOR

SAW TABLE

GUIDE

FEED

BLADE SETS IN GROOVE CUT IN GUIDE

PATTERN

WORK

PATTERN SAWING IS A SIMPLE METHOD OF CUTTING DUPLICATE PARTS WITH A PATTERN AND GUIDE

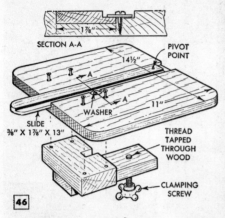

SECTION A-A

1⅞"

PIVOT POINT

14½"

11"

A

A

WASHER

SLIDE
⅜" X 1⅞" X 13"

THREAD TAPPED THROUGH WOOD

CLAMPING SCREW

46

CIRCLE-CUTTING JIG DOES PERFECT WORK, ANY DIAMETER

47

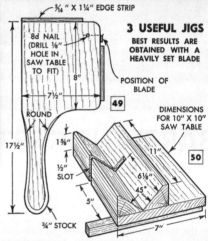

48

CORNER-ROUNDING JIG IS FAST . . . CUTS ONE SIZE ONLY

5/16" X 1¼" EDGE STRIP

8d NAIL (DRILL ⅛" HOLE IN SAW TABLE TO FIT)

3 USEFUL JIGS

BEST RESULTS ARE OBTAINED WITH A HEAVILY SET BLADE

POSITION OF BLADE

8"

7½"

ROUND

49

DIMENSIONS FOR 10" X 10" SAW TABLE

11"

17½"

1⅝"

½" SLOT

5"

6⅛"

45°

50

¾" STOCK

7"

51

V-BLOCK . . . . . IS USED FOR BEVELS AND CUTOFFS

BAR SLIDES ALONG EDGE OF TABLE

52

set must be used in order to get the free-dom of manipulation required to follow the contour of the pattern.

Useful jigs: Other than the standard fence and miter gauge, the most useful bandsaw jig is the one for circle cutting, Figs. 46 and 47. It also can be used for corner-rounding, but this work is done faster with a special corner-rounding jig, Figs. 48 and 49. However, this jig permits cutting one size only, usually about a 1⅜-in. radius. The pivot fits into a small hole drilled in the bandsaw table in line with the blade teeth. Another handy device is the V-block jig shown in Fig. 50. It is used for cutting 45-deg. bevels as in Fig. 51 and also can be used as a cutoff guide for round stock. In the latter case, the guide bar rides along the edge of the bandsaw table as in Fig. 52. It is not practical to use any kind of a fence or jig with a thin blade having a very light set as some blade leading is inevitable and the light-set blade does not cut a kerf wide enough to permit free-ing itself. A hardened blade having a fairly heavy set will make a true cut for a long time and do perfect work with any type of jig involving a fixed line-of-feed direction.

BARBECUE CART

PICNICS where you want 'em — that's the feature of this rolling outdoor grill, for not only can you wheel it to any spot in the back yard, but you can take it with you on camping trips. The frame of the cart is bent cold from rigid electrical conduit, then welded and equipped with rubber-tired coaster-wagon wheels. Both the firebox and ash pan of the original were made from metal salvaged from discarded auto hoods, making use of the hinged parts to provide folding windshields. However, the firebox can be formed from sheet metal and the windshields hinged with small butt hinges. Note that friction tabs are formed on the front windshield.

Draft holes are punched in the sloping sides of the firebox and corresponding holes are made in a draft regulator which, in use, remains inside the firebox and is shifted back and forth to control the draft. Note also that an opening is made in the bottom of the firebox for dumping the ashes. Ash pan and firebox are riveted together, and two notched posts support a spit at different heights above the coals.

Steak grill

Roasting spit

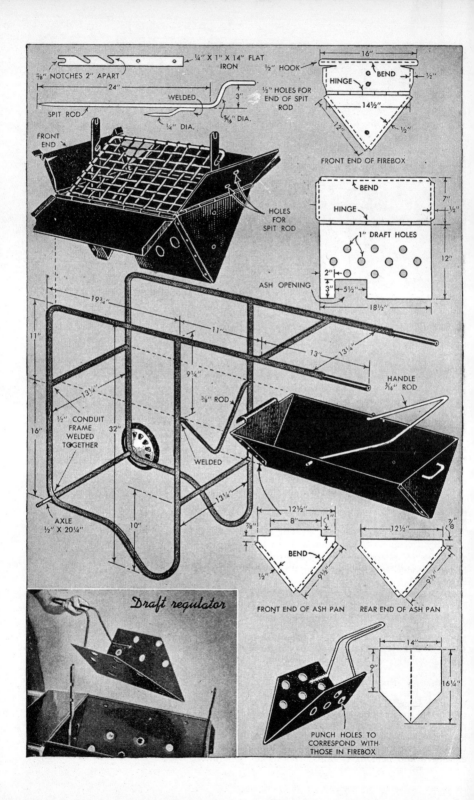

3/8" NOTCHES 2" APART

1/4" X 1" X 14" FLAT IRON

24"

WELDED

SPIT ROD

1/4" DIA.

5/16" DIA.

3"

1/2" HOOK

1/2" HOLES FOR END OF SPIT ROD

16"

BEND

HINGE

14 1/2"

1/2"

1/2"

12"

FRONT END OF FIREBOX

FRONT END

HOLES FOR SPIT ROD

BEND

HINGE

7"

1/2"

1" DRAFT HOLES

12"

2"

3"

ASH OPENING

5 1/2"

18 1/2"

19 3/4"

11"

13"

13 1/4"

11"

13 1/4"

9 1/4"

3/8" ROD

HANDLE 3/16" ROD

16"

1/2" CONDUIT FRAME WELDED TOGETHER

32"

WELDED

10"

13 1/4"

AXLE 1/2" X 20 1/4"

7/8"

12 1/2"

8"

1"

BEND

1/2"

9 1/2"

12 1/2"

7/8"

9 1/2"

FRONT END OF ASH PAN

REAR END OF ASH PAN

Draft regulator

14"

9"

16 1/4"

PUNCH HOLES TO CORRESPOND WITH THOSE IN FIREBOX

If your basement is leaky or so damp and musty that you cannot get the benefit of this desirable space for recreation or other purposes, it is not too difficult to eliminate these conditions by waterproofing

BASEMENT MOISTURE PROOFING

BEFORE GOING TO THE EXPENSE of building rooms in your basement, it should be made relatively dry if it is subject to excessive moisture at any time during the year.

The problem of wet basements: Water from outside may get into a basement through cracks and imperfections in the walls, or it may penetrate walls because of their porosity. Undrained window wells may allow water to enter through windows. Sewers may occasionally back up. Water under a basement floor may find entry through loose joints or cracked portions of a house drain. This is apt to happen especially when the height of standing underground water, or "water table," rises above the floor level because of melting snow or excessive and prolonged rainstorms. The higher the water table is, the more pressure is exerted by the water against the basement walls and floor, permitting easier penetration. When a house is located on a hillside or on sloping ground, surface water tends to collect around basement walls on the uphill side, since the walls then act as a dam to obstruct the natural flow downhill. Water also may collect around basement walls because of leaky or clogged gutters and downspouts, or because the discharge from the downspouts is too close to the house.

Condensation of atmospheric moisture on basement walls, floors, pipes and other cold surfaces, occurs mostly during summer months in humid localities. It generally disappears when the heating plant is put into operation.

Waterproofing walls on the outside: The best way to prevent the entrance of free water through basement walls is to waterproof them on the outside and provide adequate drainage all around. This entails digging of trenches to the depth of the wall footings, but not beyond this, to expose the outer surface of the walls for treatment. First you remove all loose dirt from the surface of the wall by wire-brushing it thoroughly, and then you apply one or more coats of a suitable waterproofing compound, a number of which are available. Many of these are basically fine, portland cement to which water-repellent ingredients are added. Some of them have the desirable property of expanding in the pores of the concrete. Most of these compounds come in dry form and are dissolved in a specified amount of water for application with a brush or spray. The walls are dampened generally before application to assure proper adhesion.

Hot tar and asphalt damp-proofing compounds are also used extensively to produce water-repellent walls. These may be brushed on as shown in Fig. 1, or applied with a spray gun. The consistency of the compounds varies with the method of application. It is highly essential that the walls be entirely dry before application to assure complete adhesion.

A still more effective waterproofing job results if you apply two layers of 15-lb. asphalt-saturated felt, using asphalt damp-proofing compound as an adhesive. Strips of felt are applied horizontally, starting at the bottom of the wall and letting the first strip overlap the wall footing as shown in Fig. 2. Then successive strips of felt overlap those below for a distance of not less than 3 in. Any vertical laps should be at least 6 in. wide. All laps must be cemented so that a continuous watertight membrane results.

Concrete and masonry walls can be made highly resistant to moisture by troweling on two successive ⅜-in. layers of cement plaster. The walls must be moistened thoroughly before applying the plaster. This consists of equal parts of portland cement and fine, sharp sand, with just enough water added to give a troweling consistency. Allow the first coat to set, but not dry fully, before applying the second. Often a coating of asphalt damp-proofing compound is applied over a cement-plaster coat.

Installing drainage tile: To collect and carry away water around a foundation to a lower level, or to a sewer if this is permitted, you lay 6-in. drainage tile around the walls as shown in Fig. 2. Lay the tile alongside the footing at a slight slope of ⅛ or ¼ in. per foot. Place pieces of tar paper over the joints of the tile as in Fig. 3 to prevent soil from getting inside. Cover

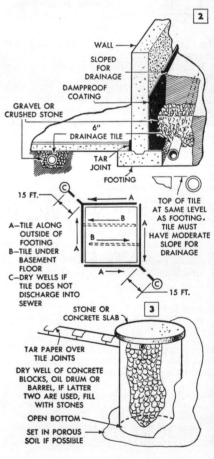

WALL

SLOPED FOR DRAINAGE

DAMPPROOF COATING

GRAVEL OR CRUSHED STONE

6" DRAINAGE TILE

TAR JOINT

FOOTING

TOP OF TILE AT SAME LEVEL AS FOOTING. TILE MUST HAVE MODERATE SLOPE FOR DRAINAGE

15 FT.

A—TILE ALONG OUTSIDE OF FOOTING
B—TILE UNDER BASEMENT FLOOR
C—DRY WELLS IF TILE DOES NOT DISCHARGE INTO SEWER

15 FT.

STONE OR CONCRETE SLAB

TAR PAPER OVER TILE JOINTS

DRY WELL OF CONCRETE BLOCKS, OIL DRUM OR BARREL, IF LATTER TWO ARE USED, FILL WITH STONES

OPEN BOTTOM

SET IN POROUS SOIL IF POSSIBLE

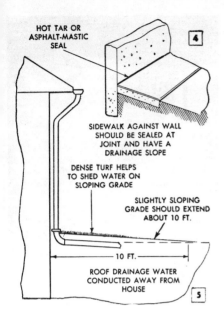

HOT TAR OR
ASPHALT-MASTIC
SEAL

4

SIDEWALK AGAINST WALL
SHOULD BE SEALED AT
JOINT AND HAVE A
DRAINAGE SLOPE

DENSE TURF HELPS
TO SHED WATER ON
SLOPING GRADE

SLIGHTLY SLOPING
GRADE SHOULD EXTEND
ABOUT 10 FT.

10 FT.

ROOF DRAINAGE WATER
CONDUCTED AWAY FROM
HOUSE

5

FIG. 6

the tile with an 18 to 24-in. layer of gravel or crushed stone.

If the basement floor is in such bad condition that it will have to be replaced, it is a good idea also to lay drainage tile under the floor at this time, as shown in the lower detail of Fig. 2. The tile is connected to the outside drainage lines which lead to discharge points at opposite corners of the building. Where collected water cannot be discharged into city sewers, it should be run to one or two dry wells as shown in Fig. 3. These should be located at least 15 ft. away from the house.

Roof and ground drainage: Water from roof drainage also may be disposed of in a similar manner. You can prevent surface water from collecting at the foundation by sloping the ground around the house away from it for a distance of about 10 ft. as shown in Fig. 5. Thick turf on the slope will help to shed water. Too dense a planting of shrubs along a foundation tends to retain moisture in the soil and keep walls from drying out.

A sidewalk that butts against a house wall should slope away from it slightly. The joint between the walk and the wall should be sealed by first tamping in oakum to within 1/4 or 3/8 in. from the top of the crack, then completing the seal with calking compound, roofing cement or hot tar as shown in Fig. 4. Then water running down the house wall will not accumulate under the walk and against the foundation.

Waterproofing walls from inside: Often basement walls can be made completely dry

by coating them on the inside with a waterproofing compound such as already discussed. These are also known as cement-water paints. The kinds that expand in the pores of the concrete will withstand considerable hydrostatic pressure from the outside of the wall. If waterproofing on the inside is not sufficient, you can still do the job on the outside.

Before applying such paint, walls should be brushed thoroughly to remove all loose particles. Then they are wetted with water to prevent the water in the paint from being absorbed too quickly, which destroys its adhesion. The paint is applied to clean, uncoated concrete or masonry, but not over previously applied coatings of paint. Scrub the paint into the pores, using a rather stiff bristle brush as shown in Fig. 6. After it has hardened, which takes from 6 to 12 hrs., the painted surface should be kept moist by repeated applications of a fine spray of water for at least 48 hrs. Generally a single coat of paint is sufficient but if this is not enough, a second coat is applied. Besides stopping water seepage, the paint produces a snow-white surface which subsequently can be painted. Figs. 7 and 8 show before and after views of such a basement waterproofing job.

Cement-water paints will not seal cracks and holes, but a paste or putty made by mixing the powder with less water can be used for this purpose. Large cracks and holes must first be undercut about 1 in. deep as shown in Fig. 10. Then the grooves are cleaned out, the concrete moistened and the cement mortar applied. This consists of portland cement, 1 part, and clean, sharp sand, 2 parts, with enough water added to make a workable mixture.

Cement-water paints on floors: When concrete floors are to be treated with cement-water paints, they must first be tested for porosity. This can be done by pouring a small amount of water on the floor and observing whether the water is absorbed within a few minutes. If not, the floor is

FIG. 7

FIG. 8

Photos courtesy Prima Products Inc.

etched with a solution of muriatic acid, 1 part, and water, 5 parts, mixed in a glass jar by slowly adding the acid to the water while stirring. Avoid getting the acid or the solution on flesh or clothes. The solution may be applied with a rubber sponge while wearing rubber gloves. After half an hour, hose the floor to remove all traces of the acid. Wipe up the free water to avoid diluting the paint, which you apply next. It must be forced well into all minute cracks. Floors thus treated should be subsequently painted or otherwise covered to protect them from abrasion. Special attention should be given to joints between floors and walls as leakage is most likely to occur here.

Joints between floor and walls: If floor-to-wall joints leak after the above treatment, a continuous tar joint is recommended. A groove can be cut with a cold chisel and hammer as shown in Fig. 9-A, but the job can be done much more easily and quickly with an air hammer. The groove should be undercut to anchor the seal. Clean out the groove and dry the concrete thoroughly with a blowtorch as in detail B. Then pour the hot tar as in detail C. Other cracks are undercut about 1 in. deep as shown in Fig. 10, then moistened and filled with cement mortar.

Resurfacing old floors: Where a floor is badly cracked, it may be easier and cheaper to resurface it with a 2 or 3-in. layer of concrete as shown in Fig. 11, than it is to make repairs. Before resurfacing, you remove the old floor drain and substitute either a longer one to compensate for the added floor height, or add a short section of soil pipe as shown in Fig. 12. It will be necessary to chip away concrete around an old drain and to melt the lead joint where it connects to the trap, which is done with a blowtorch. After removing the drain and cleaning out the bell end of the trap, a new drain is installed, calked and leaded. Where a floor drain is not to be used it can be sealed with a plug as described earlier.

Next, you cement down a membrane of

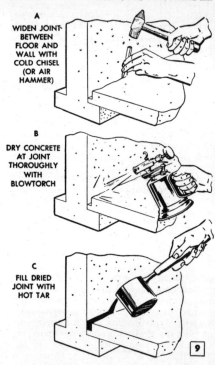

A
WIDEN JOINT-
BETWEEN
FLOOR AND
WALL WITH
COLD CHISEL
(OR AIR
HAMMER)

B
DRY CONCRETE
AT JOINT
THOROUGHLY
WITH
BLOWTORCH

C
FILL DRIED
JOINT WITH
HOT TAR

9

15-lb. asphalt-saturated felt on the floor, when it is thoroughly dry, using asphalt cement and brushing it on for each strip as you proceed. Each strip of felt is overlapped on the adjoining one about 3 in., and the joint is cemented. The felt is brought up against the walls as high as the thickness of the new floor. A membrane consisting of two layers of felt cemented together is likely to be more watertight than a single layer. The strips of the top layer are laid at right angles to those of the bottom layer. After installing the membrane the new concrete floor can be laid over it.

FIG. 10

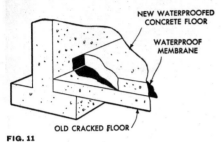

NEW WATERPROOFED CONCRETE FLOOR

WATERPROOF MEMBRANE

OLD CRACKED FLOOR

FIG. 11

FLOOR DRAIN

ADDED THICKNESS OF FLOOR

HOLE IN FLOOR AROUND DRAIN

TRAP

ADDED BELL END OF PIPE

FIG. 12

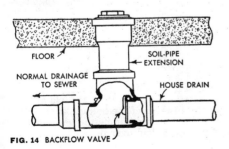

FIG. 13

FLOOR

SOIL-PIPE EXTENSION

NORMAL DRAINAGE TO SEWER

HOUSE DRAIN

FIG. 14 BACKFLOW VALVE

Backflow from sewers: The best way to prevent sewer backflow is to install a backflow valve such as the one shown in Fig. 13. It automatically closes when water from the sewer flows into the house drain, yet is normally open so that there is no interference with the usual drainage flow into the sewer. Such a valve is installed in the house drain close to its outlet as in Fig. 14. Where the drain is at greater depth, it is best to provide a concrete pit of convenient size, and close it with a cover.

You can also stop backflow water from entering the basement through floor drains by using specially made, threaded floor drains into which lengths of ordinary, 2-in. pipe can be screwed to form small "standpipes" as shown in Fig. 15. A 3-ft. length of pipe in each drain is generally sufficient. If a water closet is located in the basement, it too must be protected against overflow if an automatic backflow valve is not installed. The bowl of a water closet can be effectively plugged with a large, smooth-surface rubber ball. This is wedged in the trap opening and is held there firmly by means of a prop bearing against the ceiling, or by the weight of a sack of gravel or sand.

Window-well drainage: Wells around basement windows often become filled with snow and sometimes accumulate a considerable amount of water during heavy rainstorms. This may get into a basement through the window. Therefore, such wells should be drained. Usually enough drainage is provided by digging out the compacted earth at the bottom to a depth of about 24 in., and substituting gravel or sand as shown in Fig. 16. If this does not dispose of the water quickly, you can lead the water away through drain tile as in Fig. 17.

Condensation troubles: When warm, humid air contacts cold walls, floors and cold-water pipes, moisture forms on their surfaces. Sometimes so much water is thus produced in a basement that it is mistaken for leakage from the outside. The trouble is aggravated by laundering and drying clothes. Raising the temperature in a basement above the dew point will eliminate condensation, but heating a basement during summer is not conducive to comfort.

Condensation can be lessened to some extent by forced ventilation at night or on cool, dry days so that warm, humid air will be exhausted from the basement, and cool outside air containing less moisture will be taken in. Where this is done the basement windows and doors should be kept closed when the outside temperature rises.

Automatic dehumidification by using mechanical or chemical dehumidifiers, as shown in Figs. 18 and 19, has been found the most satisfactory method of eliminating condensation in basements. When these

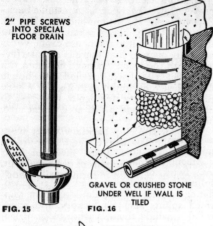

2" PIPE SCREWS
INTO SPECIAL
FLOOR DRAIN

GRAVEL OR CRUSHED STONE
UNDER WELL IF WALL IS
TILED

FIG. 15   **FIG. 16**

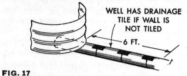

WELL HAS DRAINAGE
TILE IF WALL IS
NOT TILED

6 FT.

FIG. 17

FIG. 18   Photo courtesy General Motors Corp. Frigidaire Div.

CALCIUM-CHLORIDE
AIR DRIER
FIG. 19

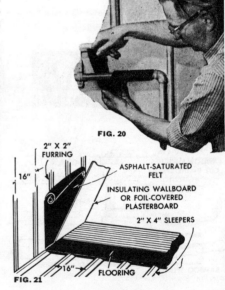

FIG. 20

2" X 2"
FURRING

16"

ASPHALT-SATURATED
FELT

INSULATING WALLBOARD
OR FOIL-COVERED
PLASTERBOARD

2" X 4" SLEEPERS

16"   FLOORING

FIG. 21

dehumidifiers are used, the basement should be kept closed as much as possible to minimize the entrance of additional moisture-laden air. Condensation usually is most apparent on cold-water pipes. To prevent water from collecting on pipes, you cover them with an antisweat, insulating material. This comes in various forms differing in effectiveness and also in cost. You can obtain asphalt-asbestos tape, Fig. 20, viscous paints containing cork granules or asbestos fiber. Also available are tubular pipe coverings that have waterproof inner liners of insulating felt. The pipe coverings are made in various sizes.

You can also prevent condensation on basement walls by installing a continuous vapor barrier on the inside as shown in Fig. 21. The installation differs from the usual above-ground installation. On above-ground walls the use of vapor barriers and insulation requires some circulation of outside air between the sheathing and the insulation. In the case of a basement vapor barrier, air from the basement circulated behind the barrier defeats its purpose and allows condensation to continue, although to a lesser degree. To stop it an excellent vapor barrier for basements is asphalt-impregnated insulating board of the kind used for perimeter insulation on concrete slab floors. This is adhered directly to the dry walls with asphalt cement, thus dispensing with the problem of air circulation. The material is concealed by the wall covering

BASKET WEAVING

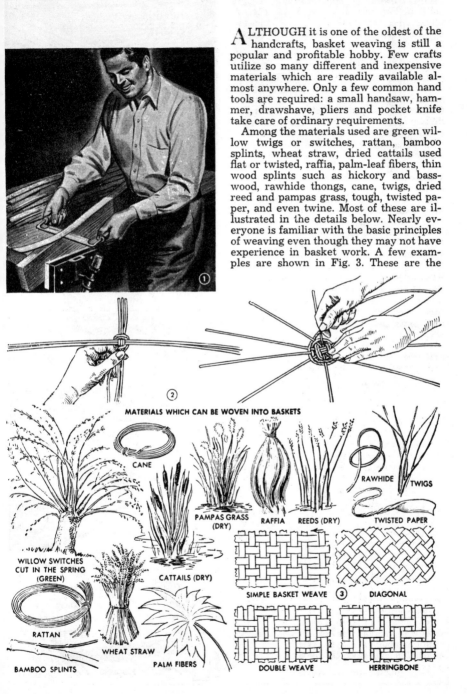

ALTHOUGH it is one of the oldest of the handcrafts, basket weaving is still a popular and profitable hobby. Few crafts utilize so many different and inexpensive materials which are readily available almost anywhere. Only a few common hand tools are required: a small handsaw, hammer, drawshave, pliers and pocket knife take care of ordinary requirements.

Among the materials used are green willow twigs or switches, rattan, bamboo splints, wheat straw, dried cattails used flat or twisted, raffia, palm-leaf fibers, thin wood splints such as hickory and basswood, rawhide thongs, cane, twigs, dried reed and pampas grass, tough, twisted paper, and even twine. Most of these are illustrated in the details below. Nearly everyone is familiar with the basic principles of weaving even though they may not have experience in basket work. A few examples are shown in Fig. 3. These are the

MATERIALS WHICH CAN BE WOVEN INTO BASKETS

CANE

PAMPAS GRASS (DRY)

RAFFIA   REEDS (DRY)

RAWHIDE   TWIGS

TWISTED PAPER

WILLOW SWITCHES CUT IN THE SPRING (GREEN)

CATTAILS (DRY)

SIMPLE BASKET WEAVE ③   DIAGONAL

RATTAN

WHEAT STRAW

PALM FIBERS

BAMBOO SPLINTS

DOUBLE WEAVE   HERRINGBONE

basket weaves done with flat strips, also willow, rattan, rawhide and similar materials adapted to tighter weaving. Several useful baskets of comparatively simple construction are illustrated in Fig. 5, along with the methods of weaving the different types. Most of this work classes as "under-over" weaving.

As a typical example, an attractive and very handy shopping bag made of dried cattails or rushes is detailed in Fig. 5. It is finished with a cotton-rope handle bound around with narrow strips of cattail stems. Gather the longest cattail stems you can find and with a razor blade guided along a straightedge, cut them in 1-in. strips after they have been thoroughly dried in a shady spot exposed to a breeze. Some of the strips are stained lightly with a brown stain, others left in a natural color to give a two-tone pattern in the finished work. When the cattail strips are thoroughly dry, weave three 38-in. strips into fourteen 29-in. strips in a simple under-over weave as in the lower left-hand detail in Fig. 5. Then bend up the strips to form sides and weave in horizontal strips until the required height is reached. Some weavers split the vertical strips, Fig. 4, and tighten the weave so that the top is smaller

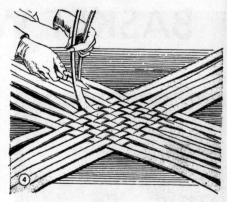

than the body of the basket. Before finishing the top edge, note that there are two horizontal strips instead of one. Ends of the vertical strips are turned over and tucked in. A cloth lining, with pockets for purse, letters, etc., will add to the convenience of the bag. The dry cattails will support any load that can be carried easily.

A neat sewing basket, suitable for many other uses, is made as illustrated in the center detail, Fig. 5. There are two methods of starting the bottom of such a basket,

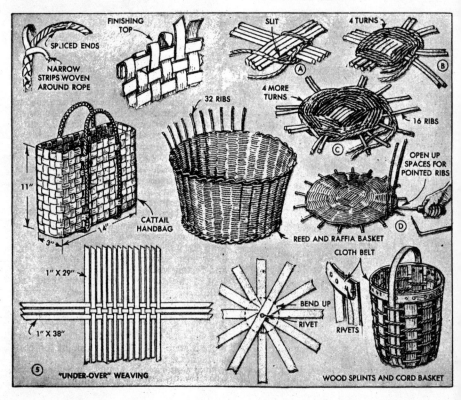

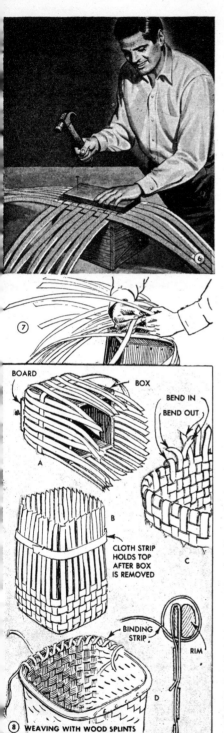

WEAVING WITH WOOD SPLINTS

one in Fig. 2, the other in details A, B, C and D in Fig. 5. Employing the latter method, use reed sticks and a bundle of raffia. Cut four of the sticks 6 in. long, and with a sharp knife make slits in each at the center, 1 in. long. Cut four more reeds the same length, sharpen the ends and insert in the slits of the other four as in detail A. These are known as spokes and form the base of the basket. Bend the ends slightly downward so that the finished base will be concave and stable on a flat surface. Double a strand of raffia at its center and put it around one of the groups of four spokes, one in front and the other strand behind as in detail B. Work around the groups of four spokes in twined weaving four times around. Then separate the spokes into pairs and weave around again four times as in detail C. Space all the spokes evenly and continue weaving another four turns, making the complete base. Push the raffia toward the center and cut off the ends of the sixteen spokes. With an awl force an opening between the top and bottom strands, each side of every spoke, and insert sharpened reeds, pushing in as far as they will go, detail D. These form the ribs. Pinch the reeds at the base or close to the circular rim of the bottom, and bend up all 32 new ribs. Continue weaving until the wall is finished, leaving about 2 in. of each rib projecting. The top ends of the spokes are bent down and bound in place in the rim.

Another easily made basket suitable for heavier loads is shown in the lower right-hand details of Fig. 5. Six long, thin wood splints, 2 in. wide, are laid one over another, spoke fashion, riveted in the center and bent up over a large pot lid, wooden disk or whatever suitable object is handy. Heavy cord or other material is then woven around the upright splints, and the top ends are riveted to a doubled strip of heavy canvas. A rope or splint handle passing entirely around the basket completes the job.

Still another similar type of basket, heavy and exceptionally strong, is made by beginning with a number of splints woven at right angles over a box slightly smaller than the base area of the basket as in Fig. 6. Lay the woven splints on top of a box and fasten with a board nailed to the bottom of the box as shown. Next, bend the splints down all around and begin weaving the walls carrying these up to a height of three or four splints as in Fig. 7 and detail A of Fig. 8. Then the box can be removed and the tops of the splints held in place by a cloth strip, detail B. Next, point the end of each splint and when the basket is as high as you wish, bend these ends over and tuck into the horizontal splint which is second or third from the top as the case requires, detail C. Make a rim of hickory, roughly trimmed to a half-round section. Lap and rivet the ends and fasten to the basket top with thin splints bound around in one direction, then other splints bound the other direction, so that they cross as in detail D. The ends are tucked under as in Fig. 9. Some weavers make hickory splints as in Fig. 1, but usually it is better to buy the splints ready-made.

Woven chair seats can be made from rawhide strips, twisted cattails, cord or rope and the old favorite, cane. A very simple rawhide job is illustrated in the upper details, Fig. 10, the strips being woven in pairs and the ends tied. Use the longest thongs you can obtain, and moisten them slightly so that they will be taut when dry. Don't soak the thongs, as in drying they may shrink and crack the rungs over which they are stretched.

Cane is commonly used in chair bottoms. A simplified pattern for the beginner is given in Fig. 10. This is easy to follow and makes a substantial seat. The conventional pattern is carried out in the various steps as shown in details A to F inclusive, Fig. 10. Holes are evenly spaced and the cane strip is brought up through a hole, second from the corner, and secured with a tapered wooden peg. Front-to-back strips are installed first, detail A, and then those at right angles, or crosswise, are completed over the first ones, detail B. Again continue with the parallel front-to-back strips and over these, the second layer of crosswise strips, detail D, securing the ends either by tying underneath or driving in a hardwood peg and cutting off the projecting end flush with the chair frame. On the diagonals the work becomes somewhat more complicated. All those running in one direction are installed first. They are followed with the strips running at right angles to the first set of diagonals. See details E and F. The cane should be soaked a short time before using, but be careful that it is merely damp, not wet. This is quite important in successful weaving.

Rush chair seats are made of dried, twisted cattails and, of course, substitutes are used. If you use cattails, cut them at the peak of growth. Dry them in a dark place and before twisting, soak in water. Ends of the reeds or stems can be joined in a square knot made only on the underside of the seat. This procedure is shown in the lower details, Fig. 10. Begin at the corners of the chair frame and work toward the center, twisting the material as you go. Before closing up the seat at the center pack the empty space between upper and lower strands with scraps of the same material to make a solid seat.

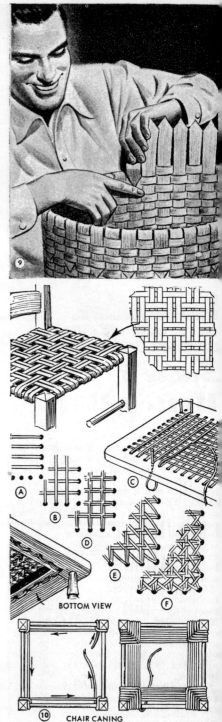

BOTTOM VIEW

(A)

(B)

(C)

(D)

(E)

(F)

⑩ CHAIR CANING

Smooth and sparkling, the walls of this luxurious bathroom are blue and white structural glass, which wipes clean easily and always looks new. Decorative figure on wall behind the tub was produced by sandblasting

Section 3
Better Bathrooms

LUXURIOUS NEW BATHROOMS can be yours when remodeling. You can modernize old bathrooms by installing smart, streamlined plumbing fixtures. These will give you better appearance, more convenience and also a much greater degree of safety. You can also add storage facilities, a vanity, and glass partitions for greater privacy. You may desire to enlarge a small bathroom, or divide a large one into two smaller ones to relieve congestion of a growing family. Or, you may need an extra bath or powder room as occasioned by the addition of a bedroom or two.

One of the improved features of modern bathroom fixtures is the elimination of most of the exposed joints and seams found in outmoded fixtures. This has been accomplished by simplified, one-piece design, and makes them more sanitary than many older-type fixtures. The newer designs also tend to conceal unsightly pipes and brackets.

How to install plumbing for economy: To reduce the cost of a plumbing installation, an extra bathroom should be located as closely to existing water-supply and drainage lines as may be possible. For example, an extra bathroom separated from an existing one by a wall often enables you to arrange the fixtures back to back on opposite sides of the wall, thus requiring only short extensions of piping. Where an extra bathroom or powder room is to be located on another floor, economy is possible by having it come directly under or over an existing bathroom. However, the convenience and comfort of a bathroom should not be sacrificed in order to save a few dollars in material and labor costs.

Bathroom arrangements: When a single large bathroom is used by an entire family, much needless congestion and waiting can be avoided by partitioning the room so that two lavatories and a shower can be used simultaneously. An excellent arrangement of this kind is the T-shaped bathroom shown in Fig. 1. A wall separates the shower stall from the two lavatories, and a counter between them offers added space. Fig. 2 shows how a large bathroom can be divided by a partition into two smaller

FIG. 1

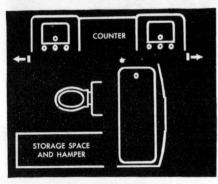

rooms, each accessible with a separate door. One room contains a bathtub or shower and may also include a lavatory, while the other room contains a lavatory and water closet.

Fig. 3 shows six basic layouts for small and medium-size bathrooms that are equipped with bathtubs. This gives the minimum spacing requirements for fixtures without sacrificing adequate elbow space. The same arrangements are applicable to larger rooms, although with these the surplus space often can be utilized for other purposes such as extra closets, cabinets and counter space.

Three examples of how large rooms not originally designed for bathrooms can be used as such are shown in Fig. 4. Detail A shows a 10 by 12-ft. room equipped with a prefabricated shower stall, two closets, a

counter and a cabinet-type lavatory. Detail B shows how a 12 by 12-ft. room was utilized as a bathroom containing a square-type bathtub. Two clothes closets of an adjoining bedroom were extended into the bathroom. An alternate arrangement, where two closets are accessible from the bathroom, is shown in detail C. In this case the bathtub and water closet were partitioned off from the lavatory section. Fig. 6 shows seven convenient layouts for single and grouped bathrooms in which shower stalls are used. With slight alterations, these arrangements also can be used where bathtubs are desired.

Important bathroom features: A single bathroom serves its purpose best usually when it is located more or less centrally in the house. A bath or powder room should be accessible from a passageway, preferably between bedrooms. An extra powder room on the first floor is a great convenience for guests. In many cases one of adequate size can be installed under a stairway. The entrance to a bathroom or powder room should not be in plain view from a dining room, living room or kitchen. If possible, don't build a bathroom where it will necessitate crossing a bedroom or other room to gain access to it. The door should be placed so that when it is opened it will not swing against a water closet or lavatory. Where space does not permit the door to swing inward as is customary, it can be swung outward.

Lighting and ventilation: Sufficient illumination and ventilation are important fea-

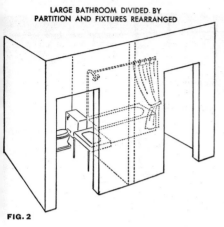

LARGE BATHROOM DIVIDED BY
PARTITION AND FIXTURES REARRANGED

FIG. 2

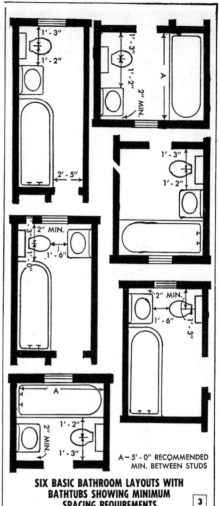

SIX BASIC BATHROOM LAYOUTS WITH
BATHTUBS SHOWING MINIMUM
SPACING REQUIREMENTS **3**

A – 5' - 0" RECOMMENDED
MIN. BETWEEN STUDS

tures in a bathroom. For maximum illumination during daylight hours, a window should be located preferably at right angles to the front of a lavatory. It should not be located over a bathtub if this can be avoided. Such a location makes it difficult to open or close the window, and the user of the tub is likely to experience cold drafts. Then also, the window should be protected with an extra shower curtain in case a shower head is installed. Should a window over a tub be the only location possible, install one of less height so that the sill will come about 4½ ft. or so above floor level.

Wall-type heating units: It is much easier to heat a small bathroom than a large one. Where it is frequently necessary to take the chill out of a cold bathroom, an auxiliary heating unit such as a gas or electric heater will be found useful. These can be obtained as built-in wall models as shown in Fig. 5. A portable, electric heater or any other electrical device should never be located within arm's-reach of a bathtub since this involves considerable danger to

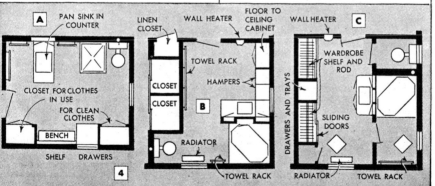

ARRANGEMENT OF PLUMBING FIXTURES AND STORAGE SPACE FOR ROOMS REMODELED TO LARGE BATHROOMS

U. S. Dept. of Agriculture illustration

FIG. 5   Photo courtesy Westinghouse Electric Corp.

SHOWER STALL USED INSTEAD OF TUB IN SMALL BATHROOM PROVIDES MORE FLOOR SPACE, AND IN THIS CASE USE OF A VANITY-TYPE LAVATORY

HERE THE USE OF A CORNER SHOWER STALL WITH DOOR AT ANGLE IN CENTER OF ROOM GIVES MOST SPACE AND MAXIMUM CONVENIENCE IN SMALL ROOM

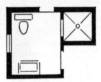

A SMALL BATHROOM CAN BE MADE LARGER BY UTILIZING ADJOINING SPACE SUCH AS A CLOSET FOR THE LOCATION OF A SHOWER STALL

TWO-DOOR ENTRANCE TO THIS BATHROOM GIVES PRIVACY IN THE SHOWER STALL, YET PERMITS SIMULTANEOUS USE OF OTHER FIXTURES

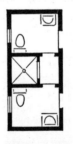

EXAMPLE OF GOOD PLANNING TO GET EQUIVALENT OF TWO BATHROOMS IN SMALL SPACE, A SINGLE SHOWER STALL BEING INSTALLED TO SERVE BOTH

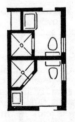

TWO SMALL BATHROOMS REPLACING A SINGLE LARGER BATHROOM WITH TUB, FOR THE GROWING FAMILY. BACK-TO-BACK ARRANGEMENT IS MOST ECONOMICAL

GROUP OF THREE BATHROOMS —A SEPARATE ONE ADJOINING A BEDROOM AND TWO WITH CONNECTING DOOR AND HALL ENTRANCE. INCLUDES TWO SHOWER STALLS AND BATHTUB

Illustrations courtesy Henry Weis Mfg. Co.

a person taking a bath. An electric outlet should be located at the cabinet over a lavatory for shaving convenience. It may be combined with a lighting fixture.

Prevention of polluted water: Generally a bathroom remodeling job that includes the substitution of modern fixtures for obsolete ones will eliminate serious health hazards from contaminated drinking water. Such hazards are inherent in the design of many older fixtures. Examples of dangerous lavatories and bathtubs are shown in Figs. 7 and 8. Here the water-supply outlets are located below the rim level of the fixture, making it possible for them to become submerged in water used for washing. When this happens a cross connection exists between the water-supply lines and the drainage system. Contaminated water then can be sucked up into the water-supply lines through an open or leaky faucet on occasions when the water pressure falls below atmospheric pressure.

Such conditions are frequently experienced in many home-plumbing systems. They are generally caused by a heavy draw of water from a lower outlet, or may result from any temporary loss of water pressure such as is caused by a broken water main or a heavy draw on the city mains by firefighting apparatus. The condition is aggravated if the house water-supply lines are too small or are badly limed, which causes a great reduction of pressure. Just what can happen when a cross connection exists, and water pressure is temporarily lacking, is shown in Fig. 9. Then polluted water can be drawn off at a lower level and inadvertently used for drinking purposes.

Modern plumbing fixtures are designed so that backflow is virtually impossible.

FIG. 7

FIG. 10 Photo courtesy Crane Co.

FIG. 8 Photos courtesy Minnesota State Board of Health

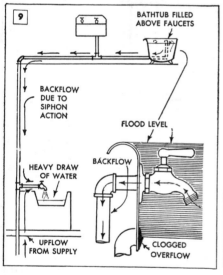

9

BATHTUB FILLED ABOVE FAUCETS

BACKFLOW DUE TO SIPHON ACTION

FLOOD LEVEL

BACKFLOW

HEAVY DRAW OF WATER

UPFLOW FROM SUPPLY

CLOGGED OVERFLOW

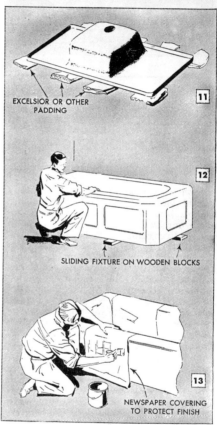

11 EXCELSIOR OR OTHER PADDING

12 SLIDING FIXTURE ON WOODEN BLOCKS

13 NEWSPAPER COVERING TO PROTECT FINISH

Faucets on bathtubs, lavatories and sinks now have their outlets projecting a sufficient distance above the flood-level rim of the fixtures, thus providing a safety air gap. Fig. 10 shows a lavatory with faucets so arranged. Often new faucets can be installed on old fixtures to provide this measure of safety, and thus save the cost of a new fixture. Water closets can be furnished with vacuum breakers or backflow preventers that eliminate the possibility of contaminated water. Many plumbing codes require such safety measures on water closets as well as suitable air gaps on other fixtures. The cost of safe, new plumbing fixtures is a worthwhile insurance to prevent water contamination and disease.

How to handle fixtures: The usual finish of bathroom fixtures is a thick coat of baked porcelain enamel. This is smooth, hard and lustrous. It is also durable and will not chip or crack unless subjected to severe strains or blows. The luster can be retained for many years if the finish is given reasonable care. Water-closet tanks and bowls are made of vitrified porcelain.

Generally crates in which fixtures are shipped are opened from the bottom by

FIG. 14 Photo courtesy American-Standard

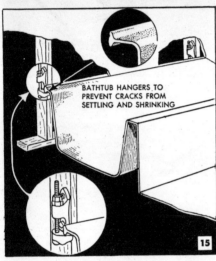

INSULATION AROUND TUB ON OUTSIDE WALL

16

17

PLASTER WALL COVERING

TUB CHANNEL MOLDING

TUB MASTIC SEAL

18 WATERPROOF JOINT WHERE WALL COVERING MEETS TUB

BATHTUB HANGERS TO PREVENT CRACKS FROM SETTLING AND SHRINKING

15

removing a few slats and blocking pieces. Take care not to strike or pry against the fixture, which may chip the finish. After uncrating a fixture, set it on protective pads of paper-covered excelsior or other resilient material as shown in Fig. 11. Never slide a fixture over a floor. The proper way to move it is to set it on wooden blocks as shown in Fig. 12. Then you can either push it slowly or get a handgrip on the under edge for lifting. When lifting one end of a bathtub, avoid forcing the opposite rim or edge against a wall or other object to prevent chipping.

When a bathtub is installed, which is done generally before the finish floor, wall covering and trim are applied, the tub should be protected from scratches and other mechanical damage. Never use a tub as a catch-all for paper wrappings, wood and other scraps likely to accumulate during construction. Often scratches are caused by persons standing on fixtures or

using them to hold tools. A good method of protecting a bathtub is to cover its surface with several layers of newspapers as shown in Fig. 13, using a special paste that comes off easily when soaked with water.

Bathtub installation: The recessed and corner types of built-in tubs are the most common. They come in square or rectangular models. A square, corner-type tub is shown in Fig. 14. The standard length of rectangular tubs is 5 ft., but shorter or longer ones also are available. Many square tubs have built-in seats. Unlike older single-shell tubs that have only a rolled edge, modern built-in tubs have an exposed apron that extends to the floor and presents a much neater appearance.

A bathtub generally is set on a subfloor covered with building paper. The bottom of the tub is often firmly bedded on a layer of sand to give firm support. The edges of the tub that are to be concealed by walls are brought snugly against the studs and

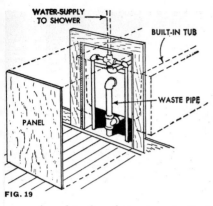

WATER-SUPPLY TO SHOWER

BUILT-IN TUB

WASTE PIPE

PANEL

FIG. 19

are anchored to them by means of adjustable supports or hangers as shown in Fig. 15. Several types of such supports are available. They are designed to prevent a crack from forming between the tub and the wall, which otherwise may result because of settling and shrinkage. Such supports assure uniform contact at various points, which is almost impossible with the use of wooden cleats nailed across studs as formerly practiced. Where bathtubs are installed against outside walls, be sure to fill the space between tub and wall with insulation as shown in Fig. 16.

After a tub has been installed, the wall covering is brought down to join it. Some tubs have upturned edges on wall sides, which go under the plaster as shown in Fig. 17. When any kind of wall covering such as linoleum or flexible tile is used, the edges joining the tub are made leakproof by using tub channel molding which is filled with a mastic sealer as shown in Fig. 18. The sealing compound remains somewhat flexible and maintains a tight, waterproof joint.

The floor covering then is brought up to the tub and the joint between the two is also sealed. The piping of a built-in tub should be accessible, usually through a paneled opening in the opposite side of the partition as shown in Fig. 19. As a rule, a shower outlet is installed over the head of the tub. The hot and cold-water pipes to a tub and shower generally connect to a combination spout but are controlled by separate faucets or valves.

Shower stalls: Numerous types of shower stalls are available. Two examples are shown in Figs. 20 and 21. The walls of a shower stall may be of glass, tile, sheet metal or other material impervious to water. It may have hinged or sliding doors, or may simply be curtained. Special leakproof bases or "receptors" are prefabricated for use with shower stalls. They also can be made up of sheet lead and a suitable

FIG. 20

FIG. 21   Photos courtesy Henry Weis Mfg. Co.

topping of tile or concrete. The floor of a shower stall should have a slight slope toward a drain which connects to a trap and waste pipe of suitable size. Shower stalls may be built as part of a bathroom construction, or you can install prefabricated units. The latter are also convenient where shower facilities are desired in a basement. A prefabricated unit can be housed between two regular partitions to make it less conspicuous as an added unit.

Receptors, Figs. 22 and 23, are generally made of heavy-gauge sheet metal, and have a non-slip, porcelain-enameled surface. The underside often is thickly coated with

FIG. 22

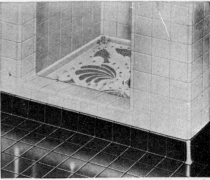

FIG. 23   Photos courtesy Henry Weis Mfg. Co.

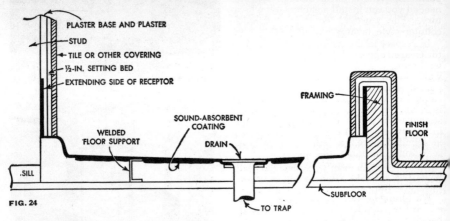

PLASTER BASE AND PLASTER
STUD
TILE OR OTHER COVERING
½-IN. SETTING BED
EXTENDING SIDE OF RECEPTOR

FRAMING

FINISH FLOOR

WELDED FLOOR SUPPORT

SOUND-ABSORBENT COATING

DRAIN

.SILL

FIG. 24

TO TRAP

SUBFLOOR

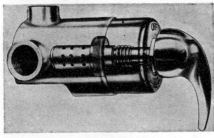

FIG. 25

Photos courtesy Symmons Engineering Co.

a sound-deadening material. In regular construction, the edges of receptors extend under the wall covering. Fig. 24 shows one installed in connection with a tile wall covering. A receptor should be set level on a floor or subfloor. In prefabricated shower stalls the water-supply and waste pipes must be installed in accordance with manufacturer's roughing-in dimensions.

Control of bath-water temperature: When using ordinary, manually controlled mixing faucets on bathtubs and showers, it is almost impossible at times to maintain the exact temperature of the water to which it was originally adjusted. In many cases water can even change to a dangerous, scalding temperature within a few seconds and before you can turn off the supply. Such annoying variations of temperature while bathing usually are caused by a heavy draw of water from another outlet in the house, usually one at a lower level. This reduces the pressure in the line leading to the bathtub or shower.

Such troubles can be avoided by installing an automatic mixing valve like the one shown in Fig. 25. This maintains the temperature of running bath water within a few degrees of the original adjustment even though there may be pressure fluctuations of as much as 90 percent in the water lines. The only time when such a device allows a change of temperature toward the cool side is when the supply of hot water in the tank has been exhausted.

Lavatories: There are many kinds of attractive lavatories, a few of which are shown in Fig. 26. Some have a raised back or shelf, while others have flat tops. Wall-hung models have a raised edge to protect the wall from splashing. Some of these are especially designed for use in corners where space is limited for more desirable positions. Where extra storage space is needed you can install a cabinet-type lavatory. For powder rooms, a small-size counter-style lavatory is often preferred.

In respect to the manner in which lavatories are supported, they may be entirely wall-hung, may be partly supported by a wall and partly on legs, or they can be supported entirely on a pedestal, counter or cabinet. The standard height of lavatories is 31 in., but the kind attached to walls or supported by adjustable legs may be varied in height somewhat to suit the users. Unless limited space is a deciding factor when selecting a lavatory, the larger sizes are most convenient, especially those having wide, flat surfaces on which you can set toilet articles.

Wall-hung lavatories, which are the least expensive, require one or two wooden backing pieces nailed securely across studs, and flush with them, as shown in Fig. 27. Determine the location of backing pieces by consulting the manufacturers' roughing-in sheets. Generally the legs of lavatories are adjustable to compensate for slight differences of floor level. Most modern lavatories have a combination spout so that water can be mixed to desired temperature by adjusting the faucets. Often the faucets and spout are combined in a single unit.

Water closets: Usually water closets for homes have a flush tank, either separate from the bowl or cast integral with it. The tank should be supported with backing pieces like wall-hung lavatories. In operation, water closets may be the "washdown" or the "siphon-jet" type. In the former, water from the tank enters the bowl through perforations in the bowl rim and often also through an extra inlet port. In siphon-jet water closets, a faster and more positive flushing action is produced by a stream of water directed into the trap, in addition to the entrance of water through the rim. Such a closet generally is less noisy but more expensive than one of the wash-down type.

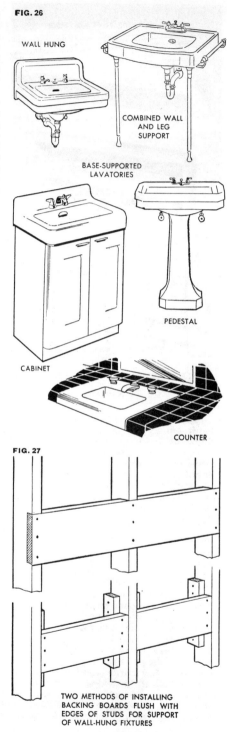

FIG. 26

WALL HUNG

COMBINED WALL AND LEG SUPPORT

BASE-SUPPORTED LAVATORIES

PEDESTAL

CABINET

COUNTER

FIG. 27

TWO METHODS OF INSTALLING BACKING BOARDS FLUSH WITH EDGES OF STUDS FOR SUPPORT OF WALL-HUNG FIXTURES

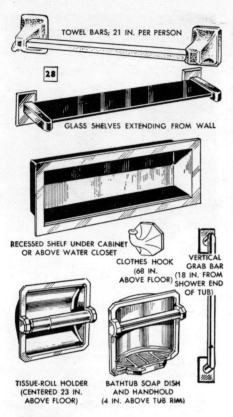

TOWEL BARS; 21 IN. PER PERSON

28

GLASS SHELVES EXTENDING FROM WALL

RECESSED SHELF UNDER CABINET OR ABOVE WATER CLOSET

CLOTHES HOOK (68 IN. ABOVE FLOOR)

VERTICAL GRAB BAR (18 IN. FROM SHOWER END OF TUB)

TISSUE-ROLL HOLDER (CENTERED 23 IN. ABOVE FLOOR)

BATHTUB SOAP DISH AND HANDHOLD (4 IN. ABOVE TUB RIM)

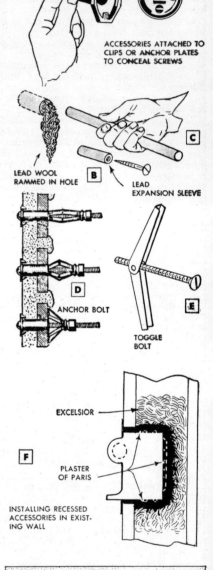

LUGS

A

SCREWS

ACCESSORIES ATTACHED TO CLIPS OR ANCHOR PLATES TO CONCEAL SCREWS

LEAD WOOL RAMMED IN HOLE

B

C

LEAD EXPANSION SLEEVE

D

ANCHOR BOLT

E

TOGGLE BOLT

F

EXCELSIOR

PLASTER OF PARIS

INSTALLING RECESSED ACCESSORIES IN EXISTING WALL

BACKING PIECE

WOOD BOX AROUND ACCESSORY

G

PLASTER OF PARIS

INSTALLATION OF RECESSED ACCESSORIES IN NEW CONSTRUCTION

Bathroom accessories: A number of bathroom accessories are shown in Fig. 28. Some of these project from the walls; others are recessed. Many, such as hooks, towel bars, shelf brackets, etc., fit on clips or anchor plates that are fastened as shown in detail A of Fig. 29, thus concealing the screw heads. As plaster easily chips and breaks loose when screws are driven into it, you put lead expansion sleeves or lead wool tightly packed in holes, after which the screws can be driven in. You can also use screw anchors. See details B, C and D of Fig. 29. Cut holes in plaster with a star drill, or other drill of proper size. A circular-motion, silicon-carbide tipped drill is used to make holes in tile. Details D and E show how anchor bolts and toggle bolts provide anchorage behind plastered walls where more holding power is required.

Towel bars should provide 21 in. of horizontal space per person. A roll-tissue holder should be centered about 23 in. above the floor. A vertical grab bar on the wall over a bathtub provides cheap insurance against slips and accidents. Locate it about 18 in. from the head of the tub—the end where faucets are located. A recessed

FIG. 30   Photo courtesy Crane Co.

FIG. 31   Photo courtesy Douglas Fir Plywood Assn.

metal cabinet over a lavatory should be centered about 62 in. above the floor. A light should be provided on either side or above the cabinet. One of the fixtures should be equipped with an outlet for shaving convenience.

Recessed fittings such as soap dishes, bathtub hand grips and roll-tissue holders require cutting a square or rectangular hole through the plaster or other wall covering at a location between studs. Make the hole just large enough to admit the body of the unit so that the flange overlaps the wall surface, thus concealing the edges of the cutout.

To install recessed accessories in existing walls, you can stuff excelsior tightly into the partition all around the unit as shown in detail F of Fig. 29. Then you smear plaster of paris into the excelsior, and also over it, so that the unit, when pushed in place, will be imbedded firmly. A thin layer of plaster smeared on the flange will seal the joint. Some accessories have extending fins to facilitate anchoring them. Others have lugs on which wire can be strung to be imbedded in the plaster. Surplus plaster is removed from the wall with a putty knife before it hardens, and the wall surface then is wiped clean with a moist rag.

To install a recessed accessory in an open wall of new construction, you build a wooden box to house it as shown in detail G of Fig. 29. The plaster edges of the wall, which will overlap the box, will generally anchor the plaster-of-paris bedding with which the unit is secured in the box. Installation is the same as described above except that excelsior is not needed. Manu-facturers provide roughing-in dimensions from which the size of the boxes can be determined.

Added conveniences and storage space: An attractive, permanent shower enclosure of glass represents an economy by eliminating the constant cost of replacements for fabric and plastic curtains of the usual type. Often it is possible to utilize the space above a shower enclosure for a spacious storage cabinet, which can be provided with either sliding or hinged doors. As the bottom is subject to dampness, this should be made of either tempered hardboard or of exterior-type plywood, which is bonded with waterproof glue to give protection against moisture.

Considerable added storage space also is possible under the usual type of wall-hung lavatory as shown in Fig. 30. This photo also shows a lavatory cabinet, wider than the usual type, and having sliding doors, two of which are mirrors. Another convenient storage cabinet for odds and ends in the bathroom is shown in Fig. 31. This one utilizes most of the space above a water-closet tank, which usually is wasted space. Such a cabinet, about 6 or 8 in. wide, can be made from ½-in. plywood, fitted with sliding doors and enameled to match the bathroom color scheme. This type of cabinet can also be used elsewhere in the home.

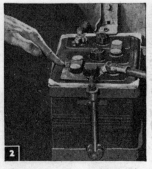

Remove white coating from battery terminals with a soda-and-water solution. Wipe dry with clean cloth

Check sealing compound for cracks. Repair with compound, using in a tarry consistency that does not run

Inspect the battery cradle for acid damage. If the cradle is in poor condition it should be replaced

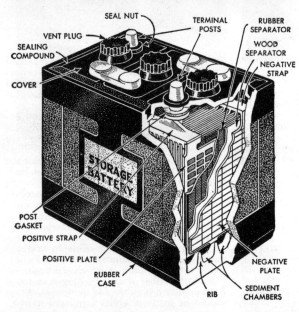

SEAL NUT
VENT PLUG
SEALING COMPOUND
COVER
TERMINAL POSTS
RUBBER SEPARATOR
WOOD SEPARATOR
NEGATIVE STRAP
STORAGE BATTERY
POST GASKET
POSITIVE STRAP
POSITIVE PLATE
RUBBER CASE
RIB
NEGATIVE PLATE
SEDIMENT CHAMBERS

BATTERY

BEFORE one attempts to service any mechanical or electrical device it's a good idea to know how it works. Being well acquainted with your car battery helps you to service it regularly.

A storage battery consists of three identical 2-volt cells connected in series, making a total of 6 volts across the terminals. Each cell has positive plates of lead peroxide and negative plates of lead, the number of plates depending upon the ampere-hour rating of the battery. An electrolyte solution of distilled water and sulphuric acid sur-

State of the charge is checked with a hydrometer. Reading should never go below recommended levels

Add water when necessary. In cold weather add water just before driving car, otherwise it may freeze

Before removing the cables from from an old battery, note and, if necessary, mark positive terminal

7 Disconnect ground terminal first. Use a puller and work carefully if clamp is "frozen" to the post	**8** When replacing battery, tighten bolts uniformly. Renew rubber washers. Don't draw nuts too tightly	**9** Worn or frayed cable should be replaced. Note bends in old cable and install new one in the same way

CARE

rounds the plates. In order to keep positive and negative plates from touching each other and shorting the battery, nonconducting separators are placed between each pair of plates. In addition, some batteries have Fiberglas sheets to retard the loss of active material from the plate grids. The case is of hard rubber with a space in the bottom for sludge deposits and the cover is a separate piece held in place by sealing compound.

The plates are not solid, but consist of a framework or grid composed of an alloy of lead and antimony. The mesh of the positive plate is filled with lead peroxide and that of the negative plate with sponge lead. These fillers are porous to allow the electrolyte to penetrate them freely. When the battery is in use, lead peroxide and sponge lead gradually drop off the grids and fall to the bottom of the battery case. The speed with which this happens depends upon how nearly the battery charge is kept normal, how it is charged and how used. To get the

most out of a battery, the active material must be kept on the grid or framework as long as possible, the separators must be kept in good condition and the case protected from damage and leakage.

When the electrical circuit is closed between the positive and negative terminals of the battery, as when the lights are turned on or the car is started, the sulphuric acid in the electrolyte combines with the material on the plates, both negative and positive, to form lead sulphate. Electric current then flows through the electrolyte to the positive terminal and out to the electrical system. As this happens, the amount of acid in the battery solution decreases. This action gives the basis of testing battery strength with a hydrometer, which measures the amount of acid in the solution in proportion to the water present, by the difference in the specific gravity of these two liquids. There is no change in volume of liquid in the battery, as the absorbed acid is replaced by water in the

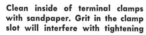

Clean and brighten terminal posts with a wire brush. Be careful not to get dirt into the cell-cap vents	Clean inside of terminal clamps with sandpaper. Grit in the clamp slot will interfere with tightening	Apply mineral grease or white petroleum jelly to battery posts and terminal clamps. Cover thoroughly

10	**11**	**12**

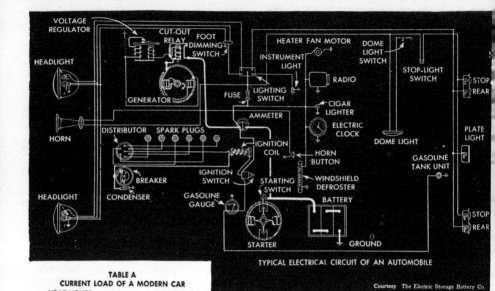

TYPICAL ELECTRICAL CIRCUIT OF AN AUTOMOBILE

Courtesy The Electric Storage Battery Co.

Courtesy The Electric Storage Battery Co.

TABLE A
CURRENT LOAD OF A MODERN CAR

HEAD LIGHTS	14.0 AMPS.
IGNITION	1.7 AMPS.
INSTRUMENT LIGHTS	0.8 AMPS.
TAILLIGHTS	1.2 AMPS.
LICENSE LIGHT	0.6 AMPS.
HEATER AND DEFROSTER	7.0 AMPS.
RADIO	7.5 AMPS.
	32.8 AMPS.

SUMMER STARTING....125 TO 300 AMPS.*
WINTER STARTING......300 TO 700 AMPS.*
*Varies with engine size and oil viscosity

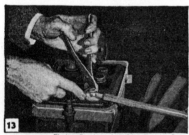

13

Photos Courtesy Auto-Lite Battery Corp.

Above, tighten clamp nuts with battery pliers. Make sure that the clamp is pressed down on the post as far as it will go. Below, ammeter should read discharge when light switch is on

14

Take a minute to study this typical wiring diagram and you'll have a better idea of the heavy load on your car battery

chemical process. A fully discharged battery contains nothing but water, with the acid completely absorbed in the plates as lead sulphate.

Charging simply reverses this process, and by this means the battery can be restored to full charge, provided the lead sulphate has not been allowed to remain on the plates too long. When it is impossible to recharge a run-down battery, it's usually because the plates have remained sulphated too long, or the active material has dropped off the plates.

When you buy a battery rated at 100 ampere-hours, this theoretical rating means that the battery will deliver 100 amperes of current for one hour, or one ampere for 100 hours. Normally, careful testing and charging of a battery is a job for a fully equipped service station, but a hydrometer to test the strength of the electrolyte is inexpensive to own and easy to use. Make a test only when the battery solution is thoroughly mixed, never immediately after adding water. Hydrometer readings are set for one temperature, usually about 80 deg. F. A temperature correction of "4 points" of gravity must be made for each 10 deg. of variation from 80 deg. F. Add for above 80 deg. and subtract for below 80 deg. For example, the gravity of a fully charged battery, at 80 deg. F., is 1.280. At 100 deg. F., it will be about 1.288. At 10 deg. F., it will be 1.252. These are battery-solution temperatures, not air temperatures.

Figs. 1 to 14 picture the steps necessary in ordinary periodic care of a battery. Table A lists the average current requirements of a modern car with the usual accessories and the detail directly above table A shows a typical wiring diagram.

Electric Motor Mounted on Board Recharges Auto Battery

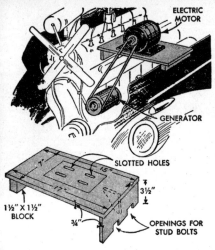

ELECTRIC MOTOR

GENERATOR

SLOTTED HOLES

3½"

1½" X 1½" BLOCK

¾"

OPENINGS FOR STUD BOLTS

To keep an auto battery charged, a small electric motor belted to the car generator can be installed in a few minutes. The motor must rotate in the same direction as the generator, and is mounted on a board long enough to extend from the engine to one side of the hood. The board is slotted for motor mounting bolts and provided with end cleats high enough to keep it level when in use. It may be necessary to notch the end cleat resting on the engine block to fit over studs; however, installation will vary on cars of different design. To use the unit, remove the fan belt and slip the drive belt over the generator pulley to connect it to the motor. Correct tension is obtained by adjustment of the mounting bolts. In no case should the motor be used on automobiles not having current and voltage regulators unless the battery is watched closely for overcharging.

Washers Prevent Clamp Sticking

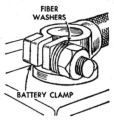

FIBER WASHERS

BATTERY CLAMP

If fiber washers are inserted between the nut and clamp when connecting the cable to a battery terminal, the cable will be easier to remove later. Corrosion tends to make the nut stick to the clamp but the washers will prevent this. When the battery is removed, the washers are pried outward to loosen the clamp. It may be necessary to use a longer bolt and acid resistant washers.

Extending Auto-Battery Life

Automobile-battery life can be extended considerably if the battery is cleaned and refinished every six months. Remove the battery from the car and plug the small vents in the caps with match stems. Then thoroughly wash the entire casing. If corrosion is difficult to remove, use a soda-water solution to clean it. After this cleaning, any small cracks such as those frequently caused by overtightening of the mounting bolts will be discernible. Mend them by applying a soldering iron to the cracked area until sufficient melting of the hard-rubber casing occurs to fill the crack. Finally, coat the casing with rubber paint of the type used on tires. The battery will look like new and unnecessary damage by corrosion to both the battery and battery cables will be avoided.

Ammonia Frees Battery Terminal

For removing corroded battery terminals that are stuck tightly to the post, apply a small amount of ordinary household ammonia, letting it soak in for a few minutes. The terminal then can be lifted off easily, after which it should be wiped clean and dry.

Cutter Removes Battery Straps Without Damaging Elements

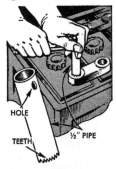

HOLE

TEETH

½" PIPE

Instead of sawing off the posts to remove the connecting straps of a storage battery, use a hole saw to cut the strap from the post. To make the saw, file teeth in one end of a piece of thin-wall pipe or tubing and drill a hole at the other end for a handle. To use, press the cutter down on the strap where it fits over the terminal post and turn the cutter back and forth until the ring is cut through. The straps can then be lifted off, and may be placed over the posts of a new cell and soldered tight.

BEACH EQUIPMENT
Part One

The whole family will enjoy bathing if the youngsters can be towed to deeper water in this floating playpen. Four auto inner tubes prevent tipping

Sturdy aquaplane shown below will bring endless thrills to the more experienced swimmer. Rubber mats at rear provide nonslip footing for rider

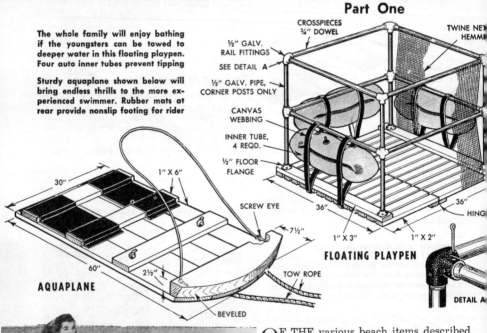

CROSSPIECES ¾" DOWEL

TWINE NET HEMM

½" GALV. RAIL FITTINGS

SEE DETAIL A

½" GALV. PIPE, CORNER POSTS ONLY

CANVAS WEBBING

INNER TUBE, 4 REQD.

½" FLOOR FLANGE

SCREW EYE

7½"

36"

36"

HING

1" X 3"

1" X 2"

FLOATING PLAYPEN

DETAIL A

30"

1" X 6"

60"

2½"

AQUAPLANE

TOW ROPE

BEVELED

OF THE various beach items described on this and the next three pages, the diving raft, knockdown pier and lounging chair are the only ones which require a considerable amount of work. Most of the remaining articles can be built in a few hours and feature simplicity of construction along with maximum portability. For example, the floating playpen detailed above comes apart merely by removing the pins which hold the rails in place. After the rails are pulled from the netting, the inner tubes deflated and the pipe uprights unscrewed from the floor flanges, the hinged platform can be folded and the entire unit then packed neatly in the trunk of a car.

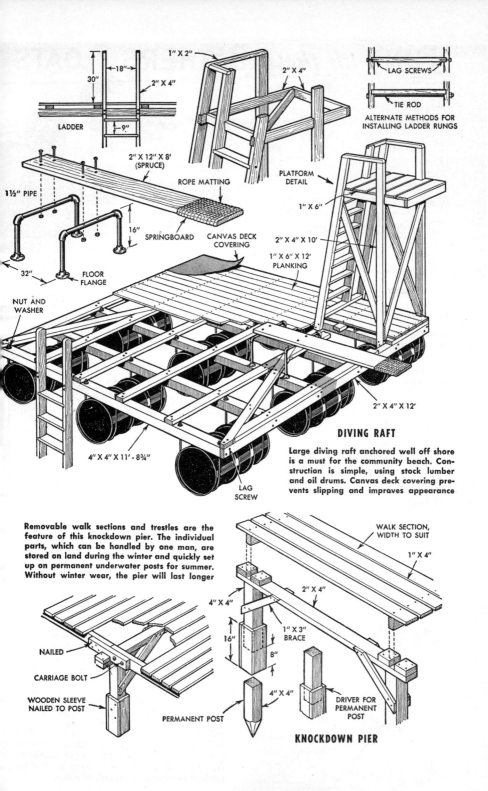

18"

30"

2" X 4"

LADDER

9"

1" X 2"

2" X 4"

LAG SCREWS

TIE ROD

ALTERNATE METHODS FOR
INSTALLING LADDER RUNGS

2" X 12" X 8'
(SPRUCE)

ROPE MATTING

PLATFORM
DETAIL

1½" PIPE

16"

1" X 6"

SPRINGBOARD

CANVAS DECK
COVERING

2" X 4" X 10'

1" X 6" X 12'
PLANKING

32"

FLOOR
FLANGE

NUT AND
WASHER

2" X 4" X 12'

4" X 4" X 11' - 8¾"

LAG
SCREW

DIVING RAFT

Large diving raft anchored well off shore
is a must for the community beach. Construction is simple, using stock lumber
and oil drums. Canvas deck covering prevents slipping and improves appearance

Removable walk sections and trestles are the
feature of this knockdown pier. The individual
parts, which can be handled by one man, are
stored on land during the winter and quickly set
up on permanent underwater posts for summer.
Without winter wear, the pier will last longer

WALK SECTION,
WIDTH TO SUIT

1" X 4"

4" X 4"

2" X 4"

1" X 3"
BRACE

16"

8"

NAILED

CARRIAGE BOLT

WOODEN SLEEVE
NAILED TO POST

PERMANENT POST

4" X 4"

DRIVER FOR
PERMANENT
POST

KNOCKDOWN PIER

FUN *with these* BATHERS' FLOATS

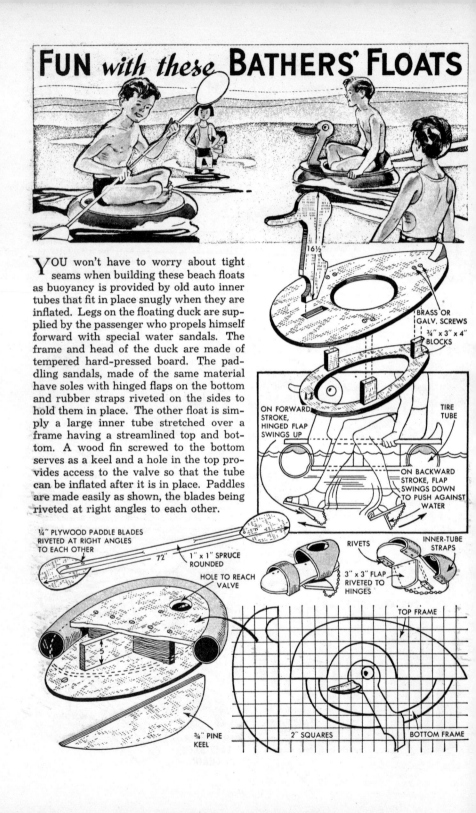

YOU won't have to worry about tight seams when building these beach floats as buoyancy is provided by old auto inner tubes that fit in place snugly when they are inflated. Legs on the floating duck are supplied by the passenger who propels himself forward with special water sandals. The frame and head of the duck are made of tempered hard-pressed board. The paddling sandals, made of the same material have soles with hinged flaps on the bottom and rubber straps riveted on the sides to hold them in place. The other float is simply a large inner tube stretched over a frame having a streamlined top and bottom. A wood fin screwed to the bottom serves as a keel and a hole in the top provides access to the valve so that the tube can be inflated after it is in place. Paddles are made easily as shown, the blades being riveted at right angles to each other.

16½"

BRASS OR GALV. SCREWS

¾" x 3" x 4" BLOCKS

ON FORWARD STROKE, HINGED FLAP SWINGS UP

TIRE TUBE

ON BACKWARD STROKE, FLAP SWINGS DOWN TO PUSH AGAINST WATER

¼" PLYWOOD PADDLE BLADES RIVETED AT RIGHT ANGLES TO EACH OTHER

72"

1" x 1" SPRUCE ROUNDED

HOLE TO REACH VALVE

RIVETS

INNER-TUBE STRAPS

3" x 3" FLAP RIVETED TO HINGES

5

¾" PINE KEEL

TOP FRAME

2" SQUARES

BOTTOM FRAME

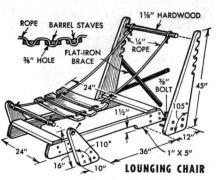

ROPE · BARREL STAVES · 1⅛" HARDWOOD
⅜" HOLE · FLAT-IRON BRACE · ¼" ROPE
24" · ⅜" BOLT · 45" · 105° · 1½" · 110° · 12" · 1" X 5" · 24" · 16" · 10" · 36"

LOUNGING CHAIR

This lounging chair for the private beach is just the thing to help you spend those lazy summer afternoons in solid comfort. It's adjustable to four different positions so you can sit up to read or lie down to relax while basking in the sun

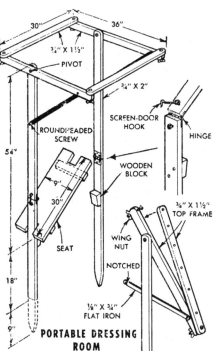

30" · 36" · ¾" X 1½" · PIVOT · ¾" X 2" · SCREEN-DOOR HOOK · HINGE · ROUNDHEADED SCREW · WOODEN BLOCK · 54" · 9" · 30" · ¾" X 1½" TOP FRAME · SEAT · WING NUT · NOTCHED · 18" · ⅛" X ¾" FLAT IRON · 9"

PORTABLE DRESSING ROOM

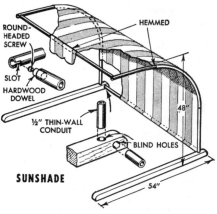

ROUND-HEADED SCREW · HEMMED · SLOT · HARDWOOD DOWEL · ½" THIN-WALL CONDUIT · BLIND HOLES · 48" · 54"

SUNSHADE

Thin-wall conduit forms the frame for the generously proportioned sunshade shown above. Two lengths of wood support the frame. Below, lazy-back chair with pocket for sundries has handle for carrying. Cushions are used on seat and back

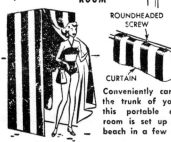

ROUNDHEADED SCREW · GROMMET · CURTAIN

Conveniently carried in the trunk of your car, this portable dressing room is set up on the beach in a few minutes

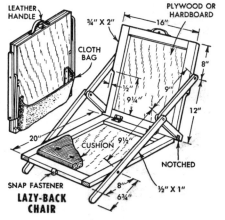

LEATHER HANDLE · PLYWOOD OR HARDBOARD · ¾" X 2" · 16" · CLOTH BAG · 8" · ½" · 9" · 9¼" · 12" · 20" · CUSHION · 9½" · NOTCHED · SNAP FASTENER · 8" · 6¾" · ½" X 1"

LAZY-BACK CHAIR

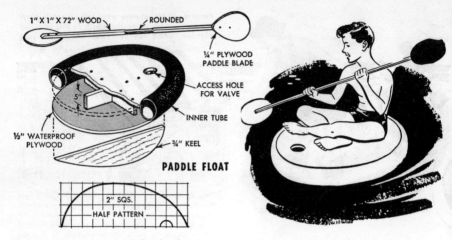

1" X 1" X 72" WOOD — ROUNDED

¼" PLYWOOD PADDLE BLADE

ACCESS HOLE FOR VALVE

INNER TUBE

5"

½" WATERPROOF PLYWOOD — ¾" KEEL

PADDLE FLOAT

2" SQS.
HALF PATTERN

There's real adventure in the shallow beach water for the young mariner who is master of his own paddle float, above. Drive the stakes for the picnic table, below, place the top over them, and you're all set. For easy handling, the top folds together and the stakes fit in cloth loops

¾" X 36" X 36" PLYWOOD

2" X 2" X 24" LEG (6 REQD.)

CLOTH LOOPS

PICNIC TABLE

HANDLE

BUTT HINGE

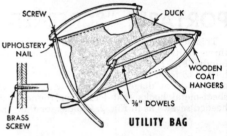

SCREW

DUCK

UPHOLSTERY NAIL

WOODEN COAT HANGERS

⅜" DOWELS

BRASS SCREW

UTILITY BAG

The utility bag shown above is made from wooden coat hangers. The surfboard, below, is simply a pine board with rounded ends. Hardwood cleats glued in grooves on the underside prevent warping

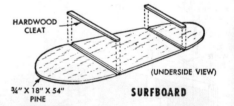

HARDWOOD CLEAT

(UNDERSIDE VIEW)

¾" X 18" X 54" PINE

SURFBOARD

If the 12 x 12-ft. diving raft, which is floated on tightly sealed oil drums, is too large, the basic construction can be adapted readily to a smaller and less pretentious raft. The cross members are spaced to rest near the edges of the drums and are held tightly in place with hangers of threaded ½-in. iron rod. Should extra buoyancy be needed, additional drums are easily installed. Note that the diving platform and spring-board can be located to straddle any pair of the 4 x 4-in. cross members.

The knockdown pier may be built in as many sections of a conveniently handled size as are required to attain the desired length. When assembling the pier, the trestles are slipped over permanent posts set below water level.

Bringing a large canoe across a sandy beach is almost effortless if the boat is lashed to this nail-keg dolly. A reamed floor flange at each end of the keg serves as a bearing for the axle

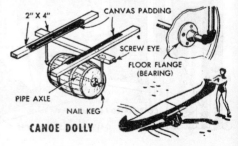

2" X 4"

CANVAS PADDING

SCREW EYE

FLOOR FLANGE (BEARING)

PIPE AXLE

NAIL KEG

CANOE DOLLY

Parents will feel at ease when baby is safely playing in the yard or on the beach in this screened playpen, which can be folded flat for carrying

PORTABLE "SCREENED PORCH" FOR BABY

This screened playpen consists of only three units which fold into a compact bundle, Fig. 1. The side and end walls are hinged to form two separable units, which are joined at diagonal corners with flat sheet-metal hooks that lock over round-headed screws as in Fig. 2. Frames for the walls are constructed with mortise-and-tenon corner joints and covered with 14-mesh wire screen. The gable ends, made from pine, are hinged on the outside and wooden turn buttons on the inside hold them erect when the pen is set up. A notched ridgepole supports the awning.

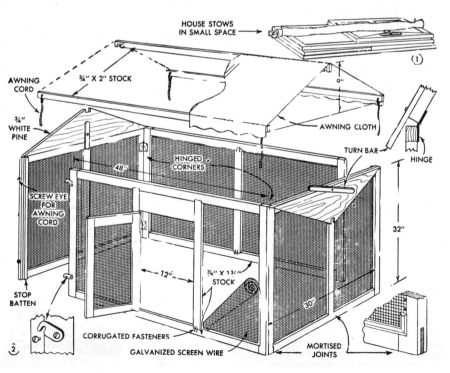

HOUSE STOWS IN SMALL SPACE

AWNING CORD

¾" X 2" STOCK

0"

AWNING CLOTH

¾" WHITE PINE

TURN BAR

HINGE

48"

HINGED CORNERS

SCREW EYE FOR AWNING CORD

32"

STOP BATTEN

12"

⅞" X 1¾" STOCK

30"

CORRUGATED FASTENERS

GALVANIZED SCREEN WIRE

MORTISED JOINTS

Part Two

BEACH EQUIPMENT

WITH a few yards of cloth and some scrap wood, you can make a beach dressing room that can be assembled or taken apart in a few minutes and carried under your arm. It consists of a wooden frame pivoted to two uprights and held by flat-iron supports; a seat, which rests on blocks screwed to the uprights, and a drape, which is fitted with grommets that slip over projecting round-head bolts in the frame, as shown in the left-hand detail. The circular detail shows how the frame is jointed to fold against the uprights, which are hinged also for ease in carrying. They are held open by screen-door hooks and screw eyes, as indicated in the right-hand detail.

WING NUT
36"
30"
¾" X 2"
¾" X 1½"
⅛" X ¾" IRON
HOOK
HINGE
SEAT
54"
18"
9"
¾" X 1½" TOP FRAMING
⅛" X ¾" FLAT IRON
¾" X 2" POST

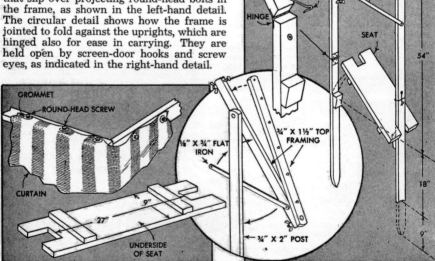

GROMMET
ROUND-HEAD SCREW
CURTAIN
9"
27"
UNDERSIDE OF SEAT

"FROG MEN"
SWIMMING PADDLES

ONCE you get used to wearing them, these "frog feet" will enable you to swim greater distances at speeds you couldn't achieve otherwise. Although good swimmers will be able to use them to advantage in a number of swimming strokes, many users probably will find the side crawl the least tiring for long-distance work. Details below show how to make the paddles, each of which consists of two parts: a shoe, or sandal, and a hinged flap, or wing, which is cloth-covered. The wing is hinged in such a way that it can swing in an arc of only about 50 deg. However, this is sufficient to allow it to "feather" properly on the return stroke when swimming. The cloth covering or web of lightweight canvas is stretched over a wire frame, sewed as indicated, then treated with airplane dope, which waterproofs and shrinks the cloth tight on the wire frame. The sandal is cut from waterproof plywood and is fitted with a "counter" cut from an old inner tube. Web straps attached to the counter tie over the ankle. Notice that the sandal is covered with leather or rubber of about the same thickness as the toe strap. This prevents chafing. Edges of the plywood are sanded smooth and all exposed parts are given two coats of shellac or spar varnish.

DIRECTION OF TRAVEL

LOOKING DOWN ON SWIMMER
USING THE SIDE CRAWL TO
SHOW ACTION OF "FROG FEET"

STRAP

ENDS OF PLYWOOD
BEVELED

COTTON OR LINEN CLOTH
COATED WITH MODEL
AIRPLANE DOPE

LEATHER SAME
THICKNESS AS
STRAP COVERS
BOTTOM OF SHOE

½" STRAP WIRED
TO SHOE

SEAM

6"   6"   HOLE

¼" WATERPROOF
PLYWOOD

⅛" X ¼"
FLAT IRON

HINGE
2 REQ'D

½" WEB
STRAP

³⁄₁₆" STEEL
ROD

FISHLINE ALLOWS
PADDLE TO SWING 50°

1½"

CROSS WIRE DRAWN
TIGHTLY, TWISTED
AND SOLDERED

⅛"
HOLE

SPRING HOLDS WEB
AGAINST SHOE

¼" WOOD
HEEL

NOTCHED FOR
CROSS WIRE

¹⁄₁₆" X ½" X 1"
SHEET METAL

Here is a bedroom suite whose beauty lies in modern lines matched by simplified construction appealing to any craftsman

BEDROOM FURNITURE

Part One

PICTURE in your home this beautiful bedroom ensemble in honey maple, limed oak or rich walnut and then try to talk your way out of building it. Mom will want it by tomorrow, and if there is a teen-age daughter in your home she will say, "It's simply out of this world." Designed for flexibility the pieces are functional and can be arranged, re-arranged and interchanged to her heart's content.

All pieces are coordinated in size to fit together in sectional groups—chest, night stands and bed are all the same height. The group features a most practical bed which incorporates built-in storage space in the headboard. The front of it opens wide to reveal a spacious compartment for extra bedding and a roomy drawer pulls out at

each end of the headboard to provide storage for shoes. The chest-on-chest unit can be stacked to serve as a five-drawer highboy, or a pair of base units can be built and placed end-to-end under a large mirror to obtain the popular Mr. and Mrs. dresser. A novel three-piece vanity consists of two twin end units bridged with a separate top unit which opens to expose a cosmetic compartment and make-up mirror.

A product of a basement shop, the original furniture was built with the power tools shown. Only two tools, a saw and jointer, actually are required as the construction involves just simple,

Right, edges of the plywood are mitered with the saw table tilted at a 45-deg. angle and planed accurately on the jointer to obtain a perfect fit

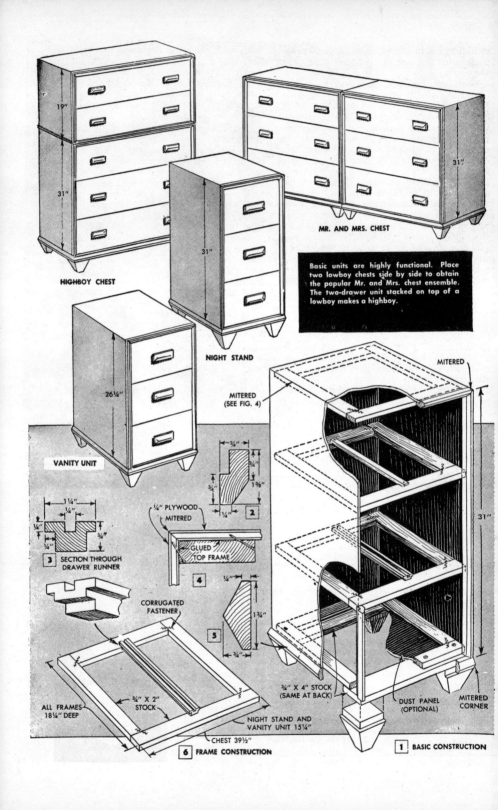

HIGHBOY CHEST

19"

31"

MR. AND MRS. CHEST

31"

NIGHT STAND

31"

Basic units are highly functional. Place two lowboy chests side by side to obtain the popular Mr. and Mrs. chest ensemble. The two-drawer unit stacked on top of a lowboy makes a highboy.

VANITY UNIT

26¼"

MITERED (SEE FIG. 4)

MITERED

31"

2 ¾" ⁹⁄₁₆" ¾" 1⅜" ¼"

¼" PLYWOOD MITERED

GLUED TOP FRAME

4

¼"

5 1¾" ¾"

3 SECTION THROUGH DRAWER RUNNER

1¼" ¼" ¼" ¾" ¼"

CORRUGATED FASTENER

¾" X 4" STOCK (SAME AT BACK)

DUST PANEL (OPTIONAL)

MITERED CORNER

ALL FRAMES 18¼" DEEP

¾" X 2" STOCK

NIGHT STAND AND VANITY UNIT 15¼"

CHEST 39½"

6 FRAME CONSTRUCTION

1 BASIC CONSTRUCTION

straight cuts in dimensional stock and incorporates the use of plywood to simplify the work.

Basic construction of the night stands, chests and vanity units is exactly the same. It's merely a case of increasing the over-all height and width as given for each respective cabinet. Fig. 1 shows the extreme simplicity of construction. Each unit, with the exception of the two-drawer chest, requires three drawer frames and a top frame, four in all, which are made exactly alike as detailed in Fig. 6. Pine or other softwood will do for the frames, although the front rail of each frame can be of hardwood, if you wish. The top frame is of ½-in. stock while the others are ¾-in., and if the bottom frame is to be fitted with a dust panel, a groove is centered in the edge of the members to take a ¼-in. plywood panel. Otherwise, the frame pieces are merely butted, glued and joined together with corrugated fasteners.

The next step is to glue and screw the bottom frame to two ¾ x 4-in. base pieces. These pieces, which are placed across the front and back, are made the same length as the frame. Note that at the front the frame is placed 1⅛ in. in from the edge, while at the back the frame is glued flush with the edge of the base piece. Now, a 1¾-in. molding, Fig. 5, is mitered and glued to the edges of the base pieces so that it is flush with their top surfaces. The molding along the sides is cut ¼ in. longer than the depth of the base to allow for a ¼-in. plywood back. Glue blocks along the sides, plus screws driven at an angle through the edges of the base pieces from the inside, are used to anchor the molding.

The edging which conceals the laminated edges of the plywood at the front is ripped from ¾-in. stock according to Fig. 2. This is mitered and glued together as a separate assembly. The top piece of the edging is cut ½ in. longer than the width of the frame to allow for the side panels. Glue the pieces together on a flat surface and place a temporary brace across the bottom. Next, the top frame is glued to the edging. The frame is kept flush with the rabbeted edge and is fastened with long screws driven through the edge of the frame from the inside. Now, you are ready to attach the edging-and-frame assembly to the base, but first the back panel should be made ready as this is installed at the same time. The plywood back panel is made the same width as the frames and is cut ¼ in. less than the length of the edging. Nail the panel to the back edges of the top and bottom frames and then coat the ends of the edging strips with glue and clamp to the base with bar clamps. After the glue has dried, drill a pilot hole up into the end of each strip and drive a 1½-in. No. 9 flat-headed screw. The re-

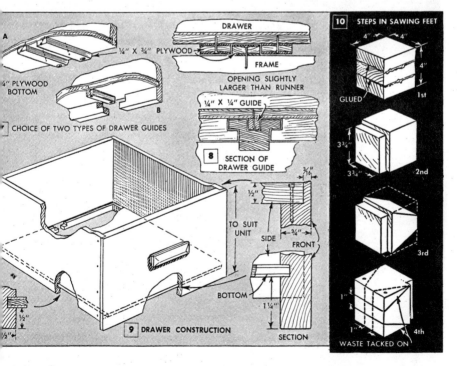

A

¼" X ¾" PLYWOOD

¼" PLYWOOD BOTTOM

B

CHOICE OF TWO TYPES OF DRAWER GUIDES

DRAWER

FRAME

OPENING SLIGHTLY LARGER THAN RUNNER

¼" X ¼" GUIDE

8 SECTION OF DRAWER GUIDE

½"

TO SUIT UNIT

SIDE

¾"

FRONT

BOTTOM

1¼"

9 DRAWER CONSTRUCTION

SECTION

10 STEPS IN SAWING FEET

4"   4"

4"

GLUED   1st

3¾"

3¾"   2nd

3rd

1"

1"   4th

WASTE TACKED ON

maining two frames are spaced equally be-tween the top and bottom ones. These are fastened to the inside of the edging strips with small screws. Pockets are formed for the screws by drilling and counterboring holes through the frame at an angle.

Now, the framework is ready to be cov-ered with ¼-in. plywood. Fit and install the top piece first. In addition to obtaining a well-fitting mitered joint, it also is im-portant to get a tight fit where the plywood abuts the rabbet of the front edging. Use bar clamps to draw this joint tightly and C-clamps to clamp the plywood firmly to the frame. Brads can be used here, as indi-cated in Fig. 4, although a good resin-type glue will hold sufficiently. Like the top piece, the sides fit flush with the outer face of the edging and the molding at the bot-tom. Clamps should be used to draw the mitered joint together. Brads can be used to reinforce the joint and to nail the ply-wood to the edge of the joint.

Steps in sawing the feet are given in Fig. 10. In most cases, the blocks for these will

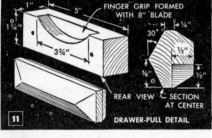

11 DRAWER-PULL DETAIL

have to be glued up using three or more pieces. The front feet require a ¼ x 1-in. rabbet on two adjacent edges, while the rear ones need a rabbet only along one side. The feet taper to 1 in. square at the bottom. After sawing two sides, the waste is re-placed and held with either brads or cellu-lose tape so that a flat surface will be had to complete the sawing.

Typical drawer construction is detailed in Fig. 9. The method of fitting the bottom differs somewhat with the type of drawer runner used. Note that the lower edge of each drawer extends to cover the drawer frame. Drawer handles are detailed in Fig. 11. A choice of two types of drawer guides is given. One features a T-shaped runner, Fig. 3, over which the back of the drawer hooks to prevent the drawer from dropping down when all the way open. The runner is grooved for a ¼-in.-square guide, which is nailed to the underside of the drawer bottom as shown in Fig. 7, detail B. Note that the T-slot in the drawer, Fig. 8, is made slightly larger than the cross section of the runner. A more simple guide is pic-tured in Fig. 7, detail A. This is formed merely by nailing two strips of plywood to the drawer bottom to form a track for a plywood runner nailed to the frame. Fig. 1 shows both types of runners in place.

Construction of the highboy (two-draw-er) chest unit, Fig. 12, differs from the other units in one respect; the bottom drawer frame is screwed to a mitered base frame which is beveled to match the edging.

12 CONSTRUCTION OF HIGHBOY-CHEST UNIT

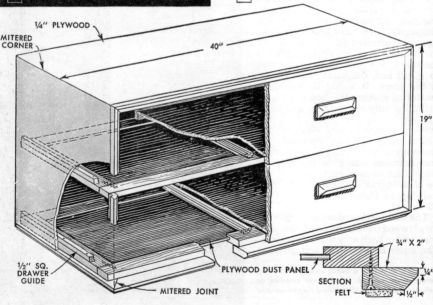

BEDROOM FURNITURE

WITH THE night stands, chests and vanity units completed as described earlier, you can tackle the bed. In addition to its pleasing simplicity, it features a built-in storage compartment in the headboard for bedding and two roomy drawers for shoes. If twin beds are preferred to a full bed, the basic construction is the same. It would be merely a matter of making the bed narrower, installing only one drawer and eliminating the center partition in the storage compartment. Most of the bed is made of ¼-in. plywood. On the original bed, the lid of the storage compartment was a ¾-in.-plywood panel, but to save cost, this too can be of ¼-in. material by gluing it to a half-lapped frame as shown in Figs. 13 and 14.

The bed footboard consists of a ¼-in. plywood panel which is framed on three sides with a ¾ x 2-in. molding. The latter is chamfered and grooved

Right, a jointer plus a bench saw are the only power tools needed. Here, base molding is being run on jointer after being ripped on saw

A roomy drawer opens at each end of the bed headboard to provide storage space for seasonal footwear. Being concealed when the headboard is flanked with night stands, the drawers also provide a safe place for personal papers and jewelry

Another feature of this headboard is a convenient built-in storage compartment for bedding. If you wish, the compartment can be lined with aromatic, red cedar to protect woolen blankets from moths. Open, the lid rests on the bed

⅜ in. deep on its inside face to fit over the edge of the plywood. The panel is faced across the bottom with a ¾ x 1¾-in. molding which matches the molding on the night stands, chests and other pieces. This molding is glued to the plywood so that it overlaps the bottom edge ½ in., sectional detail Fig. 16, and then five rabbeted cleats, 6 in. long, are spaced along the inside and screwed to the molding. Note that the molding is mitered at the ends and returned at the corners for a distance of 4 in., Fig. 16. Note also that the lower ends of the grooved molding, which covers the edges of the plywood, are chamfered on two adjacent outside edges to fit flush with the bottom molding and the upper ends are mitered. The feet are made the same as detailed earlier, except that here the shoulder must measure 1¼ in. long instead of 1 in. The feet are rabbeted on two adjacent sides and glued into the corners formed by the molding to bring them flush.

The headboard is built around a framework of scrap wood, Fig. 15. Start each end assembly with a ¾ x 4 x 11½-in. base piece and screw a ¾ x 2½ x 15-in. upright piece to it, ¼-in. in from the front edge. Note that the upper end of this piece is notched for a cross member. Another piece, ¾ x 1½ x 30¾ in., is attached vertically to the base piece, ¼ in. in from the rear edge. This piece is joined to the front piece with a cross member located 10 in. up from the top surface of the base, forming the drawer opening. Both end assemblies of the framework are joined together as shown, fitting a ¾ x 1-

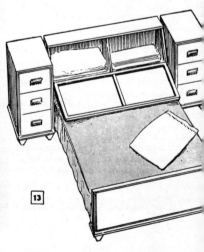

13

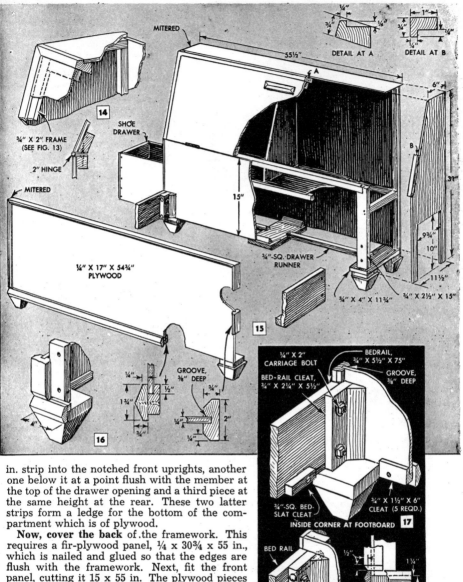

MITERED

DETAIL AT A

DETAIL AT B

¼"

¾"

¼"

1"

¾"

¼"

¼"

55½"

A

¾" X 2" FRAME
(SEE FIG. 13)

2" HINGE

MITERED

SHOE
DRAWER

14

6"

B

31"

15"

¼" X 17" X 54¾"
PLYWOOD

¾"-SQ. DRAWER
RUNNER

9¾"

10"

11½"

¾" X 4" X 11¾"

¾" X 2½" X 15"

15

16

¼"

½"

GROOVE,
⅜" DEEP

1¾"

¾"

¾"

4"

¼"

¾"

2"

¼"

¼" X 2"
CARRIAGE BOLT

BEDRAIL,
¾" X 5½" X 75"

BED-RAIL CLEAT,
¾" X 2¼" X 5½"

GROOVE,
⅜" DEEP

¾"-SQ. BED-
SLAT CLEAT

¾" X 1½" X 6"
CLEAT (5 REQD.)

INSIDE CORNER AT FOOTBOARD

17

BED RAIL

½"

1¼"

4¼"

GLUE
BLOCK

18

¼" X 4"
CARRIAGE BOLTS

INSIDE CORNER AT HEADBOARD

in. strip into the notched front uprights, another one below it at a point flush with the member at the top of the drawer opening and a third piece at the same height at the rear. These two latter strips form a ledge for the bottom of the compartment which is of plywood.

Now, cover the back of the framework. This requires a fir-plywood panel, ¼ x 30¾ x 55 in., which is nailed and glued so that the edges are flush with the framework. Next, fit the front panel, cutting it 15 x 55 in. The plywood pieces covering the ends of the headboard taper to 6 in. at the top from a point 15 in. up from the bottom. These are made right and left hand, selecting the best face of the plywood for the outside, and mitered at the top. After the ends are glued in place, the drawer-runner assembly is installed. The runners are simply ¾-in.-square strips, notched at each end to hook over the base pieces and a center piece fastened to the plywood with glue blocks.

Fit the panel forming the bottom of the bedding

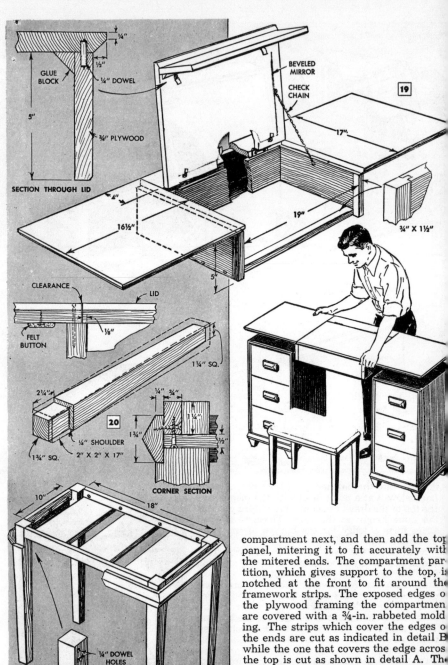

SECTION THROUGH LID

GLUE BLOCK
¼"
½"
¼" DOWEL
5"
¾" PLYWOOD

BEVELED MIRROR
CHECK CHAIN
17"
19
¾" X 1½"

4"
16½"
19"
5"

CLEARANCE
LID
FELT BUTTON
⅛"
1¼" SQ.
2¼"
¼" 3⁄4"
1¼"
1¾"
½"
20
¼" SHOULDER
2" X 2" X 17"
1¾" SQ.
CORNER SECTION

10"
18"
¼" DOWEL HOLES
21 ASSEMBLY OF VANITY STOOL

compartment next, and then add the top panel, mitering it to fit accurately with the mitered ends. The compartment partition, which gives support to the top, is notched at the front to fit around the framework strips. The exposed edges of the plywood framing the compartment are covered with a ¾-in. rabbeted molding. The strips which cover the edges of the ends are cut as indicated in detail B, while the one that covers the edge across the top is cut as shown in detail A. The molding is mitered at the corners and glued and clamped to the plywood. A base molding, matching that used on the footboard, is fitted around the outside corners, gluing and clamping it to the edges of the base pieces of the framework

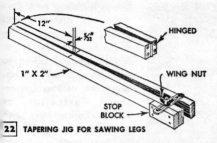

The compartment lid is hinged as shown in the sectional detail, Fig. 14, and drawers and handles are made as described in Part I. Bedrails are attached to the head and footboard as detailed in Figs. 17 and 18.

The separate top, Fig. 19, which merely rests on two base units to form a vanity, is made of ¾-in. plywood and solid stock. The top requires a panel 17 x 52½ in. Three edges are chamfered on the underside and then the panel is cut into four pieces. The cosmetic compartment is made like a box. The sides and back are screwed to a plywood bottom and a fourth piece is installed to support the narrow fill-in piece to which the lid is hinged. Note how end grain of the side and bottom members of the compartment is concealed with edging strips, tongued and grooved. The outboard panels are nailed and glued to the top edges of the compartment ⅛ in. in from the inner faces to provide a shoulder for the lid. This is shown in the detail above Fig. 20. The front apron is attached to the lid with dowels and a triangular glue block is placed on the inside. The lid can be leaned against the wall when opened or a check chain can be used to hold it at the right angle.

Assembly of the vanity stool is detailed in Fig. 21. First make the legs by cutting a ¼ x 2¼-in. rabbet on two adjacent faces of each one. The legs taper from 2 in. square at the shoulder to 1¼ in. square at the bottom, Fig. 20. Before tapering the legs, bore holes in adjacent inner faces as shown for doweling ¾ x 1¼-in. rails flush with the face of the rabbets. A jig like the one shown in Fig. 22 may be used to rip the taper on each face, after which the cut is dressed smooth on a jointer. The corner-section detail at the right of Fig. 20 show how a mitered face molding is attached to the rails with screws from the inside. A choice of two methods for upholstering the stool is given in Fig. 23. If tow or hair is used, the seat is supported by three ½-in. pieces spaced as in Fig. 21. If foam rubber is used, the bottom of the stool is covered with a piece of ¼-in. plywood held by cleats screwed to the rails.

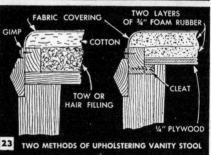

23 TWO METHODS OF UPHOLSTERING VANITY STOOL

When building new furniture or restoring old pieces, each step of the finishing process, from bleaching and filling to varnishing or lacquering, is of the utmost importance. Perfection, of course, comes only with practice, but the following information will get you off to a good start

AFTER COMPLETING the bedroom furniture described in the previous two parts, it's time for the all-important job of finishing it, because right here you can either flatter or ruin the appearance of the furniture.

No doubt, you have built the furniture of a wood suitable to take the particular finish desired, whether it be harvest wheat or heather mahogany, ambered walnut or limed oak. Naturally, the kind of wood used is a determining factor as, for instance, one cannot expect to obtain a limed-oak finish on birch. The finishing schedules presented below give a condensed procedure to follow in producing

BEDROOM FURNITURE
Part Three

a number of the popular, modern finishes, but, if the final results are to compare with finishes seen on store furniture, the finishing operation demands the same careful attention that you put into the cabinet work. Brushes and materials, as well as the room where the work is done, must be clean. Finishing should not be attempted in a cold room and the materials should not be cold. These precautions are important

Sanding: Perhaps the most important

FINISHING SCHEDULES

FINISH	APPLICATION
Ambered walnut	Bleach. Stain with amber stain. Apply sealer coat of thin lacquer. Fill with natural filler. Finish with clear lacquer.
Old-World walnut	Bleach. Seal. Fill with natural filler lightly tinted with burnt umber. Seal. Shade with brown wiping stain. Finish with clear lacquer.
Honeytone maple or birch	Tone with blond toner, using 1 part white lacquer to 4 parts clear, flat lacquer. Finish with water-white lacquer.
Pickled pine	Bleach. Stain with gray stain for pine. Finish with water-white lacquer or clear varnish.
Limed oak	Bleach. Seal. Fill pores with white paste wood filler. Finish with water-white lacquer.
Harvest-wheat mahogany	Bleaching will give required wheat color. Fill with natural filler lightly tinted with raw-sienna color in oil. Finish with lacquer.
Tweed mahogany	Bleach. Seal. Fill pores with red paste wood filler. Finish with water-white lacquer or clear varnish.
Heather mahogany	Bleach. Seal. Fill pores with white paste wood filler. Finish with water-white lacquer or clear varnish.

step in producing a beautiful, flawless finish is the sanding of the wood. Application of any number of finishing coats will not compensate for a careless job of sanding, but only tends to emphasize defects. Power sanders of the oscillating or belt types take the work out of sanding; however, if these are not available, you can do a satisfactory job of sanding by hand, wrapping the paper around a flat, felt-covered block and working with progressively finer grades of garnet paper from medium down to 5-0 grade.

Bleaching: Practically all of the so-called blond finishes are produced by first bleaching the wood to remove its natural color. This is done to obtain such popular mahogany finishes as harvest wheat, heather and tweed, and limed oak, and ambered walnut. Mahogany, when bleached and filled with white filler, is known as heather mahogany. When filled with red filler (natural filler with red oil

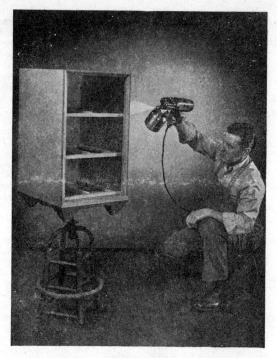

Above, a piano or draftsman's stool provides an excellent turntable when spraying lacquer on the smaller units. Below, a power sander makes play of sanding the broad, flat surfaces, but care must be used to avoid cutting through the top veneer

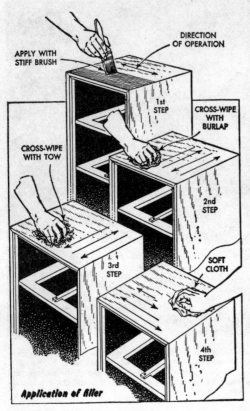

APPLY WITH STIFF BRUSH

DIRECTION OF OPERATION

1st STEP

CROSS-WIPE WITH BURLAP

CROSS-WIPE WITH TOW

2nd STEP

3rd STEP

SOFT CLOTH

4th STEP

Application of filler

the filler is applied liberally in the direction of the grain, preferably with a short-bristled brush. Do not cover more than 6 or 8 sq. ft. of surface at one time or you will get ahead of the wiping and cleaning-up operations that follow. As soon as the filler flattens, it is wiped off. This is done by wiping across the grain with a coarse cloth such as burlap, or excelsior, using a circular motion.

This is followed by cross-wiping with a fine material called tow, commonly used for upholstering purposes. This second wiping across the grain cuts the surplus filler flush with the surface of the wood.

A third cross-wiping with a soft cloth wrapped around a felt block is excellent practice. A second application of filler, somewhat thinner than the first, is sometimes required when filling mahogany or other wood having a very open grain. This is determined by noting whether the pores are completely filled.

Finally, the work is wiped lightly with the grain, using a soft cloth. This serves to remove any traces of filler missed in the towing-off operation. The filler should be allowed to dry 24 to 48 hrs. and then sanded very lightly with 5-0 waterproof garnet paper.

Toning: Toning is not successful on dark wood such as walnut, but very much so on naturally light-colored woods such as birch and maple. Toning, to some extent, takes the place of the bleaching process and is accomplished by spraying the bare wood with a semitransparent undercoat to further lighten the wood.

Toning is recommended for all extremely light finishes, as it does not obscure the grain, being almost as clear as water. Toner is made by adding white lacquer, 1 part, to clear flat lacquer, 4 or 5 parts. In the case of oak and mahogany, the toner should be made with tan-colored lacquer instead of white.

Sealing: Whether or not the bleached wood has been toned or stained, the surface must be sealed with a wash coat of shellac or lacquer before the work is filled. The wash sealer is made by cutting 1 part of clear shellac or lacquer with 6 parts of thinner. This coat is sanded lightly when dry, and then, after the grain is filled, a second sealer coat is applied. This is likewise sanded when dry, and followed with a coat of varnish or lacquer sealer. The latter coat, which fills any tiny open pores remaining, also is sanded. From here on varnish or lacquer coats are applied, using a rubbed-effect or full-gloss type.

color added), it is called tweed, because of its pleasing pink tone. Bleached and filled with natural filler, it's called harvest-wheat mahogany. After bleaching, almost any color desired can be had by giving the wood a coat of diluted stain.

Bleaching is done with a commercial chemical solution consisting of two separate solutions which are mixed together and used immediately. As all bleaching solutions are highly corrosive, they should be handled carefully. You should wear rubber gloves. Use a sponge to swab the solution on the wood and see that you wet the entire surface evenly.

One application of bleach is usually sufficient although, in any case, it is good practice to make a test on a wood sample. Let the bleach stand and dry for at least 48 hrs.

Filling: Open-grained woods, such as oak, walnut, mahogany, etc., must be filled, that is, the pores of the surface and end grain must be packed level with a prepared paste filler. Fillers are available for either lacquer or varnish finishes and require cutting with benzine or turpentine to the consistency of thick cream before applying, so that they will sink into the pores.

Combination BED-TENT
fits on car top

VACATION campers, hunters and others who prefer to "go light" on both long and short trips will appreciate the compact utility of this bed-tent. It combines the weather protection of a sturdy tent and the comfort of a four-poster bed in one unit which folds into a flat bundle easily transported on any car-top carrier. The mattress and all bedding remain inside when the unit is folded for transport. Although, as dimensioned, the bed frame will accommodate an innerspring mattress of three-quarter size, most campers will prefer an air mattress, as it is much lighter, more compact, and easier to keep clean. Other bedding in addition to the mattress can be whatever the climate and season require. It takes only a few moments to ready the unit for occupancy. There are no stakes to drive and no ridgepole to string. Merely unstrap the unit and slide it from the car carrier, open the folding legs, pull up the self-locking ridgepole and there you are.

The first step in the construction is to build the angle-steel frame shown in the plan detail below. Cut the side and end-pieces to length and square the ends with a file. Position the pieces and mark and center-punch for bolt holes at the corners. Note that the frame is assembled with the angle web up on both the sides and ends. Drill

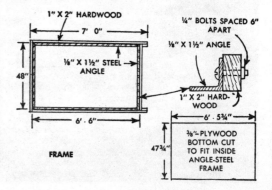

1" X 2" HARDWOOD

7' 0"

48"

⅛" X 1½" STEEL ANGLE

6' 6"

FRAME

¼" BOLTS SPACED 6" APART

⅛" X 1½" ANGLE

1" X 2" HARD-WOOD

6' 5¾"

47¾"

⅜"-PLYWOOD BOTTOM CUT TO FIT INSIDE ANGLE-STEEL FRAME

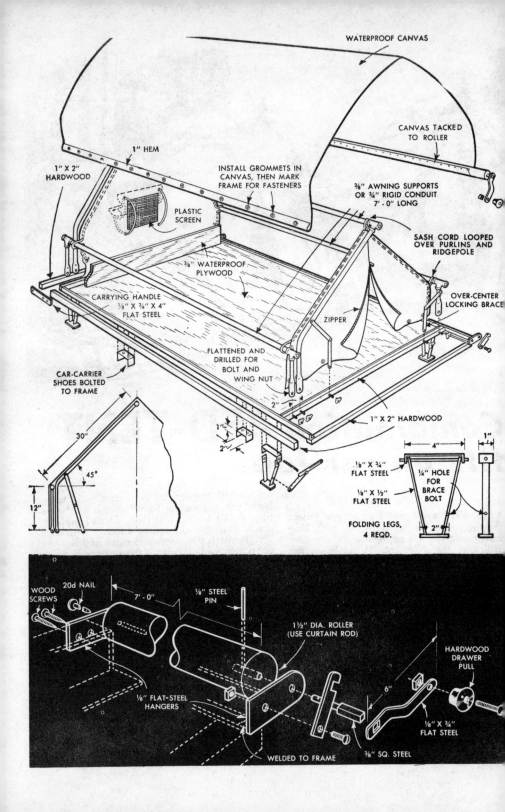

WATERPROOF CANVAS

1" HEM

1" X 2" HARDWOOD

PLASTIC SCREEN

INSTALL GROMMETS IN CANVAS, THEN MARK FRAME FOR FASTENERS

CANVAS TACKED TO ROLLER

⅜" AWNING SUPPORTS OR ¾" RIGID CONDUIT 7'-0" LONG

SASH CORD LOOPED OVER PURLINS AND RIDGEPOLE

⅜" WATERPROOF PLYWOOD

CARRYING HANDLE ⅛" X ¾" X 4" FLAT STEEL

ZIPPER

OVER-CENTER LOCKING BRACE

CAR-CARRIER SHOES BOLTED TO FRAME

FLATTENED AND DRILLED FOR BOLT AND WING NUT

1" X 2" HARDWOOD

30"

45°

12"

1"

2"

2"

1"

4"

⅛" X ¾" FLAT STEEL

⅛" X ½" FLAT STEEL

¼" HOLE FOR BRACE BOLT

2"

FOLDING LEGS, 4 REQD.

WOOD SCREWS

20d NAIL

7'-0"

⅛" STEEL PIN

1½" DIA. ROLLER (USE CURTAIN ROD)

HARDWOOD DRAWER PULL

⅛" FLAT-STEEL HANGERS

6"

⅛" X ¾" FLAT STEEL

WELDED TO FRAME

⅜" SQ. STEEL

holes for the corner bolts and also drill holes in the vertical webs for screws which hold hardwood strips. The strips are attached to the angles as detailed, using short flat-headed screws. Next, cut the plywood bottom and headboard, but, before installing the bottom, make sure that the frame is square. Then attach the plywood bottom with ¼-in. flat-headed stove bolts with the heads countersunk in the wood and the nuts turned on from the bottom so that they bear against the steel angle.

Note in the details on the opposite page that there is a headboard cut from ⅜-in. plywood and placed at the head of the bed inside the frame. Next, bolt on the wooden facing strips, noting that the carrying-handle brackets at the rear of the bed frame fit over the facing strips. Weld hanger brackets at the front and rear of the frame on the right-hand side to form bearing brackets for the roller as in the lower detail on the opposite page.

Note in the detail that the length of the ridgepole and the purlins is given as 7 ft., but, before cutting material, take careful measurements, as this dimension may vary. Flatten the ends of the conduit uprights in a vise, round the ends with a file and drill for ¼-in. bolts. Make the 45-deg. bends in the ridgepole supports. Then assemble the three units and clamp them in position on the frame so that you can locate the holes for the purlin frames, the ridgepole, and also the holes for the over-center braces. After these parts have been bolted in place —note that all bolts are provided with wing nuts — assemble the roller, or winding drum, as in the lower details on the opposite page. As will be seen from the detail, the roller is provided with a removable crank and a ratchet-type lock which permits tightening the canvas to a uniform tension and holding the adjustment.

Make four folding legs from flat steel as in the center right-hand detail on the oppo-site page. The leg brackets are bolted to the underside of the angle-steel frame at the corners and are provided with folding braces. At this stage the bed is placed on a level floor and the purlins and ridgepole are raised so that accurate measurements can be taken for cutting the canvas covering to fit. Note that the covering is attached to the frame on the left side with grommets and fasteners and that the right-hand edge is tacked to the roller. When tacking the canvas to the roller, allowance must be made for shrinkage of the fabric. The canvas closure at the head of the bed is provided with a plastic-screened opening and a separate canvas closure which is opened and closed by means of a sash, or awning, cord as shown. A slide fastener provides a double fly for opening the front of the tent covering. Both canvas ends are fastened at the bottom with grommets and are held taut with cord looped over the purlins and ridgepole. Locate the car-carrier shoes by placing the folded unit on the car-top carrier and marking pencil lines to indicate the position of the shoes. After bending to the required size from ⅛ x 1-in. flat iron, the shoes are attached to the bottom of the bed with stove bolts. Apply two coats of spar varnish to the plywood bottom, headboard and wooden rails and enamel metal parts in whatever color desired.

Tracing Legibly Onto Copper

Finding copper and brass too smooth to permit tracing legible designs onto them with carbon paper, one craftsman coats the metals with flat, white paint. Carbon transfers perfectly onto the paint, which is easily removed with turpentine after each design has been worked into the metal. Where a supply of such metals is kept in stock, time will be saved by coating a number of sheets in one operation, and storing them until used.

BENCH STOPS

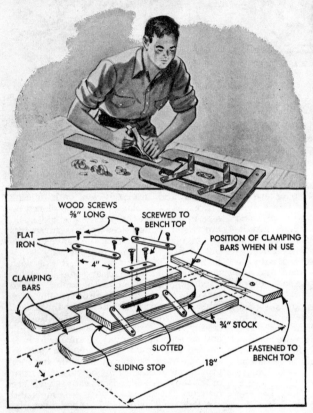

Made from two clamping bars, a sliding member or stop and a fixed piece, this bench stop adjusts itself automatically to various widths, and holds the work in a vise-like grip. Only a few general dimensions are given; the others can be determined by the size of the work to be handled. Remember that the length of the flat-iron pieces to which the clamping bars pivot, will determine the width of boards that the stop will take. After the bars and sliding member have been cut out of ¾-in. hardwood stock, assemble them as shown in the detail, fastening the pivots to the bars and the stop with wood screws ⅝ in. long. Then fasten the fixed piece in place and determine the position of the sliding stop. When this is located, screw it in place using flat-headed wood screws and a length of flat iron drilled for the screws. Since the unit is fastened to the workbench by only four screws, it is removed easily if additional space is required.

WOOD SCREWS ⅝" LONG

SCREWED TO BENCH TOP

FLAT IRON

POSITION OF CLAMPING BARS WHEN IN USE

4"

CLAMPING BARS

¾" STOCK

SLOTTED

FASTENED TO BENCH TOP

4"

SLIDING STOP

18"

PLYWOOD

NAIL TO BENCH

STAPLE

STRAIGHT CUT

BEVEL CUT

Adjustable Bench Planing Stop Is Built of Plywood

This stop is made of plywood for durability and will come in handy when planing small pieces of wood. When cutting the stop, make one side of the wedge-shaped piece parallel to the edge and saw the other at an angle. The angular side is beveled. A staple is driven through the wedge into the workbench to hold the former in place when clamping to work.

BENCH VISE

DESIGNED PRIMARILY for use at a watchmaker's bench, this tiny precision-built vise will be found equally useful by the exacting modelmaker. An excellent metalworking project in itself, the making of the vise embodies varied lathe and milling operations.

The three guide pins which are pressed in the body of the vise maintain a close sliding fit in the movable jaw to hold the jaw faces in perfect alignment. A series of removable stud pins in the tops of the jaws provides a means of clamping disks and other odd-shaped work securely. For a really fine tool, the completed parts of the vise should be carbonized, hardened and ground. You can have the hardening done at any local heat-treating shop. Specify a Rockwell hardness of 60-62 C scale. Holes for the guide pins should be made .002 undersize to allow for lapping after the vise has been hardened. This will assure a perfect fit. The drawings below detail the various parts and also show the assembly.

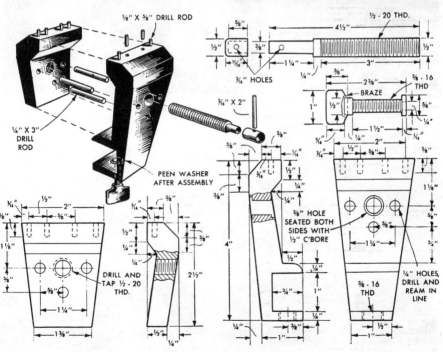

BENDING BRAKES
for Your Sheet-Metal Jobs

THESE bending brakes will simplify sheet-metal fabrication. Two designs are described, both capable of bending 24-ga. galvanized iron the width of the brake, or heavier metal when the bend is not at full 12-in. capacity. Design No. 2, Fig. 8, while more difficult to make, is somewhat superior in that it offers stronger construction and also permits partial (tab) and reverse bends which are not possible with No. 1 design.

Design No. 1: Both designs are of the folding-leaf variety, and the general features of construction are grasped easily from Fig. 3. The essential feature is that the center of hinge pin must line up exactly with the meeting edges of folding leaf and table. This is diagramed in Fig. 4. The working of the brake is shown in Fig. 1, the metal being clamped under the forming bar and then bent by pulling up on the folding leaf. The forming bar should be notched for easy removal. It is positioned exactly for duplicate work by means of two sliding

1

BENDING METAL TILE—ONE OF MANY JOBS POSSIBLE WITH BRAKE

2 SAMPLE BENDS

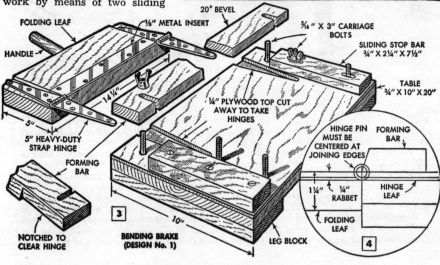

FOLDING LEAF

20° BEVEL

⅛" METAL INSERT

HANDLE

14¼"

5"

5" HEAVY-DUTY STRAP HINGE

FORMING BAR

NOTCHED TO CLEAR HINGE

¾₆" X 3" CARRIAGE BOLTS

SLIDING STOP BAR
¾" X 2¼" X 7½"

TABLE
¾" X 10" X 20"

¼" PLYWOOD TOP CUT AWAY TO TAKE HINGES

10"

3 BENDING BRAKE (DESIGN No. 1)

LEG BLOCK

HINGE PIN MUST BE CENTERED AT JOINING EDGES

FORMING BAR

1¼"

¼" RABBET

HINGE LEAF

FOLDING LEAF

4

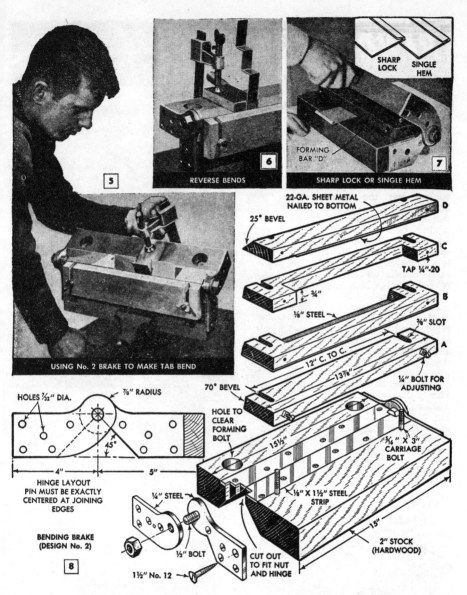

SHARP LOCK   SINGLE HEM

REVERSE BENDS

FORMING BAR "D"

SHARP LOCK OR SINGLE HEM

5

6

7

USING No. 2 BRAKE TO MAKE TAB BEND

22-GA. SHEET METAL
NAILED TO BOTTOM

25° BEVEL

D

C

TAP ¼"-20

¾"

⅛" STEEL

B

⅜" SLOT

A

12" C. TO C.

13⅞"

¼" BOLT FOR
ADJUSTING

70° BEVEL

HOLE TO
CLEAR
FORMING
BOLT

15½"

5/16" X 3"
CARRIAGE
BOLT

⅛" X 1½" STEEL
STRIP

15"

2" STOCK
(HARDWOOD)

HOLES 7/32" DIA.

⅞" RADIUS

45°

4"

5"

HINGE LAYOUT
PIN MUST BE EXACTLY
CENTERED AT JOINING
EDGES

BENDING BRAKE
(DESIGN No. 2)

8

¼" STEEL

½" BOLT

1½" No. 12

CUT OUT
TO FIT NUT
AND HINGE

stop bars, as can be seen in Fig. 3. One of these works along a fixed block to provide a guide for right-angle bends. Any kind of wood can be used for folding leaf and table, but the forming bar must be hardwood or softwood faced with metal. The hinge should not be lighter than specified and is better made a little heavier.

Design No. 2: This is shown in Fig. 8. It is a heavier and more compact design than No. 1, and requires special hinges cut from ¼-in. steel, as shown. The 45-deg. cut on the underside of leaf and table weakens the construction somewhat, but offers an arrangement that is essential for reverse bends. The four styles of forming bars shown in Fig. 8, will handle all ordinary work. Care should be taken in assembly to get the pivot points in exact alignment. This design also works out nicely with hinges made from ¾-in. plywood, pinning the bolt to the table member and providing

DOUBLE HEM   OPEN LOCK   90° FLANGE   RETURN BEND OR CHANNEL   REVERSE BEND   TAB BEND   CLOSED FORM

a brass bushing in the other to prevent wear.

Tab and reverse bends: Tab and reverse bends are worked on No. 2 brake by mounting the brake on edge in a vise and folding the leaf all the way back. A block of wood is clamped to the folding leaf and becomes the forming member. Fig. 5 shows the operation on a tab bend; Fig. 6 shows the same setup for reverse bends. Neither can be done on the No. 1 brake.

Standard operations: The sharp lock, Fig. 7, is made by using the brake in a normal position with a style D forming bar. This bend is used frequently for fastening two pieces of metal together. If the bend is at full capacity (12 in. long), it is best to form it to a flange with the stronger A or B bar and then complete the lock with the sharp-edge D bar. The single sharp lock when pressed tightly together in a vise or by hammering becomes the single hem or bend, as shown. If the single bend is hemmed again, it makes a double hem. At full capacity on a narrow hem less than ¼ in. wide, this bend offers the ultimate strength and accuracy test for your brake —a poorly made brake will fail in this double-hem operation.

Large return bends or channels are made with the standard forming bar (style A), and offer no difficulties. Smaller channels are made with the B bar, which permits working as small as ⅛-in. cross section. This operation is shown in Fig. 9. The B bar is used also for bending small closed forms, as shown in Fig. 10. As can be seen, the brake does not fully close the form on the final bend, but it is close enough so that a little springing by hand will complete it. Style C bar offers another way of working small closed forms, as shown in Fig. 11. Complete closure is possible with

"B" FORMING BAR

MAKING A CHANNEL WITH STYLE "B" FORMING BAR

"C" FORMING BAR

IRON BAR

SEAM JOINT

SEAM JOINTS ON SMALL CLOSED FORMS CAN BE MADE WITH "B" OR "C" BARS

this bar, but the work must be resprung to remove it from the bar. When the closed form has a seam joint, Fig. 12, the final bend, as in Fig. 11, is really a reverse bend and is best worked by the method shown in Fig. 5. However, the reverse caused by the narrow flange is slight and does not materially affect the bending operation. Fig. 13 shows how the seam joint is closed by hammering. This is not an easy joint to make and should be practiced before you attempt it on finished work.

Box bends: One of the most used forms of sheet-metal work is the simple square box. Like its companion in wood, it can be made a dozen different ways. Simplest way is to cut out the corners and then bend the work over a forming block, Fig. 14, or over

flange which can be riveted or soldered to the sides (a sample is shown in Fig. 2), and this style is made easily by first forming the tabs, working as shown in Fig. 5, and then bending the sides over a forming block.

Work capacity: Work capacity of both brakes described is about 12 in. No. 2 design will work satisfactorily up to about 18-24 in. No. 1 brake will not handle metal thicker than 24 ga. (usual furnace-pipe weight as obtained at tin shops); No. 2 brake will work 22-ga. material. Both will handle much thicker metal if the bend is short. Dimensions given are working specifications and can be varied.

14

MAKING A BOX WITH USE OF FORMING BLOCK

a special style A forming bar, Fig. 15. For the latter operation, the forming bar has notches cut to accommodate the flanges previously turned up. The notches (saw kerfs) do not affect the bend, and one bar can be notched many times to suit different sizes of work. The simple style of box shown, while easy to bend, presents a fair amount of work in soldering the corners. Some shapes in this style (such as lids), if shallow, are often strong enough not to require soldering. Most larger boxes make use of some kind of inside or outside

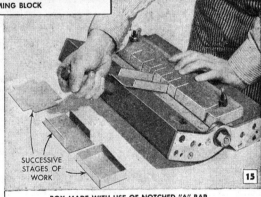

SUCCESSIVE STAGES OF WORK

15

BOX MADE WITH USE OF NOTCHED "A" BAR

Hinged Cover on Bicycle Basket Prevents Theft of Contents

One boy who made store deliveries with his bike often had packages stolen from the basket while he was inside a home delivering part of his load. To prevent this trouble, he hinged another basket to the top of the one on his bike to serve as a cover, and fitted it with a padlock. When he had to leave the bike outside with some packages in the basket he locked the cover.

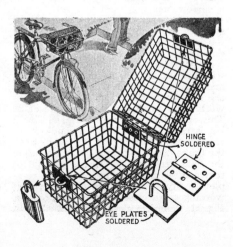

HINGE SOLDERED

EYE PLATES SOLDERED

BICYCLE BOAT

BUOYANCY and speed are two features of this bicycle boat. It consists of two pontoons and an old bicycle frame, held centrally above and between the pontoons. Propulsion is obtained by the use of a ring-and-pinion gear, bolted to the pedal sprocket, and a small three-blade propeller connected to the gears by a suitable shafting. The frames of the pontoons, both of which are exactly alike, are made of 1 x 2-in. white pine, which, when dressed, is exactly ⅞ x 1⅞ in. Dimensions for the top and bottom crosspieces and

FIG. 1

TOP

1" SQUARES

STEM

Pontoons for your bicycle boat can be made as shown or adapted from war-surplus airplane belly tanks

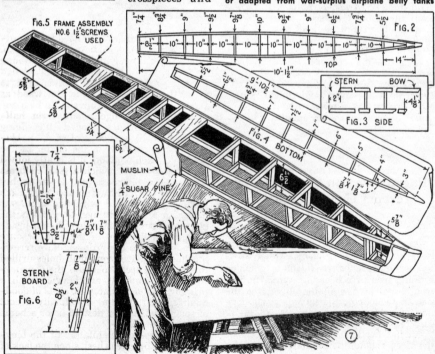

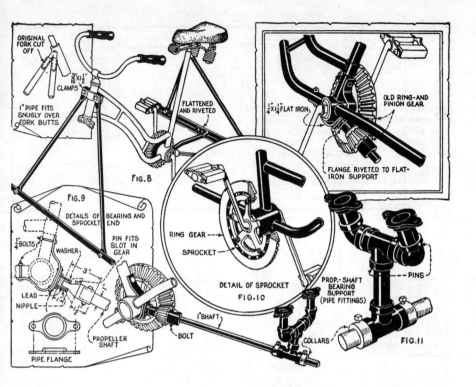

ORIGINAL FORK CUT OFF

CLAMPS

3/16" X1 1/2"

1" PIPE FITS SNUGLY OVER FORK BUTTS

FLATTENED AND RIVETED

1/4" X1 1/4" FLAT IRON

OLD RING-AND PINION GEAR

FIG.8

FLANGE RIVETED TO FLAT-IRON SUPPORT

FIG.9

DETAILS OF BEARING AND SPROCKET END

1/4" BOLTS

WASHER

PIN FITS SLOT IN GEAR

3"

RING GEAR

SPROCKET

LEAD NIPPLE

PROPELLER SHAFT

PIPE FLANGE

BOLT

1" SHAFT

DETAIL OF SPROCKET
FIG.10

PROP.-SHAFT BEARING SUPPORT (PIPE FITTINGS)

PINS

COLLARS

FIG.11

their spacing are clearly indicated in Figs. 2 and 4. Each frame consists of four pieces glued (marine glue) and screwed together, and notched to receive the longitudinal members—sheer and chine battens. Both stem and stern are set at an angle, which should be taken into consideration when building the frame (see Fig. 3). Details of the stem or nose block, which is cut from a piece of 2 x 8-in. spruce, are given in Fig. 1, part of the side being recessed ¼ in. to take the side planking. Exact dimensions and method of cutting the stern from ⅞-in. ash are given in Fig. 6. Note the additional reinforcing pieces provided across the top for the braces that support the bicycle frame, besides those that reinforce the deck directly under the rubber mats. When the frame has been finished, the side and bottom planking, which is cut from 12-ft. lengths of ¼ x 12-in. sugar pine, is screwed on after the contacting portions of the frame have been covered with marine glue. Then, with the top off, the inside of the pontoons is given an application of paint, and the top, also of ¼-in. sugar pine, is glued and screwed on, using ¾-in. flat-head brass screws. The heads of the screws should be countersunk, and the

resulting holes filled with hard water putty. After sanding each pontoon smooth, it is given a liberal application of airplane cement, and heavy muslin is stretched over the surface. A hot iron is used to press the cloth securely to the wood as shown in Fig. 7. The seam should be made along the upper edge, where ½-in. half-round molding is applied, this being screwed on. A spruce keel of ⅞ x 1¼-in. stock is screwed to the center of the bottom of each pontoon. It is neatly joined to the stem, after which a strip of brass is run over the stem and a few inches along the forward part of the keel. Each pontoon is provided with two air vents made up of pipe fittings, to prevent the pontoon from bursting when the air inside expands in the heat of the sun. Be sure to apply glue to the fittings before screwing them in place over small holes drilled through the deck, to make them watertight. The pontoons are finished with a priming coat of shellac, four coats of good-quality exterior paint and finally a coat of spar varnish. Any desired color scheme may be followed.

Next comes the adaptation of the bicycle. A girl's bicycle is best, since the lack of

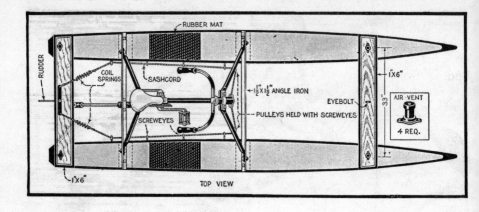

a crossbar affords more convenient mounting. Cut off the front and rear forks as shown in Fig. 8. The bracing consists of lengths of pipe, flattened at the ends and bolted to angle-iron crosspieces. At the front end, flat-iron clamps are used to hold the braces to the steering post, while the rear pipes are slipped over short stubs or butts of the original fork, directly under the seat. The pipe should fit over the stubs snugly, and it has been found best to heat and slightly flatten the joint after assembly, so that it cannot come apart. One of the horizontal frame members, originally used to support the rear wheel, is cut off nearly flush with the housing of the pedal-crank bearing so that it will not interfere with the ring gear which is to be added later. The corresponding frame member is cut off about halfway from the end, after which the cut portion is flattened and riveted to the rear angle-iron crosspiece. Fig. 10 shows how an automobile ring gear is bolted to the original pedal sprocket. It may be necessary to cut off the teeth of the sprocket to fit inside the recess of the gear. If desired, however, a brass disk may be substituted for the sprocket, in which case the disk should be the same thickness as the sprocket. A heavy piece of $\frac{1}{4} \times 1\frac{1}{4}$-in. flat iron, bolted to the frame as shown in Fig. 9, holds a bearing that supports the end of the 1-in. propeller shaft. This bearing is made from a pipe flange and short nipple filled with melted lead and drilled to receive the machined fitting on the end of the shaft. If you have no metal lathe, this fitting can be turned out quickly at any machine shop. The tapered portion should make a snug fit in the pinion gear, and a small pin, driven into the tapered portion, serves as a key for the gear. A bolt holds

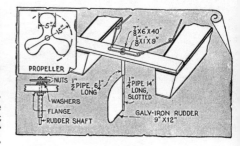

the fitting on the shaft, while the latter runs through a bearing provided directly under the rear angle-iron crosspiece. This bearing and its hanger are made up of pipe fittings as shown in Fig. 11.

The angle-iron crosspieces are fastened to the pontoons with lag screws in the approximate positions indicated in the detail above, and additional crosspieces of 1-in. stock are provided at the front and rear. The pontoons should be placed perfectly parallel, 33 in. from center to center. Steering is accomplished by means of a small sheet-metal rudder, connected with sashcord to the front-fork stub of the bicycle. If a commercial propeller is not available, one can be made from fairly heavy sheet metal. It should have a 15-in. diameter, with a hole drilled centrally to fit the shaft, end of which is threaded so that the propeller can be held securely between two nuts. Corrugated rubber mats are tacked to the deck of the pontoons on each side of the bicycle, and the craft is then ready to go.

BICYCLE DELIVERY BOXES

Saddle Boxes Improve a Bicycle Used to Make Deliveries

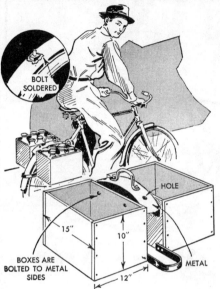

In order to make the package boxes on his bicycle removable so that they could be carried into homes when making deliveries for a store, one boy built them into a unit that rests astraddle the rear wheel. A piece of heavy sheet metal was shaped to the contour of the bicycle rear fender, and short side pieces were soldered to it, after which the boxes were bolted to these. Then, a carrying handle was fitted to the unit, and holes were drilled near the ends of the fender-shaped piece to fit over short stub bolts welded or soldered to the top surface of the bicycle fender. A U-shaped metal strip keeps the boxes spaced apart at the bottom. The entire unit is lifted from the bike and carried into the home when making a delivery.

BICYCLE LIGHTS

Generator-Operated Bicycle Light Stays Bright

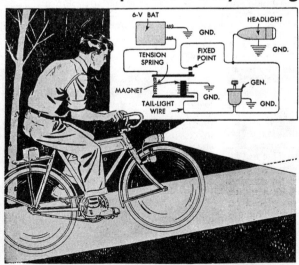

Generator-operated bicycle headlights will remain at constant brilliance when the bicycle is stopped, or slowed down to climb a hill, if a 6-volt dry battery and an automotive-type relay are wired into the circiut as shown. The relay cuts in the battery when the generator current drops. The points of the relay will have to be reversed, and when doing this be sure to insulate the fixed point from the relay case. Also, make certain that the armature and battery-lead connection is insulated from the relay tension spring.

OVERHAUL Your Bike

REGULAR OVERHAUL and replacement of worn parts not only keeps your bike in tiptop mechanical condition, but clean, well-lubricated bearings, properly inflated tires and correct wheel tension reduce bearing and road friction to the minimum. That's something to think about when there's a long hill on the paper route or on the way home from school.

Before inverting the bike to go over the wheel and crank bearings and the chain, check the handle bars and the fork stem. If there is looseness in the parts it's a good idea to remove the fork and examine the head bearing. If the bearing shows appreciable wear it should be replaced. Complete head-repair sets are available for this purpose. While you have these parts down,

If there is any looseness in the fork assembly it's a good idea to remove it and check the head bearing

To remove fork, first take off handle bars, then unscrew locknut and remove the cone and keyed washer

Special repair kits are available for replacing worn parts of the drive chain. Rollers and links which show excessive wear or rust pits should be replaced

After cleaning and reassembling drive chain, the tension is adjusted by turning in the tension-adjusting screws. Ordinarily chain is adjusted to ½-in. sag

Above, remove pedal opposite sprocket as first step in disassembling crank bearing. Then unscrew the locknut and pull off keyed washer. Slotted adjusting cone is removed with a screwdriver as shown below, or with a spanner wrench supplied for the purpose

Above, as a final part of service checkup tighten saddle bolts to uniform tension. Below, final step in disassembly of crank bearing. Note that one bearing is being held in the left hand while crank is passed through housing. Clean these parts thoroughly

remove the front wheel by unscrewing the spindle nut and sliding the wheel out of the slotted fork. To disassemble the bearing, unscrew the adjusting cone and slide the spindle assembly out of the hub. Clean the parts thoroughly in a nonflammable solvent or kerosene. Relubricate the bearing and reassemble in the wheel hub.

Now invert the bike and remove the drive chain by loosening the master link. Then remove the rear wheel by first taking out the bolt which holds the brake-arm clamp. Although close attention must be given to proper procedure, it is not difficult to remove and reassemble the coaster brake. Be careful to keep the parts in order as they are removed and cleaned. Lubricate according to the manufacturer's instructions and reassemble. To gain access to the pedal-crank bearings, remove the pedal on the side opposite the sprocket, then unscrew the locknut and remove the keyed washer. The slotted cone can be backed

out with a screwdriver or with a special spanner wrench. This releases the crank assembly so that it may slide out of the housing. Clean the parts, making sure that you keep them in order so they may be reassembled properly. If individual bearing balls show pitting or undue wear it is advisable to replace the entire cluster, or set, rather than the single ball. This also is true of wheel bearings. When reassembling wheel and crank bearings, tighten the adjusting cones only to the point where the spindle turns freely without play.

Clean the roller chain in a solvent and check carefully for worn links. Replace any links or rollers which show excessive wear or pitting. After the chain is replaced on the sprocket, adjust the tension to about ½-in. sag. Adjust the spokes of both wheels to a uniform tension with a spoke wrench. Reassemble the handle bars and adjust both bars and seat to a comfortable height.

Above, after reassembling the wheel bearing, tighten adjusting cone just sufficiently to take out all end play, yet permit wheel to turn freely. Below, adjust wheel tension with spoke wrench, drawing spokes to a uniform tension. Be sure the wheel rim is true

Above, withdraw spindle bolt carefully so that bearings do not drop out. Keep the parts in order so that they are easily reassembled. Below, before spindle nut is loosened remove bolt holding the brakearm clamp. Then release the chain-tension screws

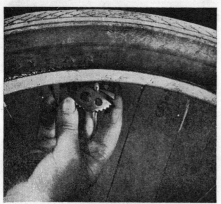

BILGE PUMP

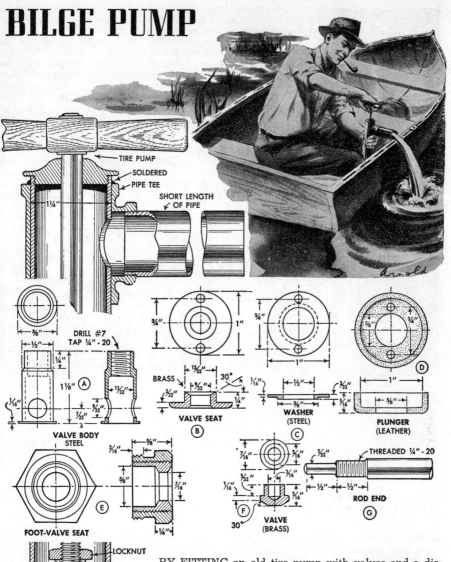

TIRE PUMP

SOLDERED

PIPE TEE

SHORT LENGTH OF PIPE

1¼"

⅝"

DRILL #7
TAP ¼" - 20

½"

¼"

1⅛" Ⓐ

¹³⁄₃₂"

¹⁄₁₆"

²⁄₃₂"

⁷⁄₃₂"

VALVE BODY
STEEL

¾" 1"
¾"
1"

Ⓓ
¾"
⅝"
¾"

BRASS

¹³⁄₃₂"
³⁄₃₂"
30°
¼"
¹⁄₁₆"
½"

VALVE SEAT
Ⓑ

³⁄₃₂"
⅝"
³⁄₃₂"
¹⁄₁₆"

WASHER
(STEEL)
Ⓒ

³⁄₃₂"
1"
⅝"

PLUNGER
(LEATHER)

⁵⁄₁₆"
⅝"
³⁄₁₆"
⁷⁄₁₆"

FOOT-VALVE SEAT

¼"

⁷⁄₁₆"
³⁄₄"
³⁄₃₂"
⅝"
³⁄₁₆"
¹⁄₁₆"
⅝"

VALVE
(BRASS)
Ⓕ
30°

⁵⁄₃₂"
THREADED ¼" - 20
½" ½"

ROD END
Ⓖ

Ⓔ

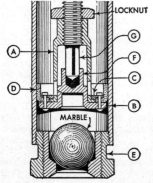

LOCKNUT

Ⓖ

Ⓐ

Ⓕ

Ⓒ

Ⓓ

Ⓑ

MARBLE

Ⓔ

BY FITTING an old tire pump with valves and a discharge spout it can be converted to an efficient bilge pump. The base and hose of the tire pump are removed and the end is threaded internally for a brass pipe bushing which is fitted with a valve seat turned from a smaller bushing. The upper end of the pump is equipped with a pipe tee that is bored out to fit over the end of the barrel and sweat-soldered. A hole is cut through the barrel for the discharge outlet. The body of the valve itself, part A, is made first, as the rest of the component parts are made to fit it. All parts are keyed with the sectional view to show assembly. Note that the small end of the pump rod keeps the valve aligned. A glass marble is used for the foot valve with a cross-wire stop being provided to keep the marble from coming completely out of the valve.

BILLIARD TABLE

A PARTMENT dwellers and small-home owners whose recreation-room facilities are limited to the kitchen or dining room now can enjoy a game of billiards with this new portable table top. It rests on an extension-type kitchen or dinette table, providing a standard home-size playing surface that is lightweight and easily stored in a closet. The cushion rubber and felt can be purchased from any billiard-supply or sporting-goods store. Use 1⅞-in.-dia. balls and 52-in. cues.

By extending the table, a clear space is provided for the side pockets, Fig. 3, and leveling the playing surface is accomplished by a "jack" fitted to one of the table legs as in Fig. 6.

The billiard top is built around a 3 x 6-ft. panel of ½-in. plywood which is available at some lumberyards. However, you may find it necessary to cut a 12-in. strip from one side of a standard 4-ft. sheet. The first step is to lay out the holes for the pockets, Fig. 2. Each corner of the panel is cut off at

a 45-deg. angle to form a flat 3¼ in. long. The axis point for the 2-in. radius is located on a center line 1 in. in from the edge. The center of the side pockets is located ¾ in. in from the edge. The holes are cut best with a coping saw and then smoothed up with a wood rasp. The sectional detail through the edge of the table top shows how 2 x 2-in. hardwood rails are rabbeted to receive the plywood panel. Note that the depth of the rabbet brings the panel flush when it is covered with muslin and felt. The rails are joined at the corners and side pockets with ⅛ x 1⅞-in. metal straps. These are fitted flush with the outer faces of the rails. Before fitting them to the rails, the straps are drilled and countersunk for oval-headed screws and then covered with sleeves of leather glued to the metal. The oval-headed screws make a neat job and prevent snagged clothing. Holes for bank markers are drilled at this time, the markers being flat-headed sleeve bolts located halfway between pockets. Measure from the center of one pocket to the center of the next one. Regular screw posts of the type used for a memo pad make excellent markers and can be purchased in any stationery store.

At this point the side and end rails can be temporarily fastened to the plywood panel. The cushion mounting plates are ripped to size from 1-in. stock. With the ends mitered to suit the corner pockets, the plates are clamped in position on the rails and three holes are drilled through each rail and countersunk on the face to take long oval-headed screws which hold the plates. To determine the height of the cushion rubber above the playing surface, two pieces of felt are placed on the plywood, one representing the felt covering the top and the other the felt covering the cushion. The center of the ball should come about 1/16 in. below the edge of the cushion. Now, hold the cushion rubber temporarily on the mounting plate, measure 1 in. up from the felt to the rounded edge of the rubber and mark along the lower edge of the rubber. Run this mark along the full length of each plate. This serves as a guide in gluing the rubber in position. Any good linoleum or tile cement can be

Using regular table for a base, top can be stored in closet

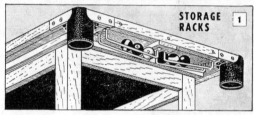

STORAGE RACKS   **1**

GLUED — 3⁄16″ X 1¼″ BIRCH

10½″

DETAIL OF BALL RACK

2

TABLE CONSTRUCTION

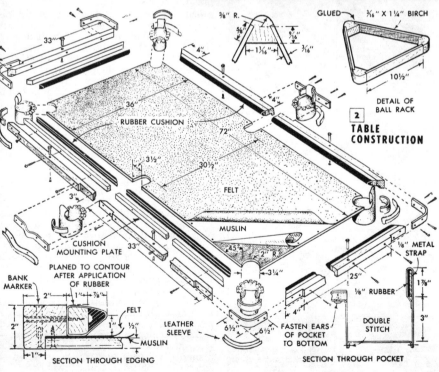

3⁄8″ R.

33″

36″

RUBBER CUSHION

72″

4″

3½″

30½″

FELT

MUSLIN

CUSHION MOUNTING PLATE   33″

BANK MARKER

PLANED TO CONTOUR AFTER APPLICATION OF RUBBER

2″   1½″   ⅛″

FELT

2″   1″   ½″

MUSLIN

SECTION THROUGH EDGING

1″

LEATHER SLEEVE

6½″   6½″

45°   2″ R.

3¼″

FASTEN EARS OF POCKET TO BOTTOM

4″

25″

DOUBLE STITCH

⅛″ RUBBER

⅛″ METAL STRAP

1⅞″

3″

SECTION THROUGH POCKET

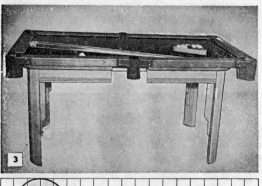

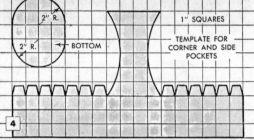

2" R.

2" R. ← BOTTOM

1" SQUARES

TEMPLATE FOR CORNER AND SIDE POCKETS

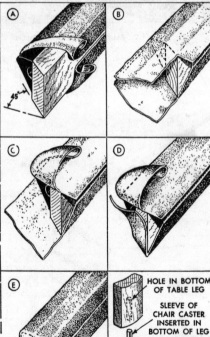

Ⓐ

Ⓑ

45°

Ⓒ

Ⓓ

Ⓔ

HOLE IN BOTTOM OF TABLE LEG

SLEEVE OF CHAIR CASTER INSERTED IN BOTTOM OF LEG

¼" NUT BRAZED TO BOTTOM OF SLEEVE

¼" STOVE BOLT, BRAZE AND SMOOTH THE SLOT

used and, after it dries, the inside edges of the plates are shaped to conform to the contour of the rubber strips. With the ends of the rubber cushions mitered to match the ends of the plates at the pockets, the cushions are covered with felt. In cutting the strips, allow enough felt to extend to the back side of the mounting plate, as in Fig. 5. The successive steps show the sequence in covering the rubber. Glue is applied to the wood surfaces only and the felt is pulled firmly from the top toward the bottom. The felt at the mitered ends of the cushions is double lapped and the end tucked under as in step E.

When all the cushion members are covered, felt is applied to the playing surface. First remove the rails which were temporarily fitted and apply two coats of shellac to the plywood, sanding each when dry. Next, stretch muslin over the plywood and tack it along the outer edges, letting the muslin cover the holes for the pockets. The felt is glued to the muslin and it is best to work a small area at a time to prevent the glue from drying before the felt can be rolled out smoothly. The felt should be large enough to overhang the top all around so that it can be pulled and stretched tautly should any wrinkles remain after gluing. In the final stretching, the felt is tacked to the plywood all around the edges. The felt, which now covers the openings for the pockets, is cut into ½-in. strips. These are tapered slightly to form gussets so that, in bringing them down around the edge of the hole, adjacent edges of the strips will butt together. Drive tacks through the felt tabs and into the edges of the plywood and then tack the ends to the underside.

Fig. 4 gives a pattern for the leather pockets. The detail in Fig. 2, showing a sectional view through the pocket, indicates how each pocket is hung from the metal strap joining the rails. Note that the inner face of the metal is lined with a strip of ⅛-in. rubber glued in place to cushion the balls. After the pockets are stitched and slipped over the metal straps, they are tacked to the underside of the plywood, nailing through the tabs provided.

Finish the rails with two coats of shellac, sanding each one lightly, and then apply paste wax. The underside of the plywood should be covered with felt to prevent marring the finish of the table. Fig. 1 suggests a simple ball rack that can be installed at one end of the table, using towel bars.

BIRDBATH

CAST INEXPENSIVELY from concrete, this birdbath forms an eye-catching lawn ornament that will attract many of the songbirds in your vicinity. The base and pedestal are poured, while the bowl is molded from a stiff concrete mix. The bowl can be replaced with a sundial or metal sphere if either of these is preferred to the birdbath.

The pedestal is poured in a tapered form which is built as shown in the center details below and greased to prevent sticking. Note that the bottom of the form is drilled to allow four 31-in. reinforcing rods to extend below the pedestal. After the pedestal has hardened, the bottom is removed from the form and the pedestal, still in the form, is supported with a framework over a form for the 3½ x 10-in. base. If preferred, the base may be poured first with the reinforcing rods embedded in the center. Then the pedestal form, minus the bottom, is set over the reinforcing rods and the pedestal poured. Note that a 6-in. hardwood dowel is embedded in the top of the pedestal in order to engage the hole in the center of the bowl.

The concrete bowl is molded on a square wooden platform. This is drilled to receive a dowel or metal rod of the same diameter as the supporting dowel embedded in the pedestal. Wooden or sheet-metal templates pivoted on the center rod are used to form the contours of both inner and outer surfaces of the bowl. A clay core, built up on the platform and shaped with the smaller template, is allowed to dry, and then a 1-in. layer of stiff concrete is troweled over the clay. Wire mesh is placed over the concrete and a second layer is troweled over this. Finally, the concrete is shaped with the larger template. When the bowl dries, it is set on top of the pedestal and the center hole is filled with concrete. On soft turf, the birdbath is set on a concrete footing.

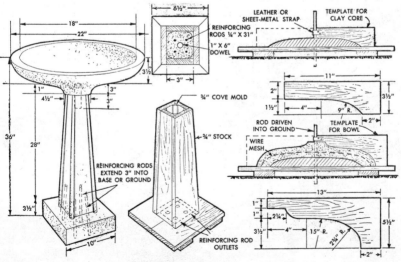

Bird-Cage Novelty

Assembled from strips of bamboo without using glue or nails, this novel bird cage can be made tiny enough to fit in the palm of the hand or proportionately larger. Bowed side strips are passed through the corner frame members to hold them in place. A bamboo perch supports a balsa bird

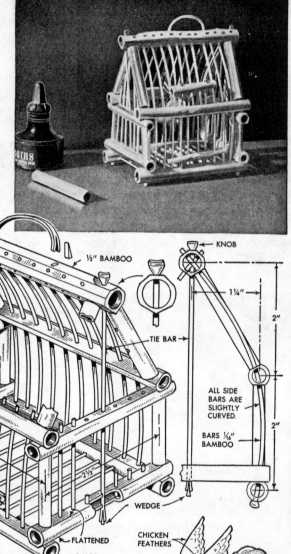

3/8" BAMBOO

2"

2"

3 1/2"

2 1/2"

1/2" BAMBOO

TIE BAR →

KNOB

1 1/4"

2"

2"

ALL SIDE BARS ARE SLIGHTLY CURVED.

BARS 1/16" BAMBOO

WEDGE →

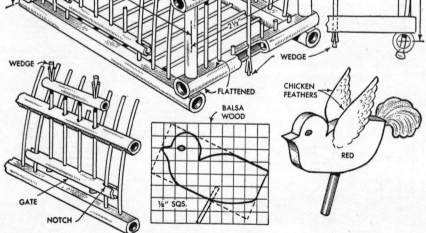

WEDGE

FLATTENED

WEDGE

GATE

NOTCH

BALSA WOOD

1/8" SQS.

CHICKEN FEATHERS

RED

Bird Feeders Hold Grain or Vegetable Scraps

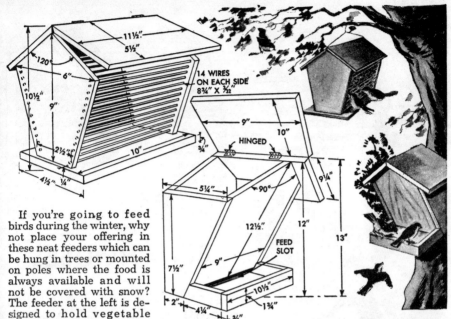

If you're going to feed birds during the winter, why not place your offering in these neat feeders which can be hung in trees or mounted on poles where the food is always available and will not be covered with snow? The feeder at the left is designed to hold vegetable scraps and bread crumbs, and the one on the right is for grain. The roof of the vegetable feeder is mitered at the peak, but on the grain feeder one side overlaps the other for hinging and therefore must be slightly wider. As only one side need open for filling the hopper, the other is nailed or screwed in place per-manently. Although either type of feeder may be mounted on a post, the vegetable feeder can be hung from the branches of a tree by hooking a wire through the gable ends, allowing birds to feed from both sides at once.

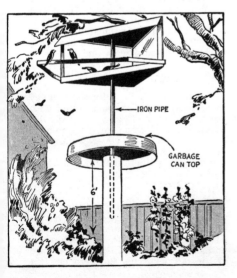

Bird Feeder Is Made Cat Proof By Can Lid on Standard

One homeowner, who had a bird feeder on a post in his back yard, found that cats were climbing the post and catching the birds. To stop this trouble he mounted a garbage-can lid on the post, as shown. This guard also keeps squirrels from stealing grain from the feeder.

CHICKADEE, NUTHATCH, TITMOUSE DOWNY WOOD PECKER
①
RAFFIA OR DRY GRASS, ALL SEEDS REMOVED
1¼" OR 1½" HOLE
9"
SPLIT WILLOW
FIREWOOD SLABS
GREEN BARK

③ PURPLE MARTIN
④ WREN HOUSE
1½"
6"
1½"
6"
8"
5½"   5½"
¾" STOCK
SCREWED FOR REMOVING BOTTOM

DRY GRASS ANCHORED WITH TWIGS
BARK
② ROBIN BARN SWALLOW
6" 6"
8"

1½" HOLE
6½"
4"
⑤ BLUE-BIRD, TREE SWALLOW, AND VIOLET-GREEN SWALLOW
⅜" PERCH
¾" STOCK USED
SPLIT TWIGS
12" HOLLOWED SECTION
3" X 14" SLAB
HOLE IN LOG ENLARGED BY BURNING
PARTITION ARRANGEMENT
⑥ FOUR-FAMILY APARTMENT

BIRD HOUSES

BIRDS are more likely to occupy houses if the nesting cavities are adapted to their requirements. A chart of inside dimensions for houses is shown on the opposite page. After deciding which species of birds you wish to attract, make the houses to suit them. The hanging log house in Fig. 1 is an attractive ornament even when birds are not in residence. To make it, split a seasoned log with a handsaw, chisel out the inside to the dimensions given and bore the proper size entrance hole. Then bolt the log together at the ends so that it can be taken apart for cleaning.

Robins and barn swallows require a fairly large house with one side open as in Fig. 2. This is easy to make if firewood slabs are available. Thin bark is used for the purple-martin house in Fig. 3, the bark being wrapped halfway around two end disks and bound with green willow, split and secured with brads. Fig. 4 shows a simple design built of ¾-in. material and covered with bark taken from dead logs.

Bluebirds will like the little thatched-roof cabin shown in Fig. 5. Walls are covered with split twigs, and straw or grass is used for the thatching, which is held down with anchor poles. If you can find a hollow log, most of the work on the four-family apartment house in Fig. 6 is done, except for the slabs on top and bottom. Bore holes of the required size and install partitions and perches. If a

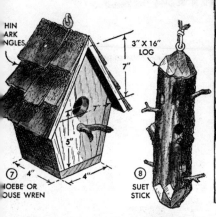

HIN
ARK
NGLES

3" X 16"
LOG

7"

7"

5"

⑦   4"   4"

OEBE OR
USE WREN

⑧

SUET
STICK

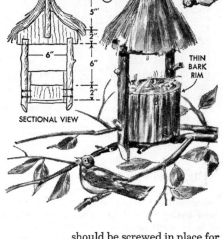

SONG
SPARROW

⑨

5"

2"

6"

6"

2"

THIN
BARK
RIM

SECTIONAL VIEW

log has only a small hole in the center it can be enlarged by burning it out.

The song sparrow isn't so exclusive as most birds and likes a house with all sides open like the miniature summer house in Fig. 9. It can be set on the end of a tree branch, provided it is not over 3 ft. above ground. On the other hand, the flicker and redheaded woodpecker demand privacy and considerable depth. Homes for them are illustrated in Figs. 10 and 11. They are merely wooden boxes covered with bark and attached to a tree trunk. The fronts

NESTING BOX DIMENSIONS IN INCHES					
Species	Floor plan	Depth	Entrance above floor	Dia. of entrance	Height above ground (feet)
Wren	4 x 4	6-8	1-6	1	6-10
Chickadee	4 x 4	8-10	6-8	1⅛	6-15
Nuthatch	4 x 4	8-10	6-8	1¼	12-20
Titmouse	4 x 4	8-10	6-8	1¼	6-15
Downy woodpecker	4 x 4	8-10	6-8	1¼	6-20
Bluebird	5 x 5	8	6	1½	5-10
Tree swallow	5 x 5	6	1-5	1½	10-15
Violet-green swallow	5 x 5	6	1-5	1½	10-15
Robin	6 x 8	8	One side open		6-15
Barn swallow	6 x 6	6	One side open		8-12
Song sparrow	6 x 6	6	All sides open		1-3
Flicker	7 x 7	16-18	14-16	2½	6-20
Red headed woodpecker	6 x 6	12-15	9-12	2	12-20
Phoebe	6 x 6	6	One side open		8-12
House wren	4 x 4	6-8	1-6	1	6-10
Purple martin	6 x 6	6	One side open		15-20

should be screwed in place for easy removal when cleaning time comes. The little cottage in Fig. 7 will interest the phoebe if the front wall is left out, and the house wren if it is left in. Use material surfaced on one side only, the rough side out, and shingle with strips of thin bark.

To attract birds, scatter the kind of food they like. The kinds of fruit and berry bushes around your home will determine the species of birds that will congregate there. Those that remain through the winter like suet. A suet stick fitted with perches as in Fig. 8 and suspended in a tree will be well patronized. Bore 1-in. holes in the stick and stuff them with the suet.

BLAST FURNACES

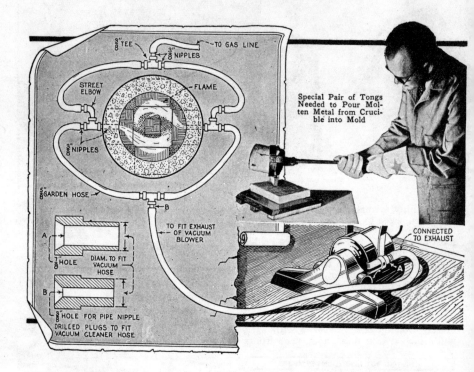

Special Pair of Tongs Needed to Pour Molten Metal from Crucible into Mold

CONNECTED TO EXHAUST

THIS double-burner blast furnace, which will quickly melt 10 to 15-lb. charges of aluminum, brass or any alloy of which the melting point is under 2,000° Fahr., can be built at very low cost. It can also be used for making alloys, for heat-treating, annealing, casehardening and many other metallurgical operations. The refractory lining is built to dimensions inside of a sheet-metal can, which serves to protect the lining and gives added strength to the completed furnace. A 5-gal. oilcan, with its top cut away and two holes drilled and reamed to admit ⅜-in. pipe nipples, was used. The burner holes were drilled in opposite sides of the can at points 3⅝ in. from the bottom. Heat-resisting lining is built up from ganister, which is a mixture consisting of equal parts of fire clay and pulverized fire brick moistened with water and worked to the consistency of

heavy plaster. Scraps of fire bricks are used as filler, which furnishes added strength and saves considerable time. The bottom of the can should be covered to a depth of 1 in. with ganister packed down firmly by ramming with a stick. Four pieces of fire brick, each 4½ in. long and 3½ in. wide, are next pressed firmly into the bottom layer of ganister as shown. Another piece of brick is set in the center to support the bottom of a crucible. The space between the supporting bricks is packed with ganister until its level is within 1 in. of the top of the bricks.

Two lengths of ⅜-in. gas pipe are inserted through the burner holes to extend to the center of the furnace, forming burner inlet holes. The pipe is removed after the ganister wall has partly dried, leaving two openings for the burners. A sheet-metal form 8 in. in diameter is now set in the can and centered. Small chips of fire

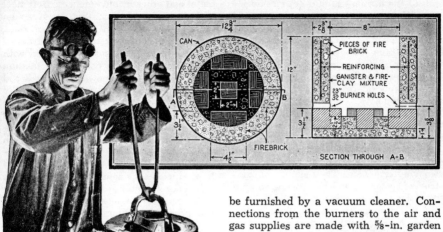

SECTION THROUGH A-B

be furnished by a vacuum cleaner. Connections from the burners to the air and gas supplies are made with ⅝-in. garden hose, which fits snugly over ⅜-in. gas pipe. The wooden adapters for connecting the vacuum cleaner to the air line are turned from hardwood. The hose of the cleaner is used to connect the exhaust, which normally opens into the bag, with the air line. When the connections have been completed and the gas feeds have been tested for leaks, a final drying should be carried out by lighting the furnace and allowing it to operate at low heat without a crucible, charge or cover for 15 or 20 min. To light the furnace, ignite a piece of paper and drop it inside of the furnace. While the paper is still burning and with the vacuum cleaner turned off, open the gas jet. Allow the gas to burn for half an hour or longer without a blast in order to dry out the fire wall. The vacuum cleaner may then be started and the hot blast used to complete the drying. At this point it will be necessary to regulate the gas until a whirl of intense flame is established inside of the furnace. Turn the gas as low as is possible to maintain good combustion. The

brick and ganister may be used to support the can in the exact center of the outside shell. This can should be smooth and free from dents to facilitate its removal after the fire wall has set. The space between the can and the shell is now packed with ganister and pieces of fire brick. In order to give added rigidity and permanence to the lining, old hacksaw blades or other similar material may be used as ribbing to reinforce the wall. Eight or ten such stays, inserted upright and centrally in the lining, will give great strength without being detrimental to the refractory value of the lining. When the wall has set sufficiently to support its weight, in about 12 hrs., remove the inner shell and the ⅜-in. pipes, and allow the assembly to dry in the air for two or three days.

The burners are built from ⅜-in. pipe and fittings. The air blast may

ends of the burners should not extend inside of the lining as the intense heat would melt them. Change their position slightly and watch for the long tongues of almost colorless blue flame which will be seen when combustion is best. To shut off the furnace, always discontinue the blast before shutting off the gas in order to prevent a "pop back." Some cracks are certain to be found after the wall has been dried out, which are filled with a putty made of fire clay and water.

A pair of tongs of the kind illustrated should be constructed for inserting and removing crucibles. They should be constructed so that it will be possible to pour from the crucible into molds while it is held in the tongs to avoid spilling molten metal. As a precaution, it is a good idea to wear thick-soled shoes when metal is poured. The work should be done on dry sand and the elevation of the ground in the room used for pouring should be so adjusted that any spilled metal will not flow against wood or other inflammable furnishings. A small shallow hole in the ground is convenient for dumping excess quantities of molten metal. The pig thus cast can be removed after it has cooled to be remelted when needed. Metal should never be allowed to freeze in the crucible.

To melt metal in the furnace light the gas and start the blast; insert the charged crucible with the tongs, cover the furnace with an asbestos board or other fireproof lid and allow the charge to melt. Inspection of the charge may be made by lifting the lid with a pair of tongs and observing the contents of the crucible through colored glasses. In melting metals a small handful of borax should be poured on the molten metal as a flux to dissolve any oxides which are formed. The scum or dross, which will come to the top, may then be skimmed off before the molds are poured.

The strap-iron stand shown may be constructed to elevate the furnace to any desired level. Crucibles made from graphite are ideal for most work although their cost and the difficulty of obtaining them sometimes make their use prohibitive for most experimenters and home-shop workers. A crucible may be constructed by fitting a malleable-iron pipe cap to a pipe nipple of suitable size. It is important that the pipe cap used in the construction of these crucibles be of malleable iron, otherwise cracks may develop resulting in a loss of metal and other inconveniences. Soft steel may be casehardened; that is, given an outer case of very hard, high, carbon steel, in this furnace. Work to be casehardened is put in a crucible and surrounded with finely powdered bone charcoal, potassium carbonate or even powdered hardwood charcoal. The crucible and its charge are then put in the furnace and heated. The higher the temperature the more rapid will be the absorption of carbon. The thickness of the case depends upon the length of time the work is kept heated. It is impossible to state the exact time required to produce a satisfactory depth, due to the difference in qualities of steel and iron; however, a few experiments will show the best procedure. When you think the work has heated long enough, turn off the heat

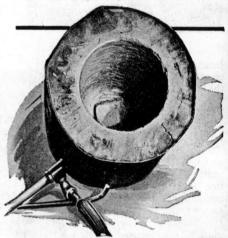

and allow the pack to cool. When cool, remove the work from the pipe crucible and brush off any adhering carbonaceous matter. The carbonized work is now ready to be hardened. This is done by heating to a cherry-red temperature and quickly immersing in a tank of cold water. While the work is in the cold water, it must be kept in constant motion to increase the rapidity of cooling.

Articles made from soft iron and ordinary steel may be given a very hard and durable surface by this treatment. Another application of casehardening involves the iron electroplating of articles made from softer metal at points where wear is likely to be encountered. These iron-plated pipes may then be casehardened as described above.

BLINKER LIGHT

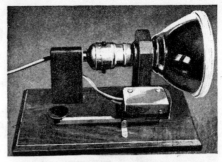

This safe blinker light utilizes a floodlight bulb of the reflector type used in show-window lighting

YOUNGSTERS engaged in back-yard war games will enjoy using this safe blinker light to work out a winning strategy. A floodlight bulb of the reflector type used in lighting show windows serves as a light source. A normally open microswitch is actuated by an improvised telegraph key to control the light, making it easy to transmit messages in blinker code. Details below show how to mount the light socket and connect the wiring from the power source to the socket and switch. Note that the switch is shielded so there is no possibility of a finger coming in contact with the open terminals on the switch. The wooden block that supports the socket is drilled at A, and hole B is drilled through the bottom, meeting hole A. Finally, hole C is drilled through into hole B. This makes it possible to fish the wiring through the block to the socket and switch. For easy operation the distance from the key knob to the pivot should be about twice that from pivot to switch button.

The socket and bulb are supported at a uniform height in separate wooden blocks attached to base

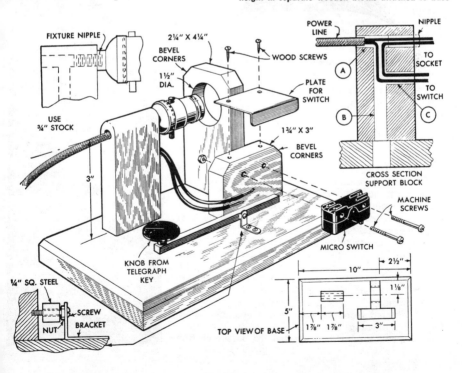

FIXTURE NIPPLE

2¼″ X 4¼″

BEVEL CORNERS

1½″ DIA.

USE ¾″ STOCK

WOOD SCREWS

PLATE FOR SWITCH

1¾″ X 3″

BEVEL CORNERS

3″

KNOB FROM TELEGRAPH KEY

¼″ SQ. STEEL

SCREW

NUT

BRACKET

MICRO SWITCH

MACHINE SCREWS

POWER LINE

NIPPLE

TO SOCKET

TO SWITCH

A

B

C

CROSS SECTION SUPPORT BLOCK

2½″

10″

1⅛″

5″

1⅞″ 1⅞″

3″

TOP VIEW OF BASE

BLOW TORCH

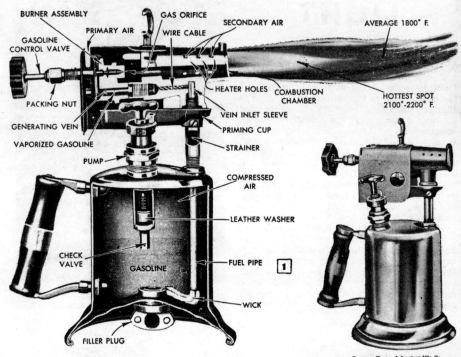

BURNER ASSEMBLY
GAS ORIFICE
SECONDARY AIR
AVERAGE 1800° F.
PRIMARY AIR
WIRE CABLE
GASOLINE CONTROL VALVE
HEATER HOLES
COMBUSTION CHAMBER
HOTTEST SPOT 2100°-2200° F.
PACKING NUT
VEIN INLET SLEEVE
GENERATING VEIN
PRIMING CUP
VAPORIZED GASOLINE
STRAINER
PUMP
COMPRESSED AIR
LEATHER WASHER
CHECK VALVE
GASOLINE
FUEL PIPE
1
WICK
FILLER PLUG

To keep your blowtorch in top operating condition, a knowledge of the principles of operation and how to clean and adjust the burner is most essential

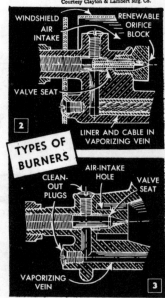

Courtesy Clayton & Lambert Mfg. Co.

WINDSHIELD
AIR INTAKE
RENEWABLE ORIFICE BLOCK
VALVE SEAT
2
LINER AND CABLE IN VAPORIZING VEIN

TYPES OF BURNERS

CLEAN-OUT PLUGS
AIR-INTAKE HOLE
VALVE SEAT
VAPORIZING VEIN
3

A BLOWTORCH is a versatile little heater and, if correctly maintained, it will give years of efficient service for hundreds of small heating jobs both around your home and in your shop. The mechanism of a torch, Fig. 1, is relatively simple, but it must be kept clean and correctly adjusted.

In operation, gasoline in the tank is forced up to the burner through the feed pipe and generating vein or fuel passage by air pressure inside the tank, which is maintained by occasional use of a small hand pump installed as a part of the tank unit. As the gasoline passes through the generating vein, it is vaporized by heat conducted from the combustion chamber when the torch is burning.

When a cold torch is to be ignited, the burner casting

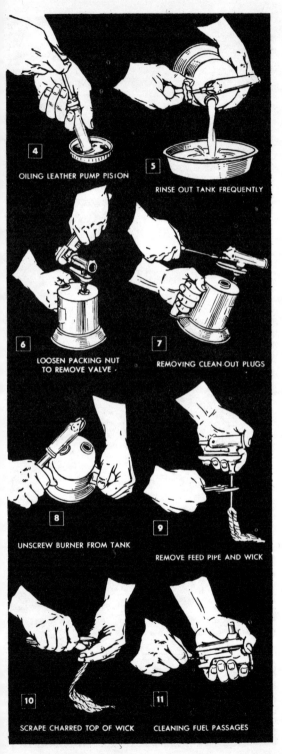

4
OILING LEATHER PUMP PISTON

5
RINSE OUT TANK FREQUENTLY

6
LOOSEN PACKING NUT
TO REMOVE VALVE

7
REMOVING CLEAN-OUT PLUGS

8
UNSCREW BURNER FROM TANK

9
REMOVE FEED PIPE AND WICK

10
SCRAPE CHARRED TOP OF WICK

11
CLEANING FUEL PASSAGES

must first be heated by burning liquid gasoline in the priming cup. The gas vapors generated in the vein emerge from the gas orifice and mix with incoming primary air. This mixture passes into the combustion chamber where it ignites and burns, causing a long, blue flame at the mouth of the burner. Secondary air passes into the flame through the heater holes in the combustion chamber to complete burning of the gas vapors. Two types of burners are used on blowtorches. The type shown in Fig. 2 has a renewable orifice block and liner and cable in the vaporizing vein. It provides a smooth flame and long-burning life before carbonizing. The type of burner shown in Fig. 3 is of the simplest construction and, therefore, the least expensive of the two. It will give a hot, blue flame and the veins are easily cleaned. Temperature of the flame, Fig. 1, is fairly constant at any given tank pressure for various torch models. However, the volume or size of the torch flame varies.

If the flame is too small and weak in force, open and close the gas-control valve several times to clear the burner orifice. If this does not return the flame to normal, the torch needs cleaning.

Allow the torch to cool before dismantling it for cleaning. Then unscrew the pump and remove and clean the check valve. Draw oil into the pump cylinder, as in Fig. 4, to lubricate the leather washer on the pump piston. Before replacing the pump, rinse out the tank, Fig. 5, with gasoline to clean out any sediment. To inspect the gas-control valve, loosen the packing nut, as shown in Fig. 6, and unscrew the control valve. Then hold the nozzle to a light and look through the fuel passage. If the orifice is enlarged, the orifice block should be replaced with a new one, if it is of the type shown in Fig. 2. Burners of the type shown in Fig. 3 should be sent to the manufacturer for repairing. Poor operation often results from carbonization of the veins. To clean the veins, remove the clean-out plugs, Fig. 7, and unscrew the burner assembly from the tank. A short length of pipe may be inserted in the nozzle, as in Fig. 8, for leverage. After removing the burner, unscrew the feed pipe containing the wick, Fig. 9. If the upper end of the wick is charred, it should be scraped clean with a pocketknife, Fig. 10. The fuel passages, or veins, can be cleaned with a drill turned by hand, as in Fig. 11. Before assembling the torch, carefully apply brown laundry soap, as shown in Fig. 12, to the threads of each part to prevent leaks. There's a trick to getting the wick back into the tank. First twist it tightly, then push it through the feed-pipe inlet with a screwdriver as in Fig. 13. When the torch is assembled, fill the tank three quarters full with clean, uncolored and unleaded gasoline. Most torches must be turned upside down, as in Fig. 14, to fill. After checking to make sure the gasoline control valve is closed, pump about 20 strokes of air into the tank for starting pressure, Fig. 15. The torch can be tested without lighting it by pointing the nozzle toward a container and opening the control valve. If a small stream of gasoline sprays out as in Fig. 16, the torch will burn when properly generated. To start a cold torch, open the control valve slightly to allow gasoline to flow slowly into the priming cup until about three quarters full. Some torches, Fig. 17, are equipped with a priming valve for this purpose. Then ignite the gasoline in the cup. The burning gasoline, Fig. 18, will heat the burner casting to the generating temperature. When the gasoline in the cup has nearly burned, open the control valve. Often the torch will light itself from the priming flame. If not, hold a lighted match close to the heater holes or just below the nozzle as in Fig. 19. An intense blue flame should result. A yellow flame indicates the burner has not been properly generated. When this happens, shut off the torch and allow it to cool; then fill and relight the priming cup. To increase the flame volume, regulate the control valve and increase the air pressure in the tank. After shutting off the torch, back out the control valve one eighth turn to prevent jamming when it cools.

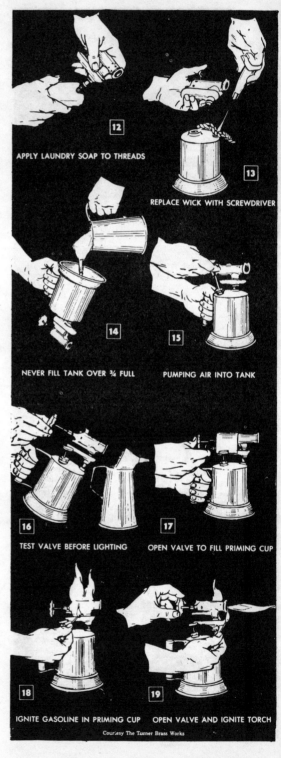

12 APPLY LAUNDRY SOAP TO THREADS

13 REPLACE WICK WITH SCREWDRIVER

14 NEVER FILL TANK OVER ¾ FULL

15 PUMPING AIR INTO TANK

16 TEST VALVE BEFORE LIGHTING

17 OPEN VALVE TO FILL PRIMING CUP

18 IGNITE GASOLINE IN PRIMING CUP

19 OPEN VALVE AND IGNITE TORCH

Courtesy The Turner Brass Works

BLUEPRINTS

READING a blueprint is much like reading shorthand. You must understand the separate meanings of signs, symbols, and lines. The particular sign, the type of symbol and the weights and types of lines used on the blueprint—all these tell a story to the machinist, just as does a music score to the musician, or a weather chart to the airman. In reading a blueprint the machinist usually notes first the location and directions of the heavy lines which show the visible outline of the object, then the dotted lines which indicate the location of parts which are invisible in the assembly. Certain full lines in parallel, dotted lines, dot-dash lines or combinations of these tell him what kind of material is to be used and where it is to be located. Other lines will give the over-all dimensions, and where necessary, the limit dimensions, and a note on the blueprint will indicate the scale reductions to which the object is drawn. If there is a repetition of parts and dimensions, the print will state how many duplicates in parts, what dimensions are duplicates, and will completely detail only one unit or its separate parts. If the object is irregular in shape the blueprint sometimes includes a perspective view to define the project more clearly in its several dimensions. Generally, projected front, side, and top or bottom views are used and sometimes these are subdivided and projected separately to make more clear to the machinist just what is to be done. Often prints detailing objects of complicated assembly will include a "bill of material" along with projected views, the parts of which are keyed with numbers or letters registering or corresponding with those on the material list so that the amount, size, and kind of materials used in the various parts can be more readily identified and calculated.

Looking at Fig. 1 and then at Fig. 2, the "alphabet" of lines, you will see how the draftsman puts these general rules into practice. Fig. 1 represents no particular mechanical device, nor are any of the parts dimensioned, but you will see at once how the visual representations of lines are car-

LINE "ALPHABET," FIG. 2

VISIBLE OUTLINE

INVISIBLE OUTLINE

CENTER LINE

$12\frac{1}{2}''$

DIMENSION LINE

EXTENSION LINE

ADJACENT PARTS

CUTTING PLANE

SHORT BREAKS

LONG BREAKS

CROSS-HATCHING LINE

ALTERNATE POSITION

LINE OF MOTION

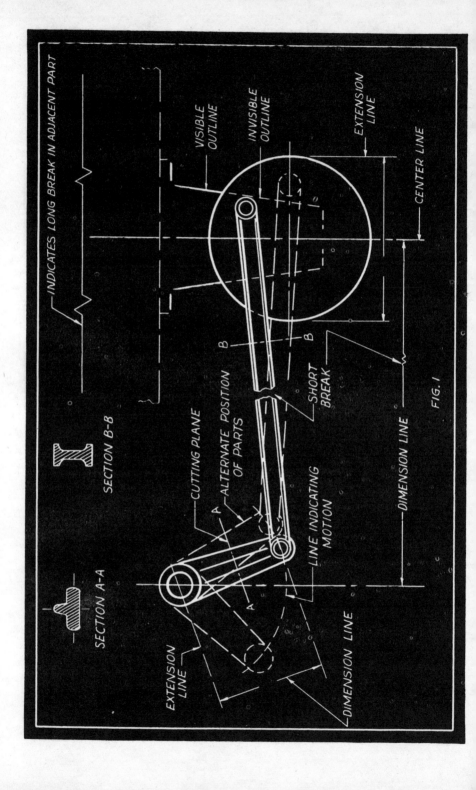

INDICATES LONG BREAK IN ADJACENT PART

VISIBLE OUTLINE

INVISIBLE OUTLINE

EXTENSION LINE

CENTER LINE

SECTION B-B

B

B

SHORT BREAK

CUTTING PLANE

ALTERNATE POSITION OF PARTS

LINE INDICATING MOTION

A

A

DIMENSION LINE

SECTION A-A

EXTENSION LINE

DIMENSION LINE

DIMENSION LINE

FIG. I

ried out. Connecting it up with the line alphabet, Fig. 2, notice first how the visible outline, Fig. 1, is made to stand out by use of heavy lines. These lines have been purposely slightly exaggerated for the sake of emphasis. And note too, that the drawing, Fig. 1, makes use of all the lines shown in Fig. 2. Extension lines from the outline of parts terminate the dimension lines, long-dash lines show the alternate position of moveable parts, lines consisting of alternating long and short dashes locate the centers, another consisting of a long dash and two short ones locates the cutting planes, while a line of short dashes indicates the line of motion. A wavy line shows the position of short breaks in parts of the mechanism, while a straight line broken at more or less regular intervals into a zigzagged section shows the location of long breaks. The draftsman uses the latter two lines to indicate that a section of the mechanism or part has been "broken away" for convenience in making the drawing or that in general, it is not essential that it be fully shown. Thus the short break in the connecting rod in Fig. 1, simply means that the rod is not shown in its full length, while the long break would indicate that the full outline of the base or overhead support to which the mechanism is to be attached is not important or that it is too large to be conveniently shown in connection with the mechanism itself. Cutting-plane lines such as A-A and B-B, Fig. 1, are used by the draftsman to indicate that figuratively the part has been cut in two at the point where the line crosses it and that elsewhere on the print you will find an end or sectional view as is the case in Fig. 1, sectional views A-A and B-B. These show the contours or outlines of the parts viewed endwise. One thing to keep in mind in connection with breaks in dimensioned parts: The dimension given always indicates the full length. Sometimes when the nature of the drawing makes it necessary or where the indication of the break is more or less obscure, the draftsman may, for the sake of emphasis, indicate the break in the dimension line also, as in Fig. 1. Otherwise, indicating a break in the dimension line generally is considered unnecessary.

Center lines are quite important to the draftsman as well as the engineer or machinist reading the finished blueprint. They are a definite aid to both neatness and legibility of the print, for they establish a geometric symmetry of arrangement and layout of the various details and units. Fig. 3 is an example of where center lines aid in laying out simple details quickly, accurately and intelligently. Here both side and end views are shown on those parts detailed at the left. Notice the varying characteristics of the indicated breaks in the four parts. The first two show breaks in round stock, as you see from the end

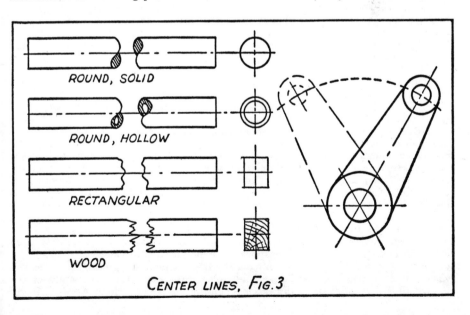

ROUND, SOLID

ROUND, HOLLOW

RECTANGULAR

WOOD

CENTER LINES, FIG. 3

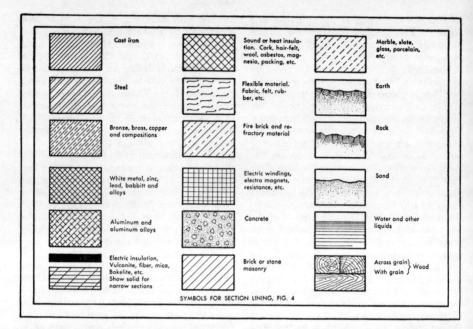

Cast iron	Sound or heat insulation. Cork, hair-felt, wool, asbestos, magnesia, packing, etc.	Marble, slate, glass, porcelain, etc.
Steel	Flexible material. Fabric, felt, rubber, etc.	Earth
Bronze, brass, copper and compositions	Fire brick and refractory material	Rock
White metal, zinc, lead, babbitt and alloys	Electric windings, electro magnets, resistance, etc.	Sand
Aluminum and aluminum alloys	Concrete	Water and other liquids
Electric insulation, Vulcanite, fiber, mica, Bakelite, etc. Show solid for narrow sections	Brick or stone masonry	Across grain ⎱ Wood With grain ⎰

SYMBOLS FOR SECTION LINING, FIG. 4

views, while the latter two show breaks in square or rectangular materials, one of them in wood.

Fig. 5 shows the commonly accepted symbols for designation of various materials by section lining. In some, one symbol refers to a single material, while others indicate any one of several materials. In the latter case the required material will be given in a material list or will be specified on the print either as a separate note or by leaving an unlined space in the cross hatching where the name of the material is lettered in.

Perspective views are coming into more general use, first because they give the blueprint reader an instant three-dimensional picture of the object, and second, despite the necessity of more freehand sketching the use of perspective views supplemented with the necessary mechanical details, actually cuts down on the amount of time necessary to prepare many prints. Fig. 5 will show more clearly what is meant. Here are two simple objects drawn much as they would appear to the eye if placed on a table. In order to give the complete overall dimensions of the first, A, it would be necessary to make at least two views, were it drawn in the conventional way. But as shown, it would be possible to give all the essential sizing dimensions on the one view, as you can see. Fig. 5, B, shows another object more complicated because it presents curved surfaces and detailed parts which are invisible. Fig. 6 shows the same object presented in three views by means of orthographic projection, also frequently referred to as third-angle projection. This latter method is more or less universal practice in drafting rooms, although the arrangement can be varied somewhat as necessity requires. No dimensions are shown in Fig. 6, only the outline of the object in the three views and the projection lines. Looking back at Fig. 5, B, you will see that it is possible to give thickness, width, length, radii, hole diameters and positions, and height and diameter of the visible boss on the right-angle arm. In fact, everything can be given except the details of the invisible boss on one arm of the casting. It is for this reason that the perspective sketch must at the present be regarded only as supplemental to the projected views of an object and as such it has a definite value in presenting a true picture of an object complicated and irregular in detail and which would be difficult to visualize in its entirety from ordinary projected views.

It is essential that a beginner in reading blueprints make a careful study of the glossary of terms included here. This will

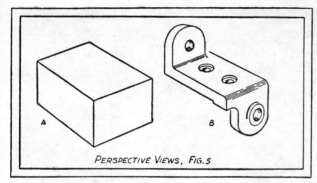

PERSPECTIVE VIEWS, FIG. 5

acquaint the tyro with the terminology in common use and a working knowledge of it will enable one to quickly grasp the meaning of detailed blueprints. Lines, symbols, and the glossary of terms are the abbreviated language of the blueprint.

Now another variation illustrated by the two simple drawings in Fig. 7, the first a perspective view of a bushing as it would appear when held a few inches below eye level, and the second a plan view or more properly, a combination of a front view and a plan, or top view. The former shows the bushing much as it would appear held flange end up at eye level, the latter or plan view, shows the same object as it would appear when seen from a point some distance directly above it. This is one thing to keep in mind when studying blueprints, that is, the position of the object in relation to the eye. Often this will help in visualizing an object otherwise difficult to picture in mind. Now to Fig. 7, add the omitted dimensions on the dimension lines, and these can be any within reasonable proportions, and you have what engineers and machinists refer to as a working drawing. Keep in mind that this one is simple in the extreme, but a working drawing it is nevertheless, for with dimensions added it contains the essential information needed by the machinist to make the part to specified size without further instruction. Now, going into it a bit farther, suppose that this bushing, or any other similar object, is required to be machined to a "press" fit, that is, dimensions are more critical than those ordinarily given in inches and the common fractions of an inch. In other words, dimensions must be expressed in decimal fractions to at least three places and the dimensions on the mechanical drawing will give the limits or tolerances within or be-

tween which the actual measurements must come.. Then the draftsman expresses the dimensions as in Fig. 8, where they show the limits to which the inside and outside diameters of the collar must be machined or finished. On smaller parts where limit gages are to be used the two values are placed one above the other and for internal dimensions the minimum limit is placed above the line, while for external dimensions the maximum limit is written above the line. Other methods of expressing limit dimensions on larger parts, where few or no gages are employed, or for other reasons, are shown in Fig. 9. When limit dimensions are given it is often necessary to indicate finished surfaces and also the kind or quality of the finish required. The draftsman does this with the symbol "V" drawn at a 60-degree angle as in Fig. 8, and inside the V he places a code letter or figure which refers to a note or table elsewhere on the blueprint. As an example, letters C and E in Fig. 8, he might designate as meaning "Rough" or "Finish Turn," while letters B and D might be designated in the table to mean "Finish Grind." The symbol V, with the point of the V touching the surface, has largely supplanted the older finish mark "f."

Fig. 10 shows a method often used to save time and labor in section lining. It is what is usually termed a "conventional" method,

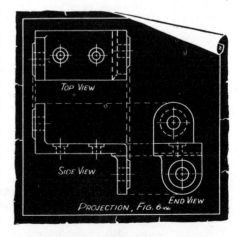

TOP VIEW

SIDE VIEW

END VIEW

PROJECTION, FIG. 6

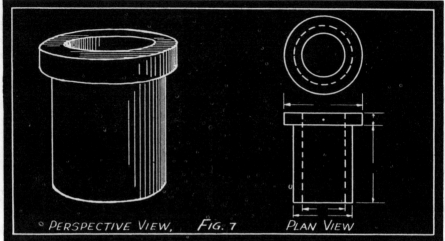

PERSPECTIVE VIEW, FIG. 7   PLAN VIEW

hence a conventional section. The section A-A along the cutting-plane line sections only the rim and hub instead of the rim, hub, and the two arms as would otherwise be necessary. Then a single oval section on one arm will serve for all six arms of the pulley, as these are identical. Also the section lining indicates that the pulley is to be made of cast iron. However, you will not find it labeled on the blueprint as you see it in Fig. 10. Instead it will ordinarily be so stated on a note elsewhere on the print. Or again, if the pulley is to be cast in brass for example, the section lining will usually be the same as the symbol for section lining of brass and a table or note on the print will give the material as brass. Fig. 10 is not a complete mechanical drawing. Certain details and the dimensions have been purposely omitted for the sake of clarity and emphasis.

There is a general tendency to simplify the intricate detailing necessary in making accurate and neat presentations of screw threads by the former method of showing the full outlines. By the latter and regular method, except in certain instances involving sections of external threads and internal invisible threads, the threads are indicated by alternate long and short cross lines at right angles to the axis, the alternate long and short lines representing the crests and roots of the thread, the short lines being heavier and representing the roots, the lighter lines the crests. These lines are simply spaced by eye and need not represent the actual pitch of the thread. See Fig. 11, D. The simplified symbol method is adopted where it is desirable or necessary to simplify and speed up drafting work. In this the threaded portion is simply indicated by lines consisting of short dashes

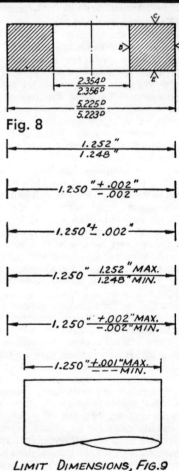

Fig. 8

LIMIT DIMENSIONS, FIG. 9

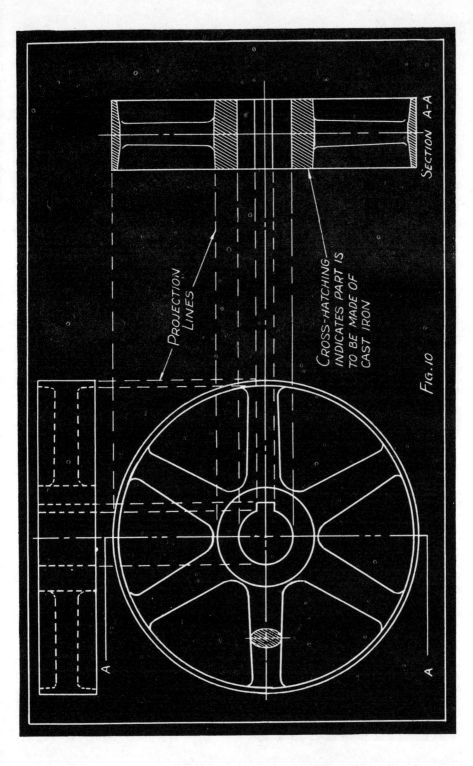

SECTION A-A

PROJECTION
LINES

CROSS-HATCHING
INDICATES PART IS
TO BE MADE OF
CAST IRON

FIG. 10

A

A

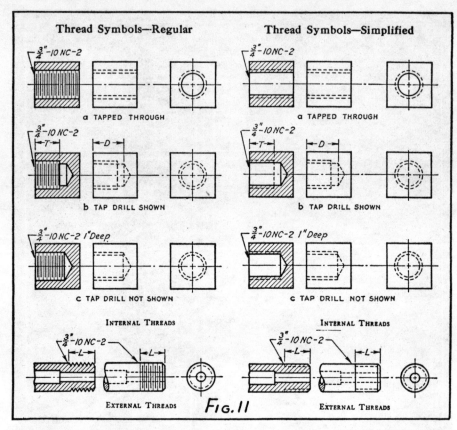

Thread Symbols—Regular

- ¾"-10 NC-2

a TAPPED THROUGH

- ¾"-10 NC-2

b TAP DRILL SHOWN

- ¾"-10 NC-2 1"Deep

c TAP DRILL NOT SHOWN

INTERNAL THREADS

- ¾"-10 NC-2

EXTERNAL THREADS

Thread Symbols—Simplified

- ¾"-10 NC-2

a TAPPED THROUGH

- ¾"-10 NC-2

b TAP DRILL SHOWN

- ¾"-10 NC-2 1"Deep

c TAP DRILL NOT SHOWN

INTERNAL THREADS

- ¾"-10 NC-2

EXTERNAL THREADS

Fig. 11

drawn parallel to the axis at the approximate depth of the thread. It should be noted that the simplified method is not recommended for either exterior or sectional views of parts assembled. Size, length of the thread and depth of tap should always be given on the drawing. Threads are considered to be right hand unless otherwise specified.

Obviously, large objects cannot be conveniently detailed full size. The outlines and other parts must be uniformly reduced in size on the drawing so that the sheets will be easy to handle and examine and also of a standard or uniform size so that they may be filed conveniently. Hence, drawings are nearly always made to a reduced scale, that is, every part is drawn to a predetermined fraction of the full size. However, there are certain comparatively rare instances where an enlarged scale must be used. In such cases a notation on the drawing will state that the details are twice actual size, three times actual size,

and so on. Continuing to consider scale reductions in size, once the draftsman has decided on a given scale reduction, such as ¾ in. equals 1 foot, he must be careful to determine beforehand whether this scale is practical, that is, that this particular scale will not reduce some parts to such small size that they are difficult to draw and to show clearly. A scale reduction within practical limits must be calculated for the smallest detailed part of the whole unit if it is of involved construction. To make this easy the draftsman uses a scale, Fig. 12, which may be a single triangular-shaped unit or a set of several scales which are like small rulers except that the edges are beveled and are graduated into various scale reductions. What the scale actually does is indicate given distances representing one foot. Then this given distance is subdivided into 12 parts by graduations, each graduation representing one inch. Then the twelfths are again subdivided into halves and quarters representing ½ and ¼ of an

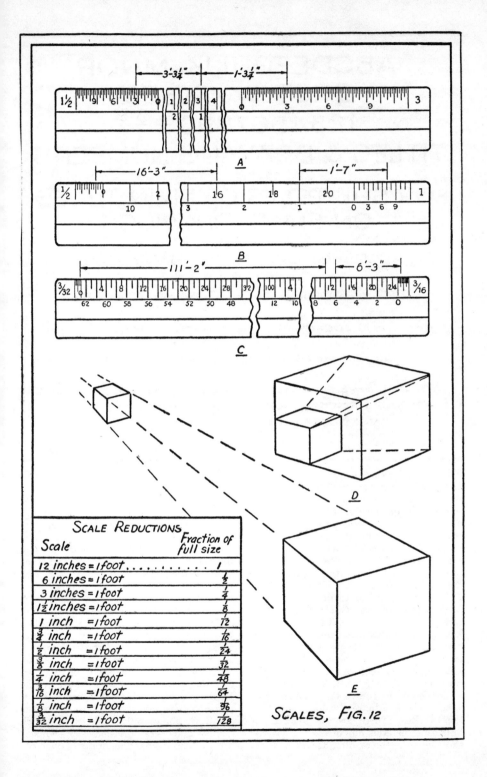

SCALES, Fig. 12

SCALE REDUCTIONS	
Scale	Fraction of full size
12 inches = 1 foot	1
6 inches = 1 foot	$\frac{1}{2}$
3 inches = 1 foot	$\frac{1}{4}$
1½ inches = 1 foot	$\frac{1}{8}$
1 inch = 1 foot	$\frac{1}{12}$
¾ inch = 1 foot	$\frac{1}{16}$
½ inch = 1 foot	$\frac{1}{24}$
⅜ inch = 1 foot	$\frac{1}{32}$
¼ inch = 1 foot	$\frac{1}{48}$
$\frac{3}{16}$ inch = 1 foot	$\frac{1}{64}$
⅛ inch = 1 foot	$\frac{1}{96}$
$\frac{3}{32}$ inch = 1 foot	$\frac{1}{128}$

ABCDEFGHIJKLMNOP
QRSTUVWXYZ&
1234567890 $\frac{1}{2}\frac{3}{4}\frac{5}{8}$
TITLES & DRAWING NUMBERS

TYPE 2
FOR SUB-TITLES OR MAIN TITLES ON SMALL DRAWINGS

TYPE 3   ABCDEFGHIJKLMNOPQRSTUVWXYZ&
1234567890 $\frac{1}{2}\frac{3}{4}\frac{5}{8}\frac{9}{32}$
FOR HEADINGS AND PROMINENT NOTES

TYPE 4   ABCDEFGHIJKLMNOPQRSTUVWXYZ&
1234567890 $\frac{1}{2}\frac{3}{4}\frac{5}{8}\frac{23}{64}$
FOR BILLS OF MATERIAL. DIMENSIONS & GENERAL NOTES

TYPE 5
OPTIONAL TYPE SAME AS TYPE 4 BUT USING TYPE 3 FOR FIRST
LETTER OF PRINCIPAL WORDS. MAY BE USED FOR SUB-TITLES
AND NOTES ON THE BODY OF DRAWINGS.

FIG. 13

inch. Now looking at detail A in Fig. 12 and reading first from right to left, you notice the figure 1½ at the extreme left. This means that this portion of the scale is subdivided in a scale reduction of 1½ inches equals 1 foot or in reality ⅛ of a foot actual foot-rule measurement, as you see by the table below. Taking a measurement from the object to be drawn, let us say, the draftsman finds that a scale reduction of 1½ inches equals 1 foot will serve the purpose of convenience. One particular part of the object he finds is 3 feet 3¼ inches long by actual measurement. He must reduce this to exact scale along with all other parts. So he looks to the right of the "O"-line on the 1½ inch division of the scale until he finds the figure 3. Then to the left of the O-line he counts three 1-inch divisions or three of those divisions representing twelfths. These are subdivided into fourths so he adds one of the fourths and this completes the reading, 3 feet 3¼ inches.

Then in detail B, Fig. 12, you see scale reductions of ½ inch equals 1 foot and 1 inch equals 1 foot. You will notice, too, that on these scales some of the graduations have been omitted for the purpose of clarity. In detail C are scales representing just about the smallest practical reductions of the standard foot measurement and fractions thereof. These reductions are used where the object or machine to be detailed is of large size with no very small parts which, in the same scale, would reduce to a size impractical to draw and dimension. In extreme cases the draftsman sometimes separates these parts and shows them in a lesser reduction and so notes the fact on the drawing so that there will be no error. Heretofore on those scales shown in Fig. 12, the reductions show 12 divisions but if you note carefully the ³⁄₃₂-inch reduction, detail C, shows only 6 divisions which means that each division represents 2 inches. The same is true of the ⅛-inch re-

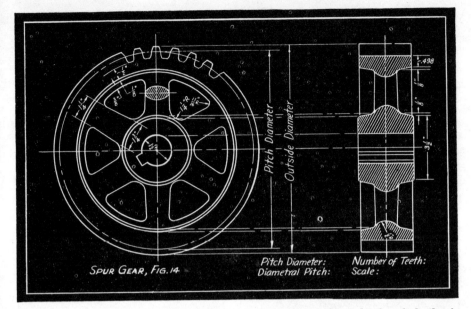

SPUR GEAR, FIG. 14

Pitch Diameter: Number of Teeth:
Diametral Pitch: Scale:

duction. Any further graduation of these reductions would make the divisions virtually invisible, hence of no practical value. The scale then is simply a reduced foot rule for laying off and determining the measurement and consequently the size of the drawing which represents the machine and its parts all reduced uniformly. The thing to keep in mind is that the dimension on the drawing is the actual measurement of the part in feet and inches or fractions of an inch. In other words the dimensions are those of the object itself, but if you measured the distance on the drawing in feet and inches, with a common foot rule, you would find it considerably less because the distance or dimension has been reduced by means of the scale, or reduced foot rule. Sketches D and E may help in visualizing the reductions more clearly. One has to think of the object itself made uniformly smaller by the scale reductions, like the same object viewed at a distance as at E.

In mechanical drawing one of the objects the draftsman is very frequently called upon to draw is a gear, Fig. 14. The latter drawing shows a front view and a vertical section of a simple spur gear, the section being a conventional one along a vertical center line. As you see, here again the arms are not shown in full section. Were the dimensions fully given this would be a complete working drawing. These would include the working depth, whole depth, number of teeth, space between teeth measured along the pitch circle, and so on. In reading blueprints having to do with the detailing of gears one of the things one must get clearly in mind is the meaning of the pitch diameter as distinguished from the true or full outside diameter of the gear blank, generally taken after the blank has been machined. After the teeth have been cut the width of each tooth and the space between will be equal when measured at the pitch circle, that is, in ordinary practice. There are exceptions, of course, on gearing made for special purposes. Now, as you will see from Fig. 14, the pitch circle, or diameter, is the circle drawn through the point at which the gear tooth comes into contact with the tooth of the companion gear or pinion which runs with it, and this of course takes place when the two tooth faces meet on the line which joins the centers of the two gears. Assuming, just as an example, that the number of teeth is to be 48 and that the pitch diameter is 12 inches, then 48 divided by 12 equals 4, which is the diametral pitch, or the figure representing the number of teeth per inch of pitch diameter. Thickness of the rim is generally shown as a decimal of three places, in this case .498 of an inch. Other minor dimensions are shown only in part.

Figs. 13 and 15 show approved specimen types of lettering in common use in draft-

ABCDEFGHIJKLMNOP
QRSTUVWXYZ&
1234567890 $\frac{1}{2}$ $\frac{3}{4}$ $\frac{5}{8}$ $\frac{7}{16}$
TO BE USED FOR MAIN TITLES
& DRAWING NUMBERS

TYPE 2 ABCDEFGHIJKLMNOPQR
STUVWXYZ&
1234567890 $\frac{13}{64}$ $\frac{5}{8}$ $\frac{1}{2}$
TO BE USED FOR SUB-TITLES

TYPE 3 ABCDEFGHIJKLMNOPQRSTUVWXYZ&
1234567890 $\frac{1}{2}$ $\frac{3}{4}$ $\frac{5}{8}$ $\frac{7}{16}$
FOR HEADINGS AND PROMINENT NOTES

TYPE 4 ABCDEFGHIJKLMNOPQRSTUVWXYZ&
1234567890 $\frac{1}{2}$ $\frac{1}{4}$ $\frac{3}{8}$ $\frac{5}{16}$ $\frac{7}{32}$ $\frac{1}{8}$
FOR BILLS OF MATERIAL, DIMENSIONS & GENERAL NOTES

TYPE 5
OPTIONAL TYPE SAME AS TYPE 4 BUT USING TYPE 3 FOR FIRST
LETTER OF PRINCIPAL WORDS. MAY BE USED FOR SUB-TITLES &
NOTES ON THE BODY OF DRAWINGS.

TYPE 6
abcdefghijklmnopqrstuvwxyz
Type 6 may be used in place of
Type 4 with capitals of Type 3,
for Bills of Material and Notes
on Body of Drawing.

FIG. 15

ing rooms. As you see, each group states its own purpose and place as commonly used on the blueprint. It should be kept in mind that the lettered notes on the descriptive drawings in connection with this article will not be found on the orthodox blueprint. A primary requirement of lettering on any blueprint is legibility. Another is simplicity, and finally, ease of execution.

Use of either the vertical, Fig. 13, of the inclined style, Fig. 15, is largely a matter of preference. Both styles are approved. Size and weight of the lettering should always be such as will produce legible prints from tracings either in pencil or ink.

Figs. 3, 4, 5, 6, 7, 11, 13, 15 abstracted from the American Standard, Drawings and Drafting Room Practice.

PLASTIC "PLANKING" renews YOUR BOAT

PLANKED ROWBOATS, outboard runabouts and other small craft that are stored during the winter months, often develop serious leaks below the waterline. This makes it necessary to recalk and presoak the planking each season before the boat can be considered safe and usable. In some cases, the individual planks or the plywood covering will be found so badly weather-checked that complete renewal is necessary. Owners of small boats can avoid seasonal labor and upkeep cost by covering the hull with glass cloth (Fiberglas) or muslin impregnated with liquid plastic, which can be applied with a brush. Properly handled, this treatment waterproofs old boats at a reasonable cost and provides a durable coating that resists scuffing and cracking, and adds considerably to the structural strength of a sound hull.

Since liquid plastic acts as a paint solvent, the first step is to remove all moldings, rub rails and other trim from the boat, and then remove the paint down to the bare wood either by scraping or by use of a paint remover. Then fill all cracks, checks and other surface defects with marine putty. After this has hardened, the hull should be sanded to remove all traces of paint and expose new wood at all points on the planking. Now, lay the glass-cloth seam strips on all the bottom seams, Fig. 1, and cut to approximate length. On some boats it will be necessary to lay strips on each side of the keel as in Fig. 2, A, and finish, after applying the cloth covering, with a ⅜-in. quarter round as in Fig. 2, B. Mix plastic with the recommended reducer, or catalyst, until the plastic is thinned to a brushing consistency. Then lift the strip of cloth over the garboard seam and apply the plastic in a uniform coating over the seam. Press the cloth into contact with the plastic coating as in Fig. 4. Proceed in the same manner with all seams on both sides of the keel, starting at the garboard seam and working outward. Roll or carry the boat into the sun and

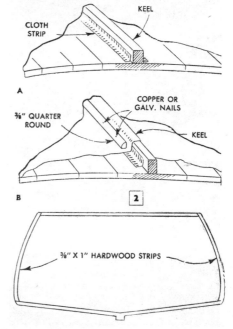

1" OR 1½" LAP   BOTTOM

A

GUNWALE MOLDING

SHEER PLANK

B

TRANSOM

CLOTH PANEL (SIDE)

MOLDING

C

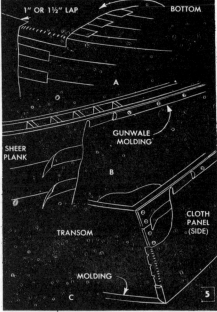

allow the plastic to set for about one hour.

While the plastic is setting, cut the cloth covering to the rough size, using either glass cloth or unbleached muslin. Then roll the boat back into the shade and apply a second coat of plastic, taking special pains to coat the strips over the seams thoroughly so that there are no·dry spots, Fig. 3. Lower the cloth over the wet surface, pull it uniformly tight and press into contact with the plastic as in Fig. 6. An ordinary squeegee can be used for working the plastic into close contact, but avoid excessive pressure as otherwise you may remove too much of the plastic coating. At the bow, the covering is fastened to the keel with copper tacks, Fig. 6. Be especially careful to work out all wrinkles that may develop over the bow, Figs. 7 and 8. Trim off excess cloth about 1½ in. above the gunwale, or spray rail.

Now, without curing the previous coat, apply a second coat of plastic to the cloth surface, Figs. 9 and 10. If you are using muslin as a covering, reduce this coat about 25 percent. Use the plastic unthinned on glass cloth. Soak the surface thoroughly and make sure that there are no blisters before curing in the sunlight. This time allow the plastic to cure so that it is sufficiently hardened to permit a light sanding with fine-grit paper. Some boatmen sand the first coat lightly, but as a rule this is not essential. This final step completes the bottom. In some cases, it will be necessary to cover only the bottom from the keel to the chines as was done on the boat pictured, but if the side planking shows signs of checking and other minor deterioration, it is best to cover the sides of the boat as well. Use the same procedure, except that in most instances a somewhat lighter cloth may be used. Details A, B and C in Fig. 5, also detail C in Fig. 2, show recommended methods of lapping the cloth covering at the chines, gunwales and transom. Special care must be taken to get a smooth lap of the cloth at the chine, detail A in Fig. 5. On some hulls it may be necessary to notch the overlapping edge of the cloth from a point near midships forward to the bow to prevent wrin-

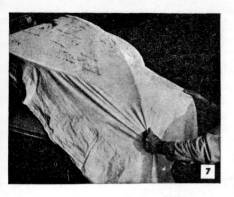

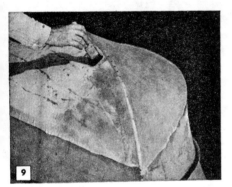

kling of the side covering. Some boatmen will want to cover the transom and this is perhaps desirable on a rowboat, but on hulls designed for outboard motors it is neither necessary nor advisable. The cloth covering is brought around the corner formed by the transom and side planking, notched if necessary to prevent wrinkling, and covered with flat hardwood strips as in Fig. 2, or with half-round molding as in Fig. 5. The job is finished with a light sanding, reinstallation of the moldings, spray rails and rub rails, and keel shoe. After the plastic is thoroughly cured, the hull may be painted any color desired. Paint must be removed in order to renew the plastic.

ONE-MAN
BOAT TRAILER

LAUNCHING a rowboat or lifting it from the water is no longer a back-breaking job if you use this underslung boat trailer equipped with a powerful hoist. The trailer will be especially appreciated if you go fishing alone, as the trailer permits handling the boat singlehandedly. The trailer frame is welded from pipe and steel channel and fitted with a lever-type hoist, as in detail A. Note in detail B how a length of chain is bolted to one of the center frames of the boat. A coil spring attached to the chain is slipped over the hoist-chain hook, the heavy spring providing a shock absorber when the boat is in riding position. A hook and eyebolt are fitted to the bow of the boat, detail C, the eyebolt being fastened to the movable clevis before the boat is raised. An angle-steel cross brace is bolted to frame after boat is in position.

Pumping lever-type hoist easily raises boat into position on trailer. Note how sheave is mounted

Movable clevis guides bow of boat to angle-steel rest at front of trailer. Hook secures bow to frame

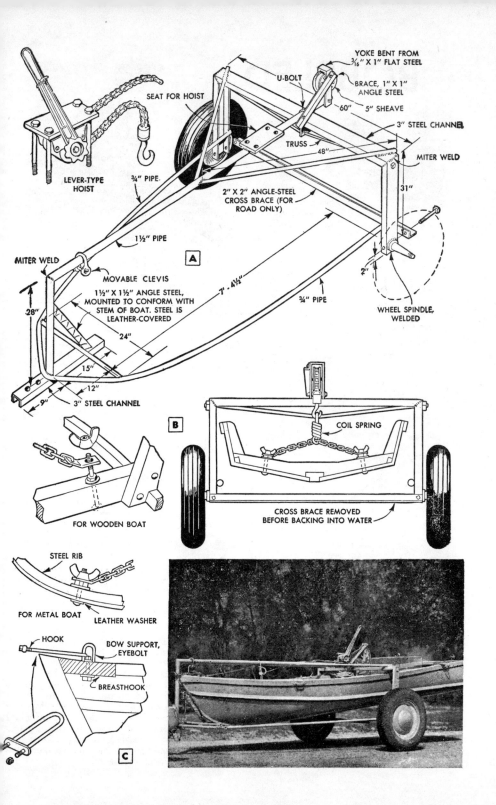

YOKE BENT FROM 3/16" X 1" FLAT STEEL

SEAT FOR HOIST

U-BOLT

BRACE, 1" X 1" ANGLE STEEL

60"

5" SHEAVE

3" STEEL CHANNEL

TRUSS

48"

MITER WELD

LEVER-TYPE HOIST

3/4" PIPE

31"

2" X 2" ANGLE-STEEL CROSS BRACE (FOR ROAD ONLY)

1½" PIPE

MITER WELD

A

2"

MOVABLE CLEVIS

WHEEL SPINDLE, WELDED

1½" X 1½" ANGLE STEEL, MOUNTED TO CONFORM WITH STEM OF BOAT. STEEL IS LEATHER-COVERED

7' 4½"

3/4" PIPE

.28"

24"

15"

12"

9"

3" STEEL CHANNEL

B

COIL SPRING

FOR WOODEN BOAT

CROSS BRACE REMOVED BEFORE BACKING INTO WATER

STEEL RIB

FOR METAL BOAT

LEATHER WASHER

HOOK

BOW SUPPORT, EYEBOLT

BREASTHOOK

C

BOBSLED

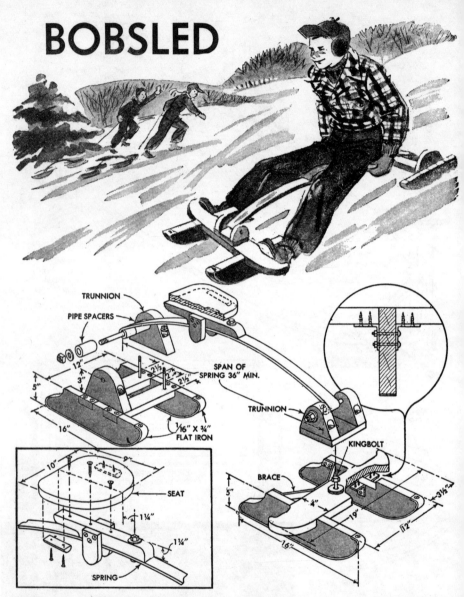

TRUNNION

PIPE SPACERS

12"

3"

5"

16"

2½"

2½"

2½"

SPAN OF SPRING 36" MIN.

¹⁄₁₆" X ¾" FLAT IRON

TRUNNION

KINGBOLT

BRACE

5"

4"

9"

16"

3½"

12"

10"

9"

SEAT

1¼"

1¼"

SPRING

THE bumpier the slide the better with this spring-bodied bobsled, which is steered with the feet so that the rider can hold on to the seat. The main leaf of an auto spring is held by lengths of iron rod set through wooden trunnions, which are bolted to cross members screwed to sled runners shod with strips of flat iron. Since the rear trunnions are widely spaced to prevent the sled from upsetting, the spring is centered on the rear rod by pieces of pipe. On the more closely spaced front trunnions these are not needed, although washers may be used between the spring and trunnion sides. Corner irons reinforce the foot rest. The seat is screwed to a support that is attached by a kingbolt through the hole in the spring. Wooden guides screwed to the support prevent side sway of the seat, and narrow cleats are attached to the underside of the seat for finger grips. Spring and runner irons are painted to prevent rusting, and the wooden parts are shellacked and varnished.

(1)

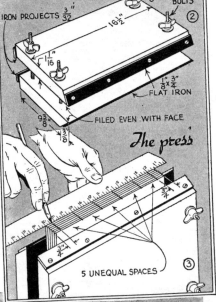

IRON PROJECTS $\frac{3}{32}$"

$\frac{3}{8}$" x 6" CARRIAGE BOLTS

(2)

16½"

$\frac{1}{16}$"

$\frac{1}{8}$" x $\frac{3}{4}$"

FLAT IRON

FILED EVEN WITH FACE

9⅜"

$\frac{3}{8}$"

The press

5 UNEQUAL SPACES

(3)

(4)

TORN, worn and faded volumes that detract greatly from the neat appearance of your library can be given new covers of leather or cloth and even improved beyond their original appearance when new. Such rebinding can be done at home by anyone. Also, when an accumulating stack of old magazines becomes a problem, why not separate the portions of them you wish to save and bind these together in yearly volumes?

Only a few simple pieces of equipment are required, namely: a press, sewing table and trimming board which are detailed in Figs. 2, 6 and 15. To bind magazines, begin by tearing off the covers and pulling out the staples as in Fig. 1. Separate the sections, being careful not to tear the backs, especially if glued. Align the edges by "jogging" the sections on the table until the back is flat and then clamp the stack in the press. Next mark lines across the back ¾ in. from the head and tail, as in Fig. 3, and divide the remaining distance into five spaces. With a fine-toothed saw make two end cuts to a depth of ⅟₁₆ in. to provide openings for inserting the needle when sewing. The other marks are undercut as shown in the circular detail of Fig. 4, to imbed heavy cords. If tapes, available at dry-goods stores, are used instead of cords, all cuts are made ⅟₁₆ in. deep, a cut being made on each side of each tape.

Now for sewing: Place the first section face downward on the bed of the sewing table. Using the saw marks as guides,

FULL BINDING →

⑤ HALF BINDING

BOOK BINDING

string the table with four vertical cords or tapes, fastening one end beneath the table with thumb tacks and tying the other end to the frame, Fig. 10. Thread a darning needle with No. 25 linen thread and begin sewing each section to the cords by holding the section open at the division and running the thread in and out around the cords as shown in the insert detail of Fig. No. 9. Leave 3 or 4 in. of thread extending at the starting hole. Then the second section is set in place and sewed from left to right with the same length of thread, after which the two ends are tied together. When the thread emerges at the left, or

Sewing table

½" DOWEL

10"

½" PLYWOOD

4"

⑥

16"

6"

8"

3" 4"

⑧ SEWING "ON-AND-OFF" STITCH

CORDS

SECTIONS SEPARATED TO SHOW DETAIL

THE "KETTLE" STITCH

⑦ A CORD → SECTIONS

"ALL-ALONG" STITCH

START

⑨

Sewing the "kettle" stitch

⑩

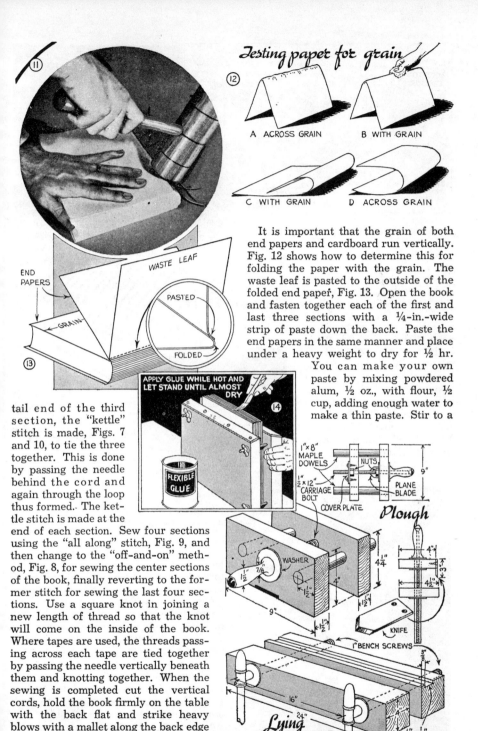

Testing paper for grain

A ACROSS GRAIN B WITH GRAIN

C WITH GRAIN D ACROSS GRAIN

END PAPERS

WASTE LEAF

GRAIN

PASTED

FOLDED

APPLY GLUE WHILE HOT AND LET STAND UNTIL ALMOST DRY

FLEXIBLE GLUE

1"x8" MAPLE DOWELS

NUTS

1/2"x12" CARRIAGE BOLT

PLANE BLADE

9"

COVER PLATE

Plough

WASHER

1/2" 7/8"

1 1/4"

4"

9"

1 1/2"

1 1/2"

KNIFE

1" BENCH SCREWS

4"

4 1/2"

3"

16"

24"

Lying press

1/4"x1 1/2" GROOVE

It is important that the grain of both end papers and cardboard run vertically. Fig. 12 shows how to determine this for folding the paper with the grain. The waste leaf is pasted to the outside of the folded end paper, Fig. 13. Open the book and fasten together each of the first and last three sections with a ¼-in.-wide strip of paste down the back. Paste the end papers in the same manner and place under a heavy weight to dry for ½ hr.

You can make your own paste by mixing powdered alum, ½ oz., with flour, ½ cup, adding enough water to make a thin paste. Stir to a

tail end of the third section, the "kettle" stitch is made, Figs. 7 and 10, to tie the three together. This is done by passing the needle behind the cord and again through the loop thus formed. The kettle stitch is made at the end of each section. Sew four sections using the "all along" stitch, Fig. 9, and then change to the "off-and-on" method, Fig. 8, for sewing the center sections of the book, finally reverting to the former stitch for sewing the last four sections. Use a square knot in joining a new length of thread so that the knot will come on the inside of the book. Where tapes are used, the threads passing across each tape are tied together by passing the needle vertically beneath them and knotting together. When the sewing is completed cut the vertical cords, hold the book firmly on the table with the back flat and strike heavy blows with a mallet along the back edge at the front and end to knock down the swelling and imbed the threads.

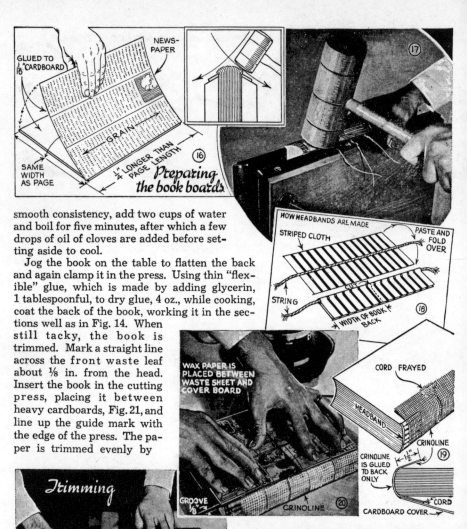

Preparing the book boards

- GLUED TO ⅟₁₆″ CARDBOARD
- NEWSPAPER
- GRAIN
- SAME WIDTH AS PAGE
- ¼″ LONGER THAN PAGE LENGTH

(16)

(17)

HOW HEADBANDS ARE MADE
- STRIPED CLOTH
- PASTE AND FOLD OVER
- CUT
- STRING
- WIDTH OF BOOK BACK

(18)

- WAX PAPER IS PLACED BETWEEN WASTE SHEET AND COVER BOARD
- CORD FRAYED
- HEADBAND
- CRINOLINE
- CRINOLINE IS GLUED TO BACK ONLY
- GROOVE ⅛″
- CRINOLINE

(19)

(20)

- CORD
- CARDBOARD COVER

Trimming

(21)

smooth consistency, add two cups of water and boil for five minutes, after which a few drops of oil of cloves are added before setting aside to cool.

Jog the book on the table to flatten the back and again clamp it in the press. Using thin "flexible" glue, which is made by adding glycerin, 1 tablespoonful, to dry glue, 4 oz., while cooking, coat the back of the book, working it in the sections well as in Fig. 14. When still tacky, the book is trimmed. Mark a straight line across the front waste leaf about ⅛ in. from the head. Insert the book in the cutting press, placing it between heavy cardboards, Fig. 21, and line up the guide mark with the edge of the press. The paper is trimmed evenly by moving the plough back and forth as the feedscrew is gradually advanced with each forward thrust. Feed the knife slowly to prevent jamming and tearing the sections.

Cut the book boards from heavy cardboard to the size given in Fig. 16. Paste a piece of newspaper to one side of each and dry under a weight. The grain of both must run vertically. Rounding and backing the book is done by first pushing in the fore edge with the thumb at the same time a drawing force is exerted with the fingers, as in Fig. 11, and then striking the back with a mallet to form "ears" along each side as in Fig. 17. Headbands of striped cloth are made as in Fig. 18 and are glued to the back at the tail and head. Apply

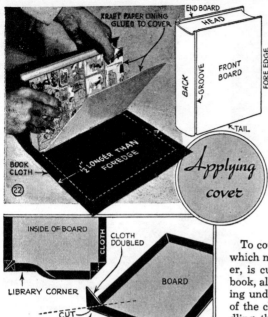

KRAFT PAPER LINING GLUED TO COVER

END BOARD

HEAD

FRONT BOARD

BACK

GROOVE

FORE EDGE

TAIL

BOOK CLOTH →

2" LONGER THAN FOREDGE

Applying cover

㉒

INSIDE OF BOARD

CLOTH

CLOTH DOUBLED

LIBRARY CORNER

BOARD

CUT

CUT CORNER

㉓

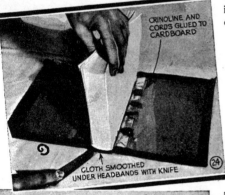

CRINOLINE AND CORDS GLUED TO CARDBOARD

CLOTH SMOOTHED UNDER HEADBANDS WITH KNIFE

㉔

CLAMPED IN PRESS 24 HOURS

㉕

TITLE GLUED TO BACK

The title, listing name, month and year, may be typed neatly on white or colored paper and glued to the back of the book as shown above, or if you prefer, it can be lettered by hand directly on the binding, using gold or silver paint applied with a pen or small brush and followed with a coat of clear shellac to keep the lettering from rubbing off

"flexible" glue to the back and lay a piece of crinoline in the glue to overhang 1½ in. on each side as shown in Fig. 19. Cut off the cords even with the crinoline backing and fray the ends. Several thicknesses of wax paper are placed over the front and back waste sheets and the frayed cords and crinoline are glued to the book covers as in Figs. 20 and 24. For this use plain glue which does not contain glycerin. The cover should project ⅛ in. at the head and tail, leaving a groove ⅛ in. wide along the back edge. Allow the book to dry thoroughly clamped in the press.

To cover the book, a piece of book cloth, which may be of buckram, paper or leather, is cut to reach completely around the book, allowing sufficient material for turning under. Make a mark down the center of the cloth on the inside and then, straddling this centerline, glue to the cloth a piece of kraft paper which is the same width and length of the book-back, including the headbands. A second piece of paper of the same width, but shorter, is glued to the back over the crinoline. Additional pieces of paper may be glued to both covers to serve as a lining as in Fig. 22. Glue the cover material first to the front board and then to the end board, and turn the cloth in over the edges of the cardboard as in Fig. 23. The sides and edges of the book are rubbed down with the rounded edge of a ruler, after which the book is covered with wax paper and clamped in the grooving end of the press where it is left for at least 12 hrs. After drying, excess cover material is trimmed away with a razor blade, leaving about ½ in. margin around the edges. The waste leaf is then torn out and the end paper thus exposed is glued down. Wax paper is placed between the covers, and the book is once again placed in the press and clamped tightly, Fig. 25. Fig. 5 shows the completed book and an example of half binding. This process is similar as described, except that the back cover material is applied first. When dry, the material is trimmed down the sides evenly, being careful not to cut the cardboard too deeply, and completed by covering the remaining portion with cloth or paper.

BOOK ENDS

INTERLOCKING cylinders of contrasting woods, such as maple and walnut, are assembled in pyramidal fashion to form this striking pair of modernistic book ends. Largely a simple lathe project, the various parts are turned in pairs, after which they are cut apart with a parting tool, Fig. 3, and shaped to nest together. Figs. 1 and 2 give the diameters and lengths of the three cylinders, A, B and C and also the dimensions of the beading and the base.

Before starting to turn the parts of the book ends, it is best to lay out a full-size pattern of the base as in Fig. 2, using a compass to mark the positions of the three cylinders. Begin the project by turning a pair of the tall, center cylinders, part A,

making them 2$\frac{9}{16}$ in. in diameter and 5$\frac{1}{4}$ in. long. The upper ends are faced-off smoothly and the edges rounded slightly. In the same way, parts B and C are turned to the sizes given in Fig. 2, their top edges also being rounded. While part A of the original set of book ends was hollowed out to receive part B as shown in Fig. 4, this part can be left intact and part B cut out instead. The latter procedure is somewhat easier, especially for the inexperienced craftsman. To do this, place the paper pattern over the end of part B and mark the contour of part A. Then, roughcut the piece a little to the right of the contour line so that enough waste stock will remain to permit sanding. If a bandsaw is available,

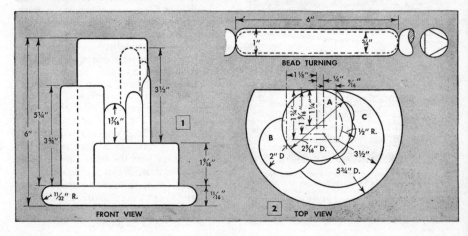

you can make this cut with the piece standing vertically. Otherwise, a gouge can be used to work the stock down to the line. Then, with fine sandpaper wrapped around part A, use the latter as a sanding block to smooth part B to a perfect fit. Part C is cut out in the same way, marking it from the paper pattern and fitting it to the contours of both parts A and B.

The bases of the book ends are 5¾-in. disks, 11⁄16 in. thick, and their edges are rounded to an 11⁄32-in. radius. The portion of each base which will be at the back of the book end is cut off flat 1⅜ in. in from the edge, and the top of the base is marked to match the paper pattern, Fig. 5. Three countersunk holes are drilled up through the bottom of the base. These are for screws which fasten the vertical members in place. The screw holes should be located near the outside edges of the scribed circles so the center of the base can be recessed and filled with lead to weight the book ends.

To add decoration, lengths of beading can be applied vertically around the center cylinder, part A. These are cut in five different lengths graduated from 1⅞ in. to 3½ in. and are arranged to form a spiral design. The beads for both book ends are cut from two sausage-shaped turnings as shown in the upper detail of Fig. 2. Sections ⅜ in. thick and ¾ in. wide are ripped from the turnings as in Fig. 6. These are cut to length and suitable flats are filed on the sides of part A to allow the beading to set flush. The top portions of the flats will have to be rounded to match the ends of the decorative beading.

To assemble the book ends, glue parts A, B and C together, clamping them by wrapping round and round with cord. Then, glue and screw these parts to the bases and glue the beading to part A. After the glue is dry, weight the book ends and glue felt to the bottoms. The units can be finished simply by waxing and polishing after final assembly.

Different sizes of cylinders for the book ends are turned in pairs and separated with a parting tool

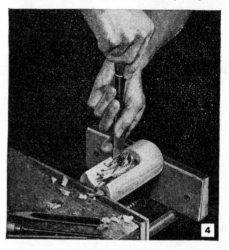

Above, center cylinder is hollowed out with a gouge to receive smaller cylinder, part B. Below, after one side of b e is cut off flat, compass is used to transfer positions of cylinders from paper pattern

Half-round strips of molding are formed by slicing sections from the sides of sausage-shaped turnings

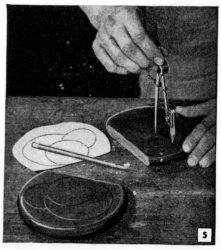